The New Science of Customer Relationships

The New Science of Customer Relationships

of Customer
Relationships

Delivering the One-to-One
Promise with AI

Thomas H. Davenport
Jim Sterne

WILEY

Tom dedicates this book to his beloved sister-in-law, Kim Bunch, who has loved and supported his entire extended family in multitudinous ways throughout her life.

Jim dedicates this book to Colleen.

Contents

About the Authors

Thomas H. Davenport is the President's Distinguished Professor of Information Technology and Management and Faculty Director of the Metropoulos Institute for Tech and Entrepreneurship at Babson College, Fellow at the MIT Initiative on the Digital Economy, and Senior Advisor to Deloitte's Chief Data and AI Officer program. He teaches artificial intelligence courses in executive programs at Babson, Harvard Business School and School of Public Health, Brown University, and MIT Sloan School.

Davenport pioneered the concept of "competing on analytics" with his best-selling 2006 *Harvard Business Review* article and 2007 book. His most recent book is *All Hands on Tech: The AI-Powered Citizen Revolution*. He wrote or edited 25 other books (including 5 other books on AI) and more than 200 articles for *Harvard Business Review*, *Sloan Management Review*, the *Financial Times*, and many other publications. He is a regular contributor to the *Wall Street Journal* and *Forbes*. He has been named one of the top 25 consultants by *Consulting News*, one of the 100 most influential people in the IT industry by Ziff-Davis, and one of the world's top 50 business school professors by *Fortune* magazine. He is the most often cited researcher in the business information systems field in the world. He was also a "Top Voice" on LinkedIn in 2016 in the education industry and in 2018 for technology.

Jim Sterne focuses his 45 years in sales and marketing on using technology for marketing. He sold business computers to companies that had never owned one in the 1980s, consulted and keynoted about online marketing in the 1990s, founded a conference and a professional association around digital analytics in the 2000s, and has lately been advising companies on the adoption of generative AI. He has written 12 books on Internet advertising, marketing, and customer service, including the humorous *Devil's Data Dictionary*. This is his second book on AI after *Artificial Intelligence for Marketing: Practical Applications* (2017).

Sterne has consulted to some of the world's largest companies and has lectured at MIT, Stanford, USC, Harvard, and Oxford. Since 2002, Sterne has remained active producing the Marketing Analytics Summit and spent 20 years with the Digital Analytics Association as co-founder and Board Chair Emeritus. He was named one of the 50 most influential people in digital marketing by one of the United Kingdom's premier interactive marketing magazines and was included in a list of the Top 25 Hot Speakers by the National Speakers Association. Sterne is on the advisory board of a variety of startups, and has served on the boards of his local library foundation, the Better Business Bureau, and the Editorial Board of the Applied Marketing Analytics peer-reviewed journal. His current passion is leveraging generative AI as a catalyst for innovation as seen in his TEDx presentation.

Acknowledgments

From Thomas H. Davenport: I want to acknowledge the energy, expertise, and enthusiasm of my co-author, Jim Sterne, whose work on various marketing-related technologies I have admired for several decades now. It's great to finally get to work with him on a book and to occasionally get to meet face-to-face in Santa Barbara.

I'm grateful to all the generous individuals who shared knowledge with us that ended up in this book—with or without their express permission— including (in no particular order) Don Peppers, Hamit Hamutcu, Jeff Goldman, Gary Loveman, Mike Thompson, Brian Ames, Giles Pavey, Fred Reichheld, Vipin Gopal, Judah Phillips, Ryan Nelson, Tom Redman, Randy Bean, Andy Palmer, Ian Barkin, and Jake Collins. We also appreciate those companies and individuals who have gone public with their case studies, surveys, analyses, musings, etc.—we hope you are happy with being in our many footnotes!

At Wiley, we'd like to thank our editor, Jim Minatel, who was positive about the book topic from the beginning and was extremely easy to work with. Kim Wimpsett was quick and helpful in project managing and editing the book, and Annie Melnick was a pleasure to collaborate with on the cover.

From Jim Sterne: My first debt of gratitude is owed to Thomas H. Davenport. He has been an inspiration, a role model, and an inveterate teacher for more than a decade. I am very grateful for his willingness to take me on as co-author and his gentle—might I say professorial way—of encouraging me to do more and better.

There are many I relied on to help me understand this new and exciting technology, including Paul Roetzer and Mike Kaput through their Marketing AI Institute and the conference where I met Jessica Hreha, Jeff Coyle, Adam Brotman, Christopher Penn, and Dale Bertrand, from whom I've learned so much.

Thanks to Jason Comier for his engaging AI Marketing Forum and to Andy Crestodina for his brilliant vision of applying generative AI to marketing. Many thanks to the innumerable people who answered my immeasurable questions about generative AI, including but certainly not limited to Kevin Davis, Kevin Lindemann, and Mike Weaver.

This last group is a curious bunch. They are podcasters, newsletter writers, and LinkedIn posters who have no idea how much they helped me. But in this age of constant and unrelenting change, classical methods of learning have given way to weekly updates. And so, my hat is off to Reid Hoffman, Kevin Roose and Casey Newton, Kara Swisher and Scott Galloway, Ethan Mollick, Nilay Patel, Sam Charrington, Brian McCullogh, and Kevin Scott. Your work is helping multitudes.

Introduction

We'll begin this book a bit unusually, with a fictional email from the near future:

To: TomSterne@gmail.com
From: New_Vehicle_Marketing@toyota.com
Date: July 20, 2026
Subject: New Toyota Offer

Dear Mr. Sterne,

You asked that we communicate with you on offers of Toyota automobiles and services, and this email is such a message. From public data and information from the Toyota Connect service on your vehicle to which you subscribe, we have observed that:

- Your 2022 RAV4 Prime is now out of warranty, though it has very low mileage of 12,343 miles over four years (as of yesterday) and a perfect service record at our service centers.
- We noted from public vehicle data that you usually purchase a new vehicle when the previous one is out of warranty.
- We also noted from the data that you have a fully electric car, a Hyundai IONIQ 6, registered in Massachusetts, and owned two fully electric cars before that.
- Your RAV4 Prime, a plug-in hybrid, is regularly plugged in to charge by you or other drivers of the car.

- Toyota Connect tells us that 92% of your trips involve fewer than 200 miles.
- Toyota Connect weight and rearward-facing visibility sensor data tells us that your car is often fully loaded.
- Most of your calls to our technical service line have involved scheduled charging at home to save on utility costs.

Given this information, we would like to offer you a reduced loyalty price on the new 2027 Highlander Platinum all-electric SUV. It has more passenger and storage capacity than the RAV4, and its electric range is well over 200 miles. It has a new, easy-to-use scheduled charging system that makes charging your vehicle at the lowest cost almost automatic. Platinum is the highest trim level on the Highlander electric, consistent with that on your current RAV4 Prime. And we understand that you see the benefits of fully electric vehicles.

Given the low mileage and service record on your RAV4 Prime, we are also prepared to offer you the highest estimated value (subject to an appraisal) on your trade-in. Combining the reduced price on the 2027 Highlander EV Platinum ($52,545) and the trade-in value on your RAV4 Prime ($35,700), you would be able to purchase the new car for less than $17,000, not including tax and licensing fees.

We would be happy to bring the new car to your home for a test drive, appraise your current car's trade-in value, and complete all administrative paperwork, all in one short visit. If this offer appeals to you, please let us know by 31 August 2026. If you have questions about it, please visit our ToyoSmart intelligent chatbot on Toyota.com or the Toyota mobile app and provide your name. It is familiar with the details of the offer, the data used to create it, and the vehicles involved.

Sincerely,
Your Friends at Toyota Motor North America

Such a highly personalized offer is technically possible today, although to our knowledge neither Toyota nor any other automobile companies (including digital native car companies like Tesla) makes such offers. We're not picking on Toyota—we both own and like their vehicles—but they market and sell cars (at least in the US) in the same nonscientific way that other companies do. Most companies in other industries also don't use these personalized and targeted approaches. But why not, given that we've been told for several decades that personalized, targeted marketing, sales, and service are the way to achieve better customer relationships? Why not, given the explosion of available data and the amazing capabilities of analytics, artificial intelligence (AI), and autonomous agents?

These are the questions that inspired us to write this book. We've both closely followed developments in the science and technology of customer relationships for the past several decades, and we've been impressed by the technological progress but underwhelmed by the lack of improvement in customer connections and engagement. It was time that the two of us explored the science of how classic data exploration, analytical AI, and generative AI can make the most of data and analytics to boost customer relationships:

Thomas (Tom) Davenport is a professor who has written many books on analytics, AI, and other business technologies, and he's been interested in how technology affects marketing and other customer-facing functions since the 1990s. However, he remains puzzled about the regular bombardments of marketing and sales materials he receives that have nothing to do with his attributes or interest. Jim Sterne has written several books on such topics as ecommerce, web analytics, and AI in marketing—and speaks and advises often on such topics—but he's also convinced that companies can do much better than they are currently doing in these domains.

Of course, technology is always changing, and it has changed a lot in the past couple of years. Jim is convinced that generative AI just might be the key that unlocks the one-to-one marketing door. Tom is certainly dazzled by what generative AI can do but isn't as sure that it will be enough to break things open. But both of us believe that it's not enough by itself to bring about effective and highly personalized customer relationships.

The science of customer relationships is also evolving rapidly. While companies have long relied on intuition and experience to understand their customers, we're now seeing the emergence of more scientific approaches that combine rigorous data analysis, controlled experiments, and reproducible results.

For example, in the case of the fictional Toyota offer in the previous email, it's likely that the content of the email will have been created by generative AI. Perhaps there might even be agents that would go out to different data sources and pull the needed data together to make the offer. But there are also business and organizational challenges that would have to be overcome before such an offer would be feasible.

For example, this fictional offer is from Toyota Motor North America, rather than a dealer. Who would make such an offer—the company or the dealer? Offers and prices are set by dealers at the moment, which is rather inefficient. It would seem that such a personalized approach made from the company overall would rival the knowledge of a dealer salesperson. And there might be no need for a showroom if cars were brought to the customer directly. Changes of this nature would involve difficult and time-consuming negotiations with the existing dealership structure, and they might never happen at all.

The offer draws on a wide variety of data sources and is processed with a variety of intelligent applications (see Figure I.1). Most of these actually exist today, but they would likely be difficult to integrate in order to create the offer. A household might have cars that are registered to different owners within it, for example. Information from service transactions might readily be captured and summarized by generative AI, but service departments collaborating with marketing and sales functions might be more challenging.

In short, it seems likely that the nontechnical changes to create such an offer might be greater than the technical challenges involved. There should be little doubt that the needed technical capabilities will be available by 2026, but the needed organizational and business capabilities may take much longer to become widespread.

Does this offer constitute customer science? We define that term as a concerted and continuous attempt to understand what customers want and

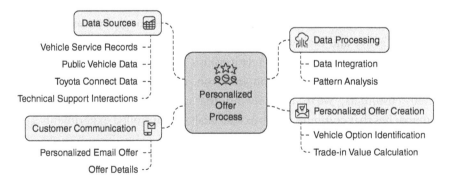

Figure I.1 The hypothetical personalized offer process.

need using data and technology, and to offer them only products, services, and advice that are targeted to meet those desires and requirements. The fictional Toyota email appears to be scientifically targeted to the customer's need for a new car. However, we can't verify that the customer wants a new car—the response or lack thereof to the email could provide clues. And we can't label it "customer science" without seeing a long-term pattern of such marketing and sales approaches. One-off experiments seldom lead to scientific breakthroughs, and one-off targeted offers don't lead to great customer relationships over time.

In this book we describe the technologies, the science, the related business issues, and the organizational and behavioral changes necessary to dramatically improve customer relationships. The one-to-one concept of personalization is discussed in detail, with reflection on why it has not come to pass in most organizations in the more than 30 years since it was defined. But we also discuss other aspects of customer-facing technologies, including the voice of the customer, automation of marketing activities, AI agents and related technologies, customer-facing operations, and many other topics with regard to customer issues. Much of the book is focused on improvements in these areas: better AI, better data, better technologies, better analytics, etc. All of these taken together—along with a sincere desire to improve the lives of customers—constitute customer science.

We've tried to strike a balance in the level of optimism about new technologies, particularly AI and generative AI. We aim to take a scientific approach, examining the evidence both for what works and for what doesn't in using technology to improve customer relationships. Even the chapters that are primarily about these technologies also mention issues of integration with the existing technology architecture, organizational adoption and absorption, and the achievement of business value.

We've also tried to provide some historical perspective, without making this book primarily about history. Since one of the motivational questions for the book is why it's taking so long to get the customer relationships that technology and technologists have long promised, we do briefly discuss the history of customer-oriented information technology, particularly in Chapter 1. But far more pages are devoted to contemporary technologies than historical ones, and we focus more on looking forward than looking backward.

The chapters in the book are briefly described here:

Chapter 1: The Broken Promise of Customer Data and Technology.
This chapter describes how customer data and technology have largely not yet produced the customer relationships every company desires. It describes the different types of customer data, the different technologies used to manage and transact with it, why one-to-one marketing hasn't come about in most organizations, and why we're more optimistic about the future.

Chapter 2: The Future Is Here, but Unevenly Distributed.   Marketers, sales managers, and customer service executives have been trying to use information technology to improve customer relationships for years. Some organizations have been successful. In this chapter we describe two prominent companies that have put data, analytics, and AI to work successfully.

Chapter 3: Better AI: Generative AI as a Catalyst for Change.
Generative AI burst into the public's consciousness only a couple of years ago, but it has transformed expectations and dialogue about how AI can impact business. In this chapter we introduce the technology, describe several ways that it could transform customer relationships, and discuss some tactics to make it more useful.

Chapter 4: Better Data.   You can't create good AI or models without good data, and there are many potential sources of data on customers. We describe the options and discuss how organizations can develop an effective customer data strategy.

Chapter 5: Better Personalization and Hyper-Personalization.   One of the key objectives of customer data and technology has been the personalization of ads, offers, and communications. In this chapter we discuss why it has taken so long and how some organizations do it well.

Chapter 6: Better Customer Voice Analysis and Action.   Customer communications go both ways, and AI increasingly makes it possible to understand and act on communications and sentiments from customers. We describe how to make the customer voice more understandable and actionable, and how to improve customer service based on it, in this chapter.

Chapter 7: Better Task Automation with AI Agents. Marketing and customer service had automation programs in the past, but they were inflexible and not data-driven. AI agents are the new cool thing, and we explore how they can and will support customer-facing applications in this chapter.

Chapter 8: Better Customer-Facing Operations. There are many departments in most companies that interact with customers. In this chapter we describe ways in which they can cooperate more effectively—often with the help of technology—to increase customer engagement and satisfaction.

Chapter 9: Better Customer Analytics and Data Science. Behind the AI models that personalize and understand customer interactions, there are analytics and data science models that make them possible. Some are old and some are new, and we discuss how to use them effectively on behalf of customers in this chapter.

Chapter 10: Better Ethics. It's great to take advantage of customer data, but there are ethical limits to what's feasible and desired by customers themselves. In this chapter we focus on how organizations can walk the line between ethical and creepy.

Chapter 11: The Customer of Tomorrow. We conclude the book with a discussion among a company's executives and their AI helpers about what kinds of customer data and technology would make for an ethical and highly effective customer experience. The hypothetical script is interspersed with real lessons about what really works for customers.

1

The Broken Promise of Customer Data and Technology

Of all the different types of data within organizations, customer data is perhaps the most important. It informs a company about what customers have bought, what kinds of people they are, and what they might buy in the future. It is the key to knowing whether customers are satisfied or dissatisfied. It reveals what products and services they might find appealing in the future. At the most basic level, customer data includes where to ship the product, how it's being paid for, and whether the customer is likely to renege on payment or return the product.

We typically think of only companies as having customers and customer data, but government agencies and nonprofits have their equivalent. Governments can apply the science of customer analysis. Knowing how constituents feel about their leaders and the services they receive is extremely important to their success. Nonprofits have both contributors and recipients of services; they're different types of customers, but keeping track of both is critical to success.

We will argue in this book that customer data and technology have often not delivered on their promises or potential. Perhaps that's a good thing for us, or you would have little motivation to buy and read these words and images. For more than 30 years, we've heard about one-to-one marketing, a 360-degree view of customers, personalization and hyper-personalization, multi- and omni-channel relationships, etc., *ad infinitum*. Despite decades of progress in the science and technology of analytics and customer modeling, the practical application of these methods has remained elusive.

If you're not skeptical of these concepts, you probably aren't paying a lot of attention to the gap between how marketing is described and how we observe it in practice. Of course, the appeal and importance of these concepts and capabilities is unquestionable. It's certainly possible to imagine a world in which customer data and technologies were used very effectively to improve the course of customer relationships. Analytics and artificial intelligence have already had a positive impact on these relationships, and generative AI and agentic technology will go much further.

If these technologies are used effectively, what will the future look like? If customer data were captured, stored, and used effectively, for example, we would know about virtually every interaction a customer has with an organization—purchases, returns, product or service usage for online offerings, web and mobile views and clicks, related social media comments, summaries of calls to the customer service center, and even subjects addressed in informal chats with salespeople or other company representatives. All of that information could be combined into customer lifetime value predictions, propensity-to-purchase models for particular products and services, churn predictions, accurate personalization of virtually every ad or offer, and detailed attribution of a customer's channel activity and path-to-purchase. Many of those analyses would be powered by traditional analytical AI based on machine learning and structured data.

Generative AI has further potential to enhance customer relationships. By harnessing the capabilities of machine learning and data integration, it could automate many textual and visual offerings to customers and provide extensive personalization of each interaction. It could analyze a customer service email or the content of a phone call or text chat, pass along relevant feedback to the individuals involved in addressing the customer need, and alert the customer about what action has been taken. The idea of standard product copy or images would become obsolete. "Agentic" AI, or a somewhat autonomous AI system that can make decisions and take actions rather than just responding to prompts, could automatically determine a customer need, make an immediate recommendation of how to address it, and complete the purchase transaction with customer approval.

Much of this glittering image of data- and technology-enhanced customer relationships is technically possible today. However, as we'll discuss later in this chapter, at various times in recent history we've been promised other revolutions in customer interaction, and we're still waiting to see them. It's a rare event for either of us, for example, to receive a marketing offer from a company for a product we really want but haven't already searched for. In the remainder of this chapter, we'll discuss the history of customer data and technology and explain why a scientific approach to customer relationships hasn't been achieved.

The Nature of Customer Data

As in any scientific endeavor, effective customer relationship management requires rigorous collection and analysis of data to generate meaningful insights. Customer data—for better or worse—is multifaceted. It consists of such elements as these:

- **Transactions:** Sales, shipments, payments, website and mobile clicks, customer support tickets, and the like.
- **Attributes:** Names and addresses, demographic information, credit card numbers.
- **Structured opinions:** Customer satisfaction ratings, net promoter scores, whether purchases are returned; web and mobile site views.
- **Unstructured opinions:** Website comments, social media comments, customer service calls, comments to salespeople.
- **Calculations:** Segmentation, engagement, acquisition cost, recency, frequency, monetary (RFM) analysis, customer lifetime value.
- **Predictions:** Recommended products or services, likelihood of attrition (churn), price the customer is willing to pay.
- **Experimental results:** A/B tests, controlled trials, and other scientific methods of testing hypotheses about customer behavior and preferences.

Customer data, then, can be a rich repository of content about one of the most important resources in business. It's hard to imagine how an organization can be very successful without managing customer data well.

Amazingly, however, most don't do it well at all. They usually manage to stay in business, but they don't prosper as much as they might if they had and used good customer data.

Why Customer Data Is Difficult to Manage

One reason customer data often isn't managed well is simply because it's complex. Vendors often speak of their "Customer 360" capabilities, suggesting that they can handle and make sense of all forms of customer data. But as you can imagine, capturing and analyzing all the different types of data we've just described can be difficult. And doing it successfully goes well beyond software alone.

Just to keep that set of customer data elements we described earlier in play, imagine the difficulty of combining all of them in a 360-degree view of customers. Customers are always changing (addresses, credit cards, opinions), so it's hard to keep up-to-date with them. Mixing structured and unstructured data is both a technical challenge and—more importantly—an analysis and sensemaking challenge. What if the customer continues to buy from us but trashes us on social media? What if they buy a lot of our product online but return much of it after purchase? What if structured data predicts churn, but the sales rep says the customer is happy? Such potential contradictions can be difficult or impossible to resolve.

There is also the difficulty of even learning who the customer is. You may have wondered, for example, why manufacturers of durable goods often package in little cards to encourage the customer to register for warranty service. It's usually not technically necessary to register to get your warranty service, but the manufacturer wants your name and address data to try to sell you additional products. Incentives and offers included in the product packaging often have the same motivation.

This is a particular challenge for consumer goods that are sold through retail channels. In such cases, the retailer knows what you have bought, but that information is seldom passed along to the manufacturer of the product because retailers want to own the relationship with the customer. This issue has bedeviled consumer packaged goods (CPG) manufacturers for decades. As we'll discuss, some CPG firms have made considerable progress in selling to—and getting data from—consumers through ecommerce channels. Not only does that usually increase their profit margins, but it also permits an ongoing marketing, sales, and service relationship with the customer.

That previous sentence suggests another difficulty with customer data: it's often captured and owned by different parts of an organization. Marketing owns personalized customer offers and perhaps leads from all channels. But to convert, those leads must be handed off to sales (inside or outside), which then owns them and customer information encountered through the sales process. Customer service is responsible for the problems that customers bring to an organization and the solutions to them. If there is a "customer success" function, it has custody of the information about how the customer is using the product or service and how they feel about it. Analytics or AI organizations may own the data used to train models and the predictions they make. If that's not enough owners, the research and development (R&D) group may own customer comments in focus groups or suggestions for new products and services.

Unless your company has an unusually friendly and collaborative culture, these different owners may clash when someone suggests pulling all the information about customers together into one database or customer data platform. And the ownership of that database or platform may be contentious as well. Those political and cultural issues can't be handled at all by software, even if it's highly flexible and functional. All of this has led many managers to give up on the 360-degree-view idea and to just try to manage the data they own or control about customers.

Perhaps the most basic problem of all in managing customer data effectively is defining the customer with precision and employing that definition around the company. Table 1.1 describes a set of alternative terms that could all be used to describe a "customer," for example. Tom has a vivid memory of this issue from a consulting engagement he performed with a computer company a few years ago. The company had two major distribution channels: direct sales to the end customer (generally businesses), or sales through distributors. The different channel organizations couldn't agree on whether a distributor counted as a customer. Even more problematically for financial reporting, they couldn't decide on what constituted a sale—if a product was sent to a distributor, did it count as a certified sale?

Table 1.1 Multiple terms that could mean the same individual

Companies	Government
User	Citizen
Visitor	Voter
Shopper	Resident
Buyer	Inhabitant
Purchaser	Constituent
Consumer	Taxpayer
Customer	Defendant
Client	Petitioner
Patron	Subject

The direct sales unit was the larger and more powerful of the two, so their definition was more likely to be employed in the organization, but the indirect sales organization didn't change their definitions—sometimes leading to multiple versions of the truth. Even with the direct sales organization, there was debate about whether a prospect should be viewed as a customer and included in the customer database. Some people included prospects; some didn't. Both of these arguments led to long delays, for example, when a new chief executive officer (CEO) asked for a list of the top 100 customers for a letter he planned to send to them upon assuming the role. As a result of these and other interactions with clients, Tom formulated a general law of common information in companies (see "Davenport's Law of Common Information").

Davenport's Law of Common Information

A couple of decades ago, Tom was researching how companies managed information. He visited several of them in a short period. When he visited American Airlines, the head of information management told him, "We have 11 different meanings of the term *airport*" and proceeded to describe some: maintenance people think that anyplace you can fix a plane is an airport, passenger-focused employees think that anyplace you can pick up or drop off passengers is an airport, the employees who work with the International Air Transport Authority (IATA) think that their list of airports is definitive, etc. Then Tom heard something similar at Union Pacific Railroad the following week: "We can't agree on what a *train* is." Some believe it's an abstract scheduling entity, some believe it has to have a locomotive, some think it's any collection of cars on a track. Then the next week someone at the US Department of Justice commented, "We have great arguments about what constitutes a *trial*." Finally, Tom got the picture. He formulated Davenport's Law of Common Information, which goes this way:

> "The more an organization knows or cares about a specific entity within its business, the less likely it is to agree on a common term and meaning for it."

Tom has seen many examples of this law in practice since he formulated it, and *customers*—being an entity that many organizations deeply care about—are one of the best examples. However, the fact that Davenport's Law of Common Information exists does not absolve organizations from trying to do something about it! Even if it's difficult, for example, to agree on a common definition of *customer*, it's important to do so, and managers should argue around a table until they agree on what it means for the entire organization. Perhaps needless to say, for IT people to create complex customer data models—some rival microprocessor circuit diagrams in visual complexity—does not generally solve the problem.

There is no right answer to these questions, but not having agreement across an organization on what constitutes a customer (and a sale to a customer) is problematic. It may be perfectly reasonable to treat prospects as customers for some purposes (marketing, for example), but in general, it's better to clearly define *customer* in a particular way (e.g. someone or some organization that has bought something from us in the past two years) and treat others as "prospects" or "lapsed customers" as their official status. Then if there is an ad or an offer that applies to more than one type of customer, the different groups can be combined temporarily for that purpose.

Organizational structures can also lead to other types of customer data problems. Take, for example, the merger or acquisition. Even if the acquired company isn't in the same industry, there may well be overlapping customer records—perhaps with slightly different data attributes. Companies have worked for decades to create integrated, high-quality "golden records" or important data types like customers, but it has been a challenging process that is rarely finished successfully.

There are AI technologies now that can help with data integration processes.[1] They typically work by using traditional machine learning to predict whether two different records are actually for the same customer. Such a system might predict with 95% confidence, for example, that "John Smith, 100 Main St., Lenexa, KS" is the same customer as "J Smith, 100 Main, Lenexa, KS." That level of confidence would generally be high enough to automatically merge the two records. These types of systems can substantially lower the time needed to integrate data, although they usually still require occasional human intervention.

Finally, there are the pernicious data quality problems that plague virtually every organization. These often originate at the front line, when a sales rep enters the customer's name, address, or other information incorrectly at first contact. Then it becomes difficult to fix the mistake. We won't go into detail on data quality issues—and there are also some partial technological solutions to the problem, like AI that identifies unlikely names or addresses that don't exist—but they continue to be found almost everywhere. Fixing them is possible but typically a labor-intensive and expensive proposition.

Where Did We Go Astray?[2]

So, customer data is hard to manage well. But as we argued at the beginning of this chapter, it's more important than just about any other type of data, so it's worth some special effort. Perhaps the real problem is that we have been overly optimistic about our ability to use technology to master customer data. Like the customer 360-degree meme mentioned earlier, there has long been a set of messages that we are just about to turn the corner on customer data management and the resulting ability to understand, act on, personalize, and profit from customer activity.

---

[1] Thomas H. Davenport and Tom Redman, "How AI Is Improving Data Management," *MIT Sloan Management Review*, 20 December 2022, https://sloanreview.mit.edu/article/how-ai-is-improving-data-management.

[2] This section draws in part on Jim Sterne and Thomas H. Davenport, "A Brief History and the Future of Customer Data," submitted to *Applied Marketing Analytics*, 2024.

Table 1.2 Technologies for customer transaction capture and execution

Mature or obsolete	Well-established	Emerging
Customer databases	Ecommerce platforms	GenAI service
CRM systems	Customer data platforms	CX platforms
Self-service kiosks	Mobile commerce platforms	Composable CDPs
Interactive voice response	Service management/ ticketing	Augmented reality
Retargeting	Data management platforms (ads)	Voice search
	Search term capture	GenAI prompt capture

Information systems have long been proposed as the answer to deeper, better, more rewarding customer relationships, and companies have been focused on this issue for decades. Various new technologies (databases, the Internet, analytics, customer relationship management [CRM] systems, etc.) have been advanced over time as the way to execute and capture customer transactions. Other technologies (descriptive customer analytics, predictive customer analytics, machine learning, and now generative AI) have been held up as the answer to all our customer insight and prediction challenges. We review the current state of these technologies in Table 1.2 (and Table 1.3 later in this chapter). They could ostensibly support greater customer awareness, understanding, affinity, engagement, conversion, and loyalty, all with the click of a mouse.

It didn't turn out that way, at least not yet. Customer transactions are no doubt easier with the Internet and mobile apps, and we have massive amounts more data about our customers than in the past. However, marketing effectively to them remains problematic. We still struggle with capturing, understanding, and acting on the behavior, sentiment, and voice of the customer. We have difficulty making high-quality offers or purchase recommendations. Post-sale customer service is hardly a pleasant experience in most cases. There is little or no evidence that our technology-enabled marketing to customers has increased customer satisfaction or lifetime value—the primary outcomes for which marketers strive. We'll next review why these technologies have not yet yielded the promised benefits to either customers or marketers.

Getting Customer Data into a Database

In the beginning, the first transactional technology for customer data was database marketing. It was to be the driver of dramatic change in the relationships among customers and their suppliers. The idea was that technology could capture—all in one place—important attributes about customers and their relationship with a company. This trend emerged in the 1980s, when companies began to compile data on how their customers transacted with them—what they bought, how much they spent, and as much demographic information as they could compile. The goal was to begin to personalize marketing offers based on historical relationships with customers and future predictions of what would appeal to them.

One early example of database marketing was at AT&T, which in 1984 created the "Opportunity Calling" marketing campaign based on a customer database. It was intended to provide personalized offers to the company's 85 million customers as it divested itself of the Bell Operating Companies.[3] The field of direct marketing was still relatively new, and the *Journal of Direct Marketing* (in which the AT&T initiative was described) began to be published in 1987.

In 1991 two marketing academics, Robert Blattberg and John Deighton, published an article discussing the possibilities for using data to personalize marketing. Like many other articles since, it could still be relevant today. It said, for example:

> To appreciate the power of a customer database, one must see it not merely as a mailing list, but as the memory of the customer relationship: a record of every message and response between the firm and each address. Add artificial intelligence and the system can design new messages, and even product offerings, at the individual level to reflect everything learned from past interactions.[4]

Although these feats sound like something requiring generative AI, they meant rule-based expert systems at the time, and neither the authors nor

---

[3] Gary F. Beck, Sherry M. Karas, and Ann E. Skudlark, "The AT&T opportunity calling program: Responsiveness and implications," *Journal of Direct Marketing* 4:1 (1990), pp. 24–29.
[4] Robert C. Blattberg and John Deighton, "Interactive marketing: Exploiting the age of addressability," *MIT Sloan Management Review,* Fall 1991, https://sloanreview.mit.edu/article/interactive-marketing-exploiting-the-age-of-addressability.

anyone else was aware of what might be done with newer forms of AI in the future. Putting all customer information in one place was certainly a good idea, but there were both organizational and technical barriers to integrating the information and using it effectively.

Our One-to-One Future, and Why It Has Been Slow to Arrive

Shortly thereafter in 1993, two consultants, Don Peppers and Martha Rogers, coined a term that has remained popular for 30 years, although it has seldom been fully realized. *One-to-one marketing* promised highly personalized offers, ads, and communications to customers based not just on their attributes and purchase histories but also on their individual interactions with the marketer.[5] They suggested that the end of mass marketing was upon us, as companies would soon be worrying less about how to sell an individual product or service to as many customers as possible, and more about how to sell an individual customer as many products or services as possible.

Since that time, marketers have struggled to achieve the one-to-one future for a variety of reasons. In addition to the problems we described earlier, customer data—particularly from third-party providers—is often inaccurate.[6] Companies don't usually have enough different offerings or messages to fully personalize them to each customer. And the individually targeted matching of customers to marketing content has been beyond the capability of the largest computers and strongest algorithms. Creating truly one-to-one content would be very labor intensive—at least until the recent emergence of generative AI.

To understand what happened with the one-to-one concept in practice, we talked with two people who were and are intimately familiar with it. Don Peppers, the co-author (with Dr. Martha Rogers) of *The One to One Future: Building Relationships One Customer at a Time* (and the author of the Foreword to this book), is justifiably impressed with his and Rogers' book's predictions but dissatisfied with actual outcomes. The book anticipated

---

[5] Don Peppers and Martha Rogers, *The One to One Future: Building Relationships One Customer at a Time* (Crown Business 1993).

[6] Alyssa Boyle, "CTV ad targeting is getting more advanced, but data quality is not," Adexchanger, 20 October 2023, https://www.adexchanger.com/tv/ctv-ad-targeting-is-getting-more-advanced-but-data-quality-is-not.

widespread personalization, a focus on customer relationship management, greater use of analytics in marketing, and even the rise of social media, remote work, and direct-to-consumer ecommerce—despite that the Internet was a largely academic resource in 1993, when the book was originally published. The first commercially useful web browser, Netscape Navigator, did not even become available until 1994.

In a conversation with Tom, Peppers laid the blame for the one-to-one future not being more broadly realized on organizational structure. Most companies, he said, are still organized by product and are effective practitioners of product management. Rarely, however, is anyone responsible for making customers happy and increasing their lifetime values, one customer at a time.

Peppers commented further:

> One of the first things we said would happen in the book is that while mass production generates economies of scale, making it possible to produce each product for less and less unit cost, one-to-one marketing generates "economies of scope," which reduce the cost of selling to any individual customer, based on the scope of a marketer's relationship with that individual customer. But one-to-one marketing requires more than interactive technology (like the internet); it also requires computer-assisted production of individually tailored products. We called it "customerizing" the product, describing a process that soon came to be called "mass customization."

Ultimately, however, Peppers says the success of any comprehensive one-to-one marketing effort depends on whether and how a company assigns responsibility within its organization for selling more products and services to individual customers (as opposed to selling their product or service to more customers, which is what product managers do). Peppers said that software-as-a-service companies are among the few that are beginning to achieve this one-to-one ideal, because not only do they treat different customers differently, customizing their offerings to specific customers, but they have also established customer success managers who are individually *responsible* for maintaining and increasing the profitability of each customer. And he predicts now that as more and more products and services are connected to the Internet, this "customer success" organization model will become more pervasive, even among consumer products.

However, Peppers' and Rogers' 1993 book had a chapter entitled "Make Money Protecting Privacy, Not Threatening It," and in other writing he has lamented the behavior of the big tech companies in general. In a 2020 blog post called "The One to One Future—Are We There Yet?" he answered the question:

> So we're *definitely* not there yet, folks. No way. Because not only has this prediction not yet become reality, but most of the "Big Tech" businesses driving so much economic growth today make their money by undermining privacy, not by protecting it.[7]

One of Peppers' and Rogers' colleagues in their consulting firm Peppers & Rogers Group was Hamit Hamutcu, who now works at the Institute for Experiential AI at Northeastern University and also runs a company focused on data science skill standards development and assessment. He was a managing partner at Peppers & Rogers Group, launching several offices globally, and at one point became the global analytics lead for the company.

When we asked him about his perspectives on the difficulties companies had with one-to-one marketing, he said there was often a gap between executive sponsorship and the reality on the ground. Client executives—typically the CEO or chief operating officer (COO)—wanted the work to be transformative and dramatic. They wanted a culture of customer centricity, with channels and marketing initiatives built around it, daily business processes designed around it, and technology to support it.

However, the easiest and most obvious changes and investments involved technology—data warehouses, CRM systems, and analytical tools. These were necessary investments, Hamutcu said, but the technology wasn't quite up to the job and was certainly not sufficient to drive the desired impact. There were no real-time analytics or machine learning models; any analytics usually had to be done after the customer transaction. There were many different repositories of data, and integrating them was always

---

[7] Don Peppers, "The One-to-One Future—Are We There Yet?" LinkedIn post, 22 July 2020, https://www.linkedin.com/pulse/one-future-we-yet-don-peppers.

challenging. Companies would define customer segments, but they would change faster than the organization could keep up and define new ones.

There were also organizational challenges, Hamutcu noted. Organizations were siloed by business unit and didn't want to collaborate on marketing or share data. The budgets and power, as Peppers told us, were often with the product organization. The consultants would devise customer-oriented actions, but deploying them consistently across a large and complex organization with a variety of goals and incentives was often hard. And the sustainability of the one-to-one focus was often a problem. A CEO makes a strategic mandate, but if the CEO changes, the next incumbent might have a different vision.

Three lessons are clear from Peppers' and Hamutcu's perspectives. One is that technology—albeit technology that is much more powerful and capable than it was in the 1990s and early 2000s—is not enough to create a customer-centered organization. Two is that organizational and cultural issues are bound to come into play within specific organizations. Three is that the one-to-one marketing organization is not a passing fancy; it must be articulated clearly, be built over time, and be a persistent goal for multiple leaders and the employees who follow their lead.

From Database to Digital

As we've noted, Peppers' and Rogers' one-to-one vision largely predated the Internet and e-commerce. But the advent of these technologies brought a resurgence of hope to the prospect of one-to-one marketing due to the enormous amount of behavioral data collected in the serving of web pages. The ability to collect information about an individual visitor's clicks, time spent on a web page, operating system, browser type, screen resolution, (approximate), geo-location of Internet Protocol (IP) addresses, and even the X–Y coordinates of their mouse movements seemed like a data dream come true.

However, data difficulties immediately surfaced that have yet to be rectified, including the following:

- Cookie deletion
- Cookie blocking
- Multiple machine browsing
- Multiple browser browsing

- Multiple people on the same cookie
- Nonhuman traffic
- Dynamic IP addressing
- Page caching
- JavaScript loading
- Pixel placement

Across a large organization, the data was further mangled by the following:

- Different tools using...
- Different date stamping routines and...
- Different methods to capture...
- Different types of data to store in...
- Different kinds of databases with a...
- Different method of data cleansing followed by...
- Different segmentation analysis to produce...
- Different kinds of reports that ended up in a...
- Different pipeline for integration into...
- Different data warehouses.

Marketers attempted to derive indicators of individual interest by reading the tea leaves of search, navigation, recency, frequency, and more. They successfully identified website friction as a signal of customer experience distress ripe for improvement, but dynamically serving content for each individual proved complex and painful, and even the best efforts failed to produce a decent return on the effort.[8]

As a result, even in a highly configurable medium like digital marketing, it is still rare for consumers to receive well-personalized marketing content from companies. One need only view the prevalence of retargeting in digital channels—assuming that if customers were once interested in a product or service, they will be interested again—to realize that we are far from the one-to-one goal.

---

[8] René Arnold, Scott J. Marcus, Georgios Petropoulos, Anna Schneider, "Is data the new oil? Diminishing returns to scale," 29th European Regional Conference of the International Telecommunications Society (ITS): "Towards a Digital Future: Turning Technology into Markets?" Trento, Italy, 1–4 August 2018, https://hdl.handle.net/10419/184927.

When social media took off, marketers saw a new data stream to attach to individuals: their own words posted in public. The sheer amount of data led to a boom in sentiment analysis companies peddling "insight" into individuals' frames of mind. But responding to a social post by hand was too labor-intensive, and doing it programmatically was seen as creepy. Then came the Cambridge Analytica debacle, and the legislation started rolling out. Not only did trying to use individuals' social posts as input for altering their opinions violate Facebook's terms of service, it violated society's sense of decency.

Today, organizations are beginning to collect and manage all types of customer feedback, including surveys, questionnaires, and reviews. This information is increasingly compiled and accessed through *customer experience platforms* (CXPs). But this is still an emerging category of customer technology, with variations involving survey-oriented feedback, service feedback, sales account feedback, customer journey mapping, and customer success tools.

From Call Centers to Chatbots

Technologies for customer service have also evolved over the years but remain frustrating to many customers. Many companies are heavily focused on the efficiency with which customer problems or questions are addressed in call or contact centers. They view customer service largely as a cost to be minimized. Therefore, they have embraced technologies that allow fewer human agents to be employed in these roles. Many organizations also outsourced customer contact to offshore providers to lower costs.

Call centers date to the 1960s, but the earliest automation tools for them—known as *interactive voice response* (IVR)—only became popular in the late 1970s. We are all painfully familiar with that technology; it involved pressing touch-tone buttons to reach different types of answers. The most popular button, of course, was 0 to reach a human agent. Later IVR technologies included some speech recognition capabilities, and customers were able to (occasionally) meet their service need by talking to the IVR system. Again, however, the most popular phrase uttered by customers was, undoubtedly, "speak to an agent." And whether the caller got to speak with an agent or not, there was usually no attempt to capture the nature of the customer's issue for later attempts at resolution. There are exceptions to this, of course—in the past typically involving pre-generative forms of AI.[9]

A further attempt to reduce human customer service assistance came with the introduction of first live human text chat and then chatbots. Chat with humans often reduced the resolution time compared to calls, and—perhaps most appealing to companies—it allowed agents to handle chats with multiple customers at once. This was often frustrating to customers who had to wait for a response.

Fully automated chatbots, also known as *virtual assistants*, made their corporate customer service debut in the 2010s. One such chatbot, Ask Jenn at Alaska Airlines, answered more than 28 million customer questions—probably with greater and lesser degrees of success. Like IVR, chatbots can be frustrating to customers, but they are slowly becoming more capable. Smart companies allow frustrated customers to reach a human agent if a chatbot can't solve their problem. Some chatbots collect customer query content to understand where the chatbot fails and to improve its performance over time.

The next phase of chatbots is clearly represented by generative AI. We are still in the early days of applying generative AI to customer service, and we'll describe that further in Chapter 6, "Better Customer Voice Analysis and Action." But customers are justifiably skeptical. We've been promised better post-sale service from chatbots, AI-based knowledge management, and previous technologies as far back as the 1990s.[10] AI-enabled or not, however, customers remain dissatisfied with machines as customer service agents. A recent survey found, for example, that only 14% of customers would prefer to speak to an AI-based service system than to wait (between 1 and 11 minutes) for a human service agent.[11] We hope that generative AI will change that preference, but it's too early to tell whether it will.

---

[9] See, for example, Thomas H. Davenport, "Extracting Customer Support Knowledge with SupportLogic," *Forbes*, 29 October 2021, https://www.forbes.com/sites/tomdavenport/2021/10/29/extracting-customer-knowledge-with-supportlogic.

[10] Thomas H. Davenport and Philip Klahr, "Managing Customer Support Knowledge," *California Management Review*, Spring 1998, https://journals.sagepub.com/doi/10.2307/41165950.

[11] Christopher Zara, "AI Agents Are Taking Over Customer Service, but Most of Us Would Rather Wait for a Human," *Fast Company*, 30 April 2024, https://www.fastcompany.com/91115626/ai-chatbots-vs-humans-customer-service-tasks-survey-ratings.

From Index Cards to Customer Relationship Management Systems

A key technology that—once again—promised to revolutionize customer focus was the customer relationship management system (CRM). Initially developed in the 1980s and early 1990s, there were two primary types of customer transactions that CRM was designed to support. One was sales processes; that technology was initially called *sales force automation* (SFA) and was eventually wrapped into CRM systems. The idea of SFA was to enable salespeople to automate many time-consuming activities—entering orders, checking available inventory, monitoring their progress against goals—to free their time up to build customer relationships. It also served a valuable function for the organizations that implemented it, in that it shifted much customer information from index or Rolodex cards to a system of record. If the salesperson left, the customer information stayed with the company. That was, of course, one factor that inhibited many salespeople from adopting it.

The other primary function of CRM systems was automating customer service transactions. They enabled service departments to create "tickets" that kept track of service requests. It was relatively rare for the information in such systems to be analyzed. Instead, the focus was on automating service transactions. By the mid-1990s, vendors like the market-leading Siebel Systems (now owned by Oracle) had combined SFA and service capabilities and began to call it CRM. Some marketing functions were included as well in CRM, but again the focus was on transactional capabilities—campaign management, outbound offer delivery, and so forth. Few CRM systems had, for example, any ability to predict what a customer might do.

However, capturing the various forms of data involved in customer relationships was a big step forward for organizations. Having all or most transaction data in one place—ecommerce transactions were often not included—made it much easier to monitor, analyze, and act on customer behavior. Since the early days of CRM, cloud-based providers like Salesforce.com have added increasing numbers of functions, including data analysis and prediction, ecommerce, mobile access, and even some AI capabilities. Enterprise resource planning (ERP) providers like SAP and Oracle also added CRM offerings to their software suites, making it possible to connect financial, supply chain, and HR information to sales and service information.

From Multiple Databases to a Customer Data Platform

Places to store customer data have proliferated over time. As we've mentioned, CRM systems ended up being one repository, but they often didn't include content such as ecommerce transactions, social media comments, and customer emails. Many companies often had separate and overlapping customer databases for sales, marketing, service, and other functions. The "360-degree view of customers" concept became an objective again when vendors began to offer "customer data platforms." There are many versions of the concept, but the overall idea is, as Forrester Research describes, "A CDP centralizes customer data from multiple sources and makes it available to systems of insight and engagement."[12] This means that customer data is extracted from the transactional systems that gather it, collected in a CDP, and analyzed there for decisions and actions. The customer identifiers may differ slightly across these different sources, so some "identity resolution" is often necessary.

CDPs have, according to surveys of marketers, achieved high levels of adoption in organizations. A 2023 Gartner survey, for example, found that 67% of marketing technology respondents in companies, technology survey said they had installed a CDP. However, only 17% of marketers reported high utilization of the CDP.[13]

There are several reasons why utilization may have lagged. The effective use of CDPs requires a high level of discipline within an organization to aggregate customer data in one place, and even more to refine it over time to maintain and improve customer data quality. They also require a high level of collaboration across customer-related functions. Marketing departments, as the most analytical customer-oriented function, tend to be the primary beneficiary of CDPs, but other functions that deal with customers have to supply data in the right formats. In addition, a lot of investment is required before companies see returns on the investment in terms of increased customer purchases or loyalty.

Although we believe CDPs are a good idea, we haven't seen them revolutionize customer relationships yet. Perhaps the low level of utilization

---

[12] See, for example, "Explore the CDP Vendor Landscape in Asia Pacific," Forrester Research website, https://www.forrester.com/blogs/explore-the-cdp-vendor-landscape-in-asia-pacific.
[13] Hana Yoo, "CDPs Are in the Gartner Hype Cycle 'Trough of Disillusionment'" AdExchanger website, 22 February 2024, https://www.adexchanger.com/data-exchanges/cdps-are-in-the-gartner-hype-cycles-trough-of-disillusionment.

found in the Gartner survey is a factor in that not happening. CDPs are best suited for business-to-consumer (B2C) companies that have substantial amounts of first-party customer data. Business-to-business (B2B) companies typically have substantially fewer customers, and some are more important than others—perhaps weakening the case for onboarding all customers into a CDP. Companies that distribute through retailers or other intermediaries to consumers (B2B2C) typically have challenges in getting detailed data on their end consumers.

Nevertheless, some B2B2C companies are making progress toward customer data integration on CDPs. The consumer products giant Nestle, for example, reported to investors in 2022 that it planned to increase the number of consumer data profiles in its CDP from 248 million halfway through 2022 to more than 400 million by 2025.[14] This increase in customer data is consistent with the company's goals for direct consumer sales through ecommerce, which it hopes will reach 25% of revenues by 2025 (from about 16% in 2022). Nestle said it was already seeing substantial benefits (measured in individual country performance) from better consumer data, including a much lower cost-per-click in digital advertising, improvement in return-on-ad-spend, and better ad recall through content personalization.

If broad utilization of CDPs for customer data management spread through more organizations, it is likely that the organizations that can afford them will see considerable improvement in customer relationships and the ability to market, sell, and service customers effectively. If Nestle—a company that historically sold through retailers and did not possess much consumer data at all—can transform itself in this fashion, many other companies can, too.

Some vendors are beginning to argue for "composable" CDPs, which don't move data into a new platform but make it accessible from existing sources. Given the challenges of moving customer data into a single location, this may be an attractive option for some companies, although it is still in the early stages. Some organizations use the broader concept of "data fabric," a virtualized data layer that allows users to access data without moving it from its original location, such as a data lake, data warehouse,

---

[14] "Accelerating Our Data-Driven Digital Transformation," Nestle investor seminar 2022 presentation, https://www.nestle.com/sites/default/files/2022-11/investor-seminar-2022-digital-transformation.pdf.

relational database, or ERP system. Data fabric can also mix and integrate data from on-premises, cloud, and hybrid cloud platforms. A composable CDP is effectively a data fabric for customer data.

From Transactions to Analytics and AI

As customer data has gotten better over time, companies and other types of organizations have begun to use analytics and AI to understand, predict, and classify customer behaviors. Now, with generative AI, they can (with some cautionary steps) communicate directly with customers using AI. This is a big step forward and a primary purpose for which much customer data was gathered in the first place.

So what's the state of customer data analytics and AI? The technology itself for this purpose is well-established. Every company has access to the cloud processing and machine learning algorithms to analyze customer data and put it to work. They're even cheaper than they were in the past—largely because of open-source algorithms and cloud processing that doesn't require a big computer purchase. Many analytical tools are now mature (Table 1.3).

Table 1.3 Technologies for customer analytics and insights

Mature or obsolete	Well-established	Emerging
Predictive purchase models	Multi-channel attribution	Automated machine learning
Descriptive customer analytics	Next best offer	Deep learning models
Spreadsheet models	Personalized content	Generative AI-based models
Rule-based segmentation	Digital attribution	Generative AI chatbots
	Dynamic pricing	Gen AI sentiment analysis
	Churn modeling	Machine learning operations
	Sentiment analysis	
	Statistical segmentation	

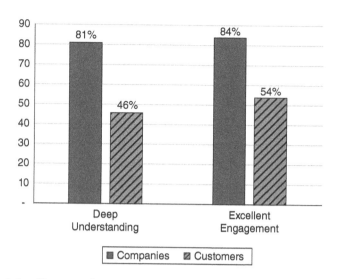

Figure 1.1 Companies vs. consumers perception gap.

Some other factors remain problematic, however. High-quality customer data, as we've discussed, is still hard to create. Data scientists— or even marketing, sales, or service professionals with a strong quantitative orientation—are still expensive and somewhat rare, at least outside of Silicon Valley. Business leaders in those domains may not be aware of what can be done in data-driven customer relationships.

The overall situation is that companies generally believe they are making considerable progress in analytics- and AI-based customer relationships, but that progress is not often noticed by customers (see Figure 1.1). For example, a 2024 survey conducted by CDP vendor Twilio found that while 81% of medium to large global companies say they have a deep understanding of their customers, less than half (46%) of global consumers agree.[15] Similarly, 84% of companies feel that they provide good or excellent customer engagement, but only 54% of consumers agree. We tend to side with the customers on this one and are only surprised that more than half are happy with the engagement level.

On the plus side, 64% of companies say they use AI to build a unified profile of every customer, and 70% say they're already using AI to personalize content and marketing offers. Among the companies that have adopted AI,

---

[15] 2024 State of Customer Engagement Report, Twilio, https://www.twilio.com/en-us/state-of-customer-engagement/report.

45% have seen improved customer satisfaction scores, 41% report better data-driven decision-making, and 41% experienced improved market segmentation and targeting.

Again, however, consumers aren't quite as bullish on AI. While 85% of the company executives surveyed "strongly/moderately" agree that AI will enhance customer engagement, only 22% of consumers share that degree of optimism. This suggests that companies attempting to measure their progress in this domain should at least occasionally ask their customers what they think about it.

Among the challenges to customer science—using data, analytics, and AI to better understand and target offers to customers—company executives mentioned "responding to changing customer needs/preferences" (44%); "connecting customer data across channels and sources" (42%); "navigating compliance and data privacy standards" (41%); and "turning data into customer insights" (40%). In other words, despite some progress, many organizations still struggle with effective customer science.

A New Era of Customer Science

Although we've described an environment for customer science that has promised great advances but delivered only spotty progress, we're optimistic about the future for several reasons. As we've discussed, organizations have been putting the foundations in place for data and its effective management. There is still more progress needed in customer data, but let's say we are halfway there. Even with the data that's already in place, companies like Nestle are making considerable progress toward more effective marketing, online sales, and customer-oriented decisions.

Another factor that gives us hope for a brighter future is artificial intelligence. It has been present in customer contexts for several decades now, but there is increased maturity and capability in traditional "analytical" AI, and now of course the highly innovative and rapidly maturing generative AI. We believe that both types of AI have a bright future in enhancing customer engagement and relationships, and we'll describe their impact throughout this book.

We're also optimistic because companies are becoming more data-driven in their cultures and decision-making. In 2024, an annual survey of data and analytics leaders in which Tom participates revealed a major change from the previous year. The percentage of company executives (primarily chief data/analytics/AI officers in large companies) reporting their organizations had "established a data and analytics culture" increased from 21 to 43% over the previous year. The organizations that had "created a data-driven organization" doubled from 24% in 2023's survey to 48% in 2024's. This was far more improvement than at any time over the 12-year history of the survey; the percentages had languished at the same level or even decreased over the previous few years. Tom and his survey colleague, Randy Bean, argued that the change was primarily driven by generative AI.[16]

However, in the thirteenth version of the survey (labeled 2025), the numbers fell back to earth a bit. In that survey, 37% indicated that they work in a data- and AI-driven organization, and 33% said that organization has a data- and AI-driven culture.[17] It appears that generative AI alone was not quite enough to create lasting cultural and organizational change. In fact, another question in the same survey asks what the principal barrier to becoming data-driven is in their companies. Ninety-two percent say that people/culture/change management issues are at fault; only 8% blame technology.

Of course, the key to success in science-driven customer relationships is to take a holistic approach across the organization. This transformation needs to encompass multiple business functions, channels, technologies, and customer-related activities if it is going to be successful. It needs to address organizational and cultural issues as much as technological ones. In the next chapter, we'll describe two companies that have addressed all of these issues and made effective use of technology for customer relationships. One did it for a while but has fallen back a bit; the other is still going strong.

---

[16] Thomas H. Davenport and Randy Bean, "Survey: Gen AI Is Making Companies More Data Oriented," *Harvard Business Review*, 15 January 2024, https://hbr.org/2024/01/surv ey-genai-is-making-companies-more-data-oriented.

[17] Data and AI Leadership Exchange, "2025 AI & Data Leadership Executive Benchmark Survey," January 2025, https://static1.squarespace.com/static/62adf3ca029a6808a6c5be30/ t/67642c0d40b42a7d7e684f49/1734618125933/2025+AI+%26+Data+Leadership+Execu tive+Benchmark+Survey+120624.pdf.

2

The Future Is Here, but Unevenly Distributed

Why do so few organizations have effective and highly customer science approaches? It's certainly not because the idea of doing so isn't well-known. As we've said, the concept of "one-to-one marketing" with technology that makes it possible has been discussed for decades. Some companies— the two we discuss in this chapter, for example—have done it well, but most have not.

What's lacking isn't the idea or a single technology—even generative AI—that would make the idea feasible. It's a long-term commitment to really knowing your customer, learning and recording the salient information about them, and using data and technology to try to make their lives better using your products and services. As we'll discuss, there are cool technologies like generative AI that can certainly make it easier to personalize your websites, ads, and offers. But a lot of underlying pieces have to be implemented before the sexy stuff can be effective.

In this chapter, we'll discuss two basic capabilities that need to be in place before you can have targeted, effective, personalized marketing. First is the infrastructure of data and technology upon which everything else must be built. Depending upon where your organization is today in building infrastructure, that can take quite a while.

Companies that are successful with customer science have also built a human infrastructure to support that objective, and a culture and organizational structure that gets it done. Because both the technical and the human infrastructure can feel somewhat abstract, we'll describe a case study at Caesars Entertainment in which both were well-constructed. For the glamorous AI and augmented reality capabilities, we will describe the customer technology and data environment at beauty products retailer Sephora. Fortunately, these two companies provide a view today (or in Caesars' case, yesterday) of what most organizations will need to be successful with these capabilities in the future.

Technical and Human Infrastructure at Caesars

Gary Loveman was a professor at Harvard Business School in 1998 (and a friend and neighbor of Tom's). His specialty was "service management," or the study of service industry companies, which was big at Harvard for a while but for no good reason no longer exists. Specifically, he and his colleagues were focused on the "service profit chain," which argued that if companies treat their employees well, they'll provide high-quality service to customers, and those customers will buy more and be more loyal, and the company will make more money. Not surprisingly for a PhD in economics from MIT, Loveman was passionate about the value of data and analytics in decision-making.

In 1998 Loveman was consulting to Phil Satre, the CEO of Harrah's Entertainment (then both a hotel and casino company), and Satre had a crazy idea. He wanted to hire Loveman as COO of Harrah's—not the type of offer that regularly comes to business school professors. Even less commonly, Satre also wanted Loveman to be chief marketing officer (CMO). He felt that Loveman might become his successor as CEO, and that the exposure to both operations and marketing functions would make Loveman a better leader of the company.

Thus began an era of change in Harrah's that would make it a customer-obsessed gaming firm that would eventually become the largest in the world. Loveman began to build both a technical and data infrastructure, and a human one as well, that would transform the company.

One of the company's problems when Loveman arrived was, in his words, "We were collecting tons of data, but not using it." Harrah's had a customer loyalty program that ultimately totaled more than 40 million members, and a database of those customers, but the program was managed locally at each casino, and Harrah's wasn't using the database beyond capturing transactions and making direct mail offers to high-rollers. The company also had another underutilized asset: a network of casinos across the United States that acted independently in terms of marketing.

Loveman expanded the network of casinos both within the United States and globally and encouraged cross-market play through promotions and incentives. The company also increased its focus on gathering and using customer information and rewarding loyal customers (see Figure 2.1). He got Harrah's to begin its focus on the history, tastes, and preferences of all its customers, not just the high spenders. It also began to offer promotions and offers that were targeted to particular customer segments and behaviors. Eventually the company would define and track hundreds of customer segments. Because marketing offers were perceived as valuable by customers, there were no complaints. "I have never had a customer complain about the information we collect and use for marketing purposes," Loveman noted in one interview with Tom.

Some of the transactional information wasn't up to the new marketing requirements, so Loveman asked his IT department to implement a new ERP system. The IT organization made the loyalty program (initially Total Gold, then Total Rewards) integrated and portable across all casinos. The company developed its own CRM system that encompassed casino play of various types, hotels, an enterprise data warehouse, analytics, and all channels and touchpoints to customers. A "closed-loop" approach to data-driven

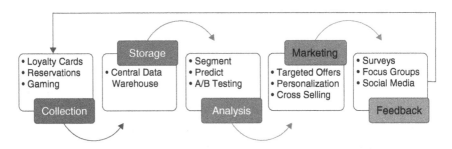

Figure 2.1 Simplified Harrah's data flow.

marketing was developed that collected all customer activity, reported on and analyzed it, predicted it, created segments with tests and control groups, drove marketing interventions, and inspired new customer activity. A new "Player Contact System" tracked all communications and interactions with loyal customers. All offers and "comped" hotel rooms could be accessed online. Support for the web and mobile apps was developed and added to the portfolio. A hotel pricing optimization system was implemented with automatic pricing discounts and availability levels based on customer spending. These infrastructural capabilities were all focused on servicing their loyal customers with a differentiated experience from initial contact through departure.

New metrics were established and made available throughout the business. In keeping with the "service profit chain" philosophy, there were multiple metrics available for financial goals, customer segmentation and promotion performance, product and program performance (including test and control reporting), and customer satisfaction.

Harrah's acquired multiple casino properties and made its largest single expansion when it acquired Caesars Entertainment in 2005, changing its name to Caesars a couple of years later. At Caesars and the previously acquired companies, Loveman and his colleagues found that there was a 10–25% increase in revenue when the Harrah's technology and data capabilities were added to the acquired properties.

A key focus was on data collection about customers. "We collect all the transactional data when customers are with us," said Gary Loveman, Caesars chairman and CEO, speaking on CNBC's *Squawk Box*. That included every purchase and gaming activity at the company's restaurants, casinos, shows, spas, and golf courses, as well as spending at other properties of the gaming and entertainment company. "We're trying to predict the things that will interest customers based on demographics and their revealed behavior," Loveman said.

The Human Infrastructure at Caesars

This capability to capture, manage, and exploit customer data required investments not only in technology but also in analytically talented people. After he came to the company, Loveman began to hire a variety of executives with an analytical bent. Fortunately, Tom came to know many of these individuals through his research at Caesars. Most had relatively little experience in the gaming industry, which despite being based on probability did not have many analytically focused leaders. Indeed, Loveman once commented to Tom that one of his greatest mistakes as CEO was retaining too many of the existing management team, rather than hiring new and data-driven leaders.

One of his first hires as chief operations and marketing officer, for example, was Tim Stanley, who became CIO and held several other senior management roles. Stanley was instrumental in making the infrastructure and technology changes we've already described. He was well-suited to the role, having previously been an airline CIO, an early ecommerce company executive, an Intel product manager, and a research scientist for a consumer products company.

Loveman also brought on Rich Mirman as VP of relationship marketing. He had an academic background in economics and math and had been a management consultant before joining Harrah's. He later became chief marketing officer and chief business development officer (overseeing acquisitions) of Caesars. He's now CEO of a firm offering "dynamic loyalty" programs to other companies.

Loveman also hired Katrina Lane, an Ivy League PhD in experimental physics who had previously been a McKinsey consultant and head of marketing for a clothing company. She describes her two roles on LinkedIn this way:

Senior Vice President and Chief Technology Officer: Responsible for the company's efforts around the creation, enhancement and utilization of technology and capabilities to drive business objectives. Specific groups include innovation, gaming, IT application development, infrastructure, security, support for customer facing systems, and all company web sites. Also responsible for key initiatives to develop new technical capabilities for the Total Rewards loyalty program. Responsible for the company's efforts around the creation, enhancement and utilization of technology and capabilities to drive business objectives. Specific groups include innovation, gaming, IT application development, infrastructure, security, support for customer facing systems, and all company web sites. Also responsible for key initiatives to develop new technical capabilities for the Total Rewards loyalty program.

VP of Channel Marketing: Responsibilities include CRM, tele-services, internet marketing, website operations, email marketing, mobile marketing, media planning and buying and marketing analysis.

Loveman also created a new role for Reuben Sigala, making him the senior vice president of enterprise analytics at Caesars. In this role, Sigala was responsible for managing the analytical functions of more than 50 Caesars properties worldwide. He worked closely with operations and shared services to identify opportunities for analytics, oversaw business development and strategic planning, and supervised a staff of 200 people. Sigala still works with Loveman at a consumer healthcare analytics company called Well.

Finally, in this list of stars, Loveman brought on David Norton as chief marketing officer. Norton had an MBA and another master's degree in technology and had worked for American Express, an analytics-driven company to which Katrina Lane moved after leaving Caesars. His LinkedIn page lists a variety of accomplishments at Harrah's/Caesars, but they include the following:

- Led the innovation of the Total Rewards program, CRM, digital marketing, VIP marketing, revenue management, sales, entertainment, brand, and media.
- VIP revenue expanded 20% to $2B in revenue, and customer satisfaction increased from 65 to 80%.
- The CEO [Loveman] tasked me with developing a sophisticated yield management system with gaming and room rates. Developed a model that granularly predicted demand and set the room rates. Evolved the model to support a market view as additional casinos were acquired. This achieved 100% adoption, which led to $50M in annual recurring EBITDA.

When times got tough at Caesars—more on that in a moment—Norton cites another achievement:

- Post-economic crisis, significant revenue declines occurred, threatening bankruptcy. I led analytics and research to understand customer behavior and a task force to redefine the VIP player experience, re-engineered marketing/operational activities, and migrated to a centralized approach to maximize profitability and drive efficiency. These efforts trimmed $200M in cost reductions, increased VIP satisfaction, and was recognized as Chief Marketing Officer of the Year (2010) by *CMO Magazine*.

Caesars had about 50,000 employees, and you'll be glad to hear that we're not going to describe all of them. But even the servers of food and drink—important in any casino—had somewhat different jobs than in most hospitality companies. The company had a very strong focus on customer satisfaction, and data analysis determined that two factors had great influence on a customer's happiness when visiting a Caesars property (other than winning at the gambling tables or slot machines, which Loveman did not want to encourage). One was the rapidity with which drinks were delivered, and the company developed a mobile device drink ordering system in which all sorts of alarms went off if a drink wasn't delivered within 5 minutes of being ordered. The other important factor was whether service personnel smiled at customers, and Caesars constantly reminded servers to smile and even measured them on this attribute.

Customer Loyalty and Segmentation

Loveman had done considerable research in his academic career on the benefits of improving customer service and loyalty, and he was initially hired in part because of his expertise in the area. The company didn't have a lot of resources at the time, and building customer loyalty was one of its few options, as Loveman explained in the CNBC interview. "We were going to take transaction data from customers, we were going to model this data using inferential methods, and we were going to use it to suggest to customers to make visits they otherwise wouldn't make, or Donald Trump was going to buy us" (and perhaps send them into bankruptcy even earlier, as he did with his Atlantic City casinos). Caesars did those things successfully and had increasingly added more functionality to the customer analytics program. For example, beginning in 2012, the program was expanded considerably to address guests' nongaming activities, including dining and entertainment.

An early focus of the analytical team was to segment customers. Conventional wisdom around the industry suggested that "whales"—big spenders—from Asia were Caesars' most profitable customers. However, detailed analysis suggested that the most profitable customers were elderly women from Philadelphia, or more generally living within an hour's driving distance of a Caesars resort. These customers had time, disposable income, and a preference for high-profit slot machines. Caesars' marketing efforts were redirected with a specific focus on this type of customer. The goal was to induce them not only to visit a close-by casino like Atlantic City but also to travel to further-away resorts in their network like those in Las Vegas.

The segmentation of customers, however, was typically based on much more than a single attribute. Customer segments, of which Caesars had hundreds, were based not only on expressed customer preferences but also on their actions while at a Caesars property, including whether they had experienced a winning day or a losing one. In many cases, the data revealed surprising, counterintuitive trends. Wealthy people might have unsophisticated culinary tastes, while less affluent patrons felt the need to try the latest fusion cuisine. One slot player liked a game that has frequent and small payouts, while another preferred the jackpot machine and had a world of patience.

Caesars was constantly experimenting and learning about its customers. A typical Caesars marketing approach was to employ particular promotions and offers as a test. An offer to visit the Caesars casino in Las Vegas, for example, would offer a certain hotel rate or inducement to attend a Kenny Rogers show. If the customer didn't respond, the next hotel rate or show inducement might be a bit more valuable. If the customer did accept the promotion at a certain level, the next promotion to that customer might be somewhat less generous. Through careful attention to what offers were made to customers and their behavior in response, Caesars could build a high level of knowledge about what customers really wanted and how much their business is worth to the company. As Loveman put it in an MIT presentation, "We're running experiments to see what people are willing to do on the margin."

As a result of these experiments, Caesars had hundreds of models built for predicting customer behavior and value to the franchise. These models were highly contextualized and could be reinvoked when similar conditions existed. For example, if certain incentives applied to visitors at Caesars' Las Vegas facilities, similar incentives were likely to work in Atlantic City when the conditions and the segment were similar.

Caesars increasingly used analytics and data to respond to customer behavior in real time for marketing and service applications. For example, the company combined data about its customers from its Total Rewards loyalty program, from web clickstreams, and from real-time play in slot machines. It had traditionally used all those data sources to understand customers, but it had been difficult to integrate and act on them in real time, while the customer was still playing at a slot machine or in the resort. The company had found that when a new member of Total Rewards had an unlucky session at a slot machine, for example, the customer was unlikely to return to Caesars. If, however, the slot machine printed an offer for dinner at a nearby buffet while the customer stood in front of it, the customer was dramatically more likely to return to Caesars for another visit.

As technology changed, Caesars' approach to data and analytics changed as well. The company embraced mobile technology and began to offer targeted real-time offers over the mobile channel. As websites proliferated, it created a unified approach to web analytics. When social media took off, Caesars began to unite information from customers coming through social channels across business units, program teams, time zones, and languages. A content-building component allowed marketers to listen in and respond in real time. Whether customer interactions originated in social media networks, from search queries, or by clicks on display ads, engagement was a key factor in moving those interactions from the top of the sales funnel to an eventual purchase.

The Decline of Caesars

Just like the Roman Empire, Caesars Entertainment eventually fell on hard times. As Norton's cost-cutting initiative suggests, visits to the company's casinos declined precipitously during the 2007–2009 financial crisis. To make matters much worse, Caesars was bought by two private equity firms in 2008 for a total price (including fees) of $31B. Caesars took on $20.5B in debt financing. Given the unfortunate timing (the deal was initially proposed in 2006, before the recession), Caesars found it difficult to pay the interest on its debt load, and one of its two business units declared bankruptcy in 2015.

Gary Loveman told Tom that although the team evaluating the private equity deal had done considerable analysis, the economy proved to be substantially worse than the team's most pessimistic estimates. He also said that he would have been fired because of a shareholder revolt if he had vetoed the deal. Loveman said one of his worst decisions at the company was not buying a license available to Caesars in the Chinese gambling mecca of Macau. The property was viewed after considerable analysis at the time as being too expensive, but in retrospect it would have been a good acquisition. The modeling that led to the decision to pass failed to anticipate the historic growth in wealth that occurred in coastal China and its impact on gaming revenues in Macau. Both of these major decisions could not ultimately be based on data analysis, since Caesars had never made previous decisions of that type.

Loveman stepped down as CEO in 2015 and remained chairman of Caesars until 2017. After he departed, there was less interest among company executives in data, analytics, and technology. One of his legacies was that the Total Rewards loyalty program was valued by bankruptcy creditors at a billion dollars—more than any other single asset at the company.

Caesars after Loveman continued to make some investments in analytics and AI, though they were relatively incremental compared to previous years. The company experimented with emotion recognition AI on customer reactions at slot machines, for example, and used AI to personalize marketing messages to customers. However, we will have to look elsewhere for examples of best practice in customer science using technologies available only in the last decade. The Caesars story reveals that one aspect of effective use of data, analytics, and AI technologies is a consistent set of priorities over the long run. In many cases that can be achieved only through consistent leadership.

Customer Science at Sephora

Our example of a company that is using customer science effectively to know and engage with their customers is the beauty and cosmetics chain Sephora (perhaps needless to say, neither of us is a customer). Like Caesars, Sephora—founded in France in 1970 and now a global retailer—has been pursuing better customer experiences and engagement with data and technology for a long time. The company launched its first website in the United States in 1999 and has been innovating with technology ever since. Sephora institutionalized a technology innovation capability when it opened its Innovation Lab in San Francisco in 2015. Still based in France, it is generally ranked the top beauty and personal care products retailer in the world.

Also like Caesars, Sephora has a loyalty program for its best customers. Called the Beauty Insider program (members are VIBs, or Very Important Beauty insiders), it is reserved for customers who spend $350 or more at Sephora in a calendar year. They receive exclusive and personalized promotions and gifts, get invitations to events, and can participate in VIB-only sales.

Sephora's industry is based on sensory and visual experience, which is difficult to create in a digital commerce setting. But AI and related tools make possible a highly personalized shopping experience. At Sephora, this translates into tools like augmented reality mirrors and mobile apps that enable customers to virtually try on products, visualize looks, and receive personalized recommendations based on their facial features and personal preferences.

For example, Sephora's Color IQ service provides a high level of personalization for customers. It employs image analysis technology to scan the customer's face (in store or online) to classify her skin tone. Based on this classification, it recommends makeup colors and types that will be a good match for the customer's skin.

Skincare IQ, a related offering, asks customers to identify their specific skin concerns (such as dark circles under eyes, dryness, visible pores) and then suggests products to help alleviate those issues. The recommendations can be received in-store or online. Sephora has announced a new skincare offering called Skincredible, a new skin diagnostic based on a mobile phone app that addresses and diagnoses a variety of facial skin issues.

Sephora's mobile app, called Sephora to Go, is the channel for the Virtual Artist offering, which allows customers to augment the appearance of their faces by adding various makeup and beauty products in thousands of different shades and styles to their images. Customers can also watch and apply beauty tutorials on their own faces digitally. If Visual Artist leads to a desire to purchase, the customer can either buy the products online or go to a store to try them on their faces IRL (in real life). Virtual Artist was launched in 2016 in collaboration with a tech start-up called ModiFace, and it has been regularly updated with new features since then.

These applications—and the products that customers actually buy—provide customers with a personalized and engaging experience, but they also provide Sephora with considerable data on the customer. That data and analysis of it can fuel an ongoing stream of personalized emails or text messages recommending new or familiar products to customers. In a broader sense, the customer data enables Sephora to identify and develop new products that are tailored to the expressed needs of customers. The company also uses the data to fuel AI-driven personalized landing pages based on search queries. If a customer mentions "sensitive skin" in the query, the landing page will focus on products for that issue.

Of course, the capture and use of this data raises both regulatory and customer privacy concerns. Sephora has to ensure that the data is used in ways that satisfy both legal obligations and customer expectations for value in exchange for data collected. In addition, the visual applications that the company offers raise challenges with regard to how skin tone and texture data is rendered on different customer technologies. If the customer's camera is of poor quality or damaged, for example, the customer could receive inaccurate recommendations for matching makeup. In addition, the recommendations made online must be consistent with those made in the store.

Sephora is also beginning to use generative AI in some countries as a means of engaging with customers. For example, the company uses that technology to send customized beauty recommendations to customers based on their purchase history and preferences. The company has also experimented with generative AI and other natural language AI technologies to create chatbots for customers, although it does not seem to have a consistent approach to chatbots globally. In France, for example, there is a chatbot intended for millennials called Ora that answers both administrative questions (store locations, order tracking, product availability, etc.) as well as acting as a virtual beauty coach with tutorials and tips. Applications such as these require not only generative AI but also linkages to solid transactional systems. Sephora's back-end technology infrastructure includes enterprise resource planning (ERP) software from SAP and customer relationship management (CRM) from Salesforce.

The Human Tech and Data Infrastructure at Sephora

We don't know the people at Sephora who make these customer science approaches happen the way we did at Caesars, but there is plenty of evidence that they are on the leading edge. Sephora's Innovation Lab in San Francisco is the hub for people who identify and develop many of the technologies we've mentioned, although there are also skilled technologists in particular countries where Sephora does business. At the Innovation Lab, a capable group—hired from the marketing, product development, and technology industries—sources, develops, evaluates, tests, and ultimately launches new offerings and technologies for shopping in the store and online. In most cases the focus is a consistent and coherent omnichannel customer experience. Innovation Lab people are focused on various technologies and topics, including machine learning, data science, systems and data engineering, web, social, and loyalty analytics, technology integration, and in-store offerings.

The Innovation Lab is also the center of efforts to build an ecosystem of external providers for leading technology capabilities. We've mentioned the partnership with ModiFace for augmented facial reality, and there are partners for chatbots, cloud services, machine learning platforms, and many other tools. Not surprisingly given its customer base, Sephora also uses or partners with social media platforms like Instagram, Facebook, Twitter, YouTube, Pinterest, Snapchat, and TikTok to build brand awareness and loyalty.

In short, Sephora has both the technical and human capabilities necessary to be successful with customer science and to generate and act on customer insights with analytics and AI. The company also has a strong understanding of both online and offline customer behavior, and it builds online and store-based engagement with a variety of leading-edge technologies. It's no wonder that Sephora dominates the category of retail beauty products.

Lessons from Caesars and Sephora

Companies that want to be good at customer science need to display a set of attributes that were present for many years at Caesars and continue to be present at Sephora. They include the following:

- **Investing in basic technology and data infrastructure:** Companies in every business need to keep up-to-date in basic infrastructure. They need to minimize technical debt, establish a high level of data integration and quality, and manage technology and data with consistency over time and across their operations.

- **Gather the data, analyze the data:** Companies need not only to gather and store customer-oriented data, but also to use analytics and AI technology to make sense of it and provide valuable offerings to customers. The skills for these two objectives are often different, but neither is valuable without the other.

- **Hire and keep the right people:** Just as important as the technology and data infrastructure is the human one to build it and maintain it over time. Particularly in the area of analytics and AI, talent is expensive and relatively scarce. Caesars and Sephora have managed to attract and retain high-quality talent that understands both their businesses and how to advance them with data and technology.

- **Every channel, omnichannel:** No matter the primary way companies begin to interact with customers, it is now important for them to address them through every channel: in-store, online, mobile, social, etc. Each possible channel has benefits and drawbacks with regard to customer relationships and communications (see Table 2.1). Since each of these channels involve different technologies, a company will need to continually involve its architectures to include them. Ideally the customer should see the same data, promotions, and offers regardless of the channel they employ.

- **Never stop personalizing:** As we've mentioned throughout this book, personalization can be approached in a variety of ways, and there are always additional personalization approaches that are possible. Offers, channels, pricing, rewards, and content can all be personalized now, and companies that don't do so will be penalized in the marketplace.

- **Don't slack off:** Caesars illustrates the importance of continual focus on technology and data by not doing it well. New management was much less focused on the issue than the team assembled by Gary Loveman had been. As a result, the company has languished a bit. Sephora has illustrated a more consistent focus on these capabilities over time and has remained at the top of its industry.

Table 2.1 Omnichannel customer communication methods compared

Channel	Primary use case	Audience reach potential	Cost (low/ medium/high)	Personalization capability	Integration complexity
Email	Customer engagement, promotions	Broad	Low	High	Medium
Social media	Brand awareness, real-time engagement	High	Medium	Medium	Medium
Website	Information hub, ecommerce	Unlimited	Medium	High	High
SMS/MMS	Timely alerts, promotions	Targeted	Low	High	Medium
Mobile app	Loyalty programs, in-app purchases	Targeted	High	High	High
Live chat	Customer support, real-time assistance	Medium	Medium	High	Medium
Call center	Customer service, complex inquiries	Medium	High	Medium	Medium

(continued)

Table 2.1 (Continued)

Channel	Primary use case	Audience reach potential	Cost (low/medium/high)	Personalization capability	Integration complexity
Direct mail	Promotions, customer loyalty campaigns	Targeted	Medium	Low	Low
In-store experience	Personal touch, upselling	Limited to store visitors	High	High	High
Push notifications	Timely updates, personalized alerts	Targeted	Low	High	Medium
Voice assistants	Hands-free interaction, FAQs	Growing	Medium	Medium	Medium
Video (YouTube)	Tutorials, brand storytelling	Broad	Medium	Low	Medium
Podcasts	Thought leadership, storytelling	Niche	Medium	Low	Low
Webinars	Lead generation, customer education	Targeted	Medium	Medium	Medium

Events (virtual)	Networking, product launches	Targeted	High	Medium	High
Events (physical)	Relationship building, brand immersion	Limited to attendees	High	Medium	High
Affiliate marketing	Third-party endorsements	Broad	Medium	Low	Medium
Online reviews	Social proof, reputation management	Broad	Low	Low	Low
Influencer marketing	Brand advocacy, niche markets	Niche	High	Medium	Medium

The following chapters will describe the specific areas and applications that will make possible this science-driven approach to improving customer relationships. We'll start with the most dramatic change of late: better AI in the form of generative AI language models. Neither Caesars nor Sephora have yet fully taken advantage of this technology, but we expect both organizations will do so eventually and that it will have transformative effects on their customer relationships.

3

Better AI: Generative AI as a Catalyst for Change

Generative AI has arrived to push the next evolution in data-informed customer relationships. It's about to turn customer communication on its head.

Generative AI (GenAI) is a transformative force that will redefine creativity and decision-making. It will bring about greater potential changes in customer relationships than any technology since the Internet. But before offering a clear explanation of what generative AI is and how it works, we need to deal with the extremes at either end of the hype spectrum.

It is our belief that generative AI is not going to become sentient anytime soon and will certainly not take over the world. It is also not going to solve all our problems and help us turn the earth into a paradise where everybody is happily pursuing self-actualization. We believe that generative AI will primarily be a tool for augmenting human work, not replacing it—though there will undoubtedly be exceptions. We think, for example, that some customer service workers are likely to be replaced by GenAI.

A great many people are working hard to implement guardrails and controls. The inherent threat of a teenager propelling a 2-ton machine at

60 miles an hour down the road with nothing between them and an oncoming teenager doing the same thing but a stripe of paint on the road terrifies every parent. But we have speed limits, seatbelts, and airbags, not to mention traffic laws and traffic cops, to mitigate the danger. Some governments are working on similar controls for AI. Unfortunately, the US Congress is not among them. We believe that's regrettable, even though we think it's unlikely that they would do a great job in crafting AI regulations. It's anyone's guess as to whether bad regulations are better than none at all.

GenAI is at the start of reshaping society and business in substantial ways. It's opening doors to creativity like never before, but with great power comes waves of uncertainty—especially in the job market. Creative roles that once seemed untouchable are now being reimagined,[1] raising questions about what it means to create and who owns the output. There's a real risk that intentional and unintentional biases and errors slip in, sometimes leading to harm.

For all its faults, fears, and flaws, generative AI is undoubtedly a power tool for improving how we attract, persuade, and serve customers. It lets companies create dynamic, context-aware text, images, voices, and videos that adapt in real time to individual customer needs and preferences, all in multiple languages. This is much more than straight machine translation. It doesn't just translate words but understands cultural nuances. It's the difference between a translator and an interpreter, like a local guide who knows the customs as well as the language.

Customer Interaction Revolution

Generative AI, despite its youth, is already revolutionizing customer contact in a variety of ways, including the following:

- **Language and culture:** From translation to culturally nuanced communication, it is enhancing global customer engagement. GenAI can bridge language barriers with nuanced, culturally aware communication. It can understand and translate idioms, slang, and

---

[1] Epstein, Z., Hertzmann, A., Herman, L., Mahari, R., Frank, M., Groh, M., Schroeder, H., Smith, A., Akten, M., Fjeld, J., Farid, H., Leach, N., Pentland, A., & Russakovsky, O. (2023). Art and the science of generative AI. *Science* 380: 1110–1111. https://doi.org/10.1126/science.adh4451.

cultural references more accurately, preserving the original meaning and tone unlike simple machine translation. That ensures that marketing messages, customer support, and product information resonate authentically with diverse audiences worldwide. "To help more people get jobs, Indeed evolved its content production pipeline from a fully human workflow to one that begins with AI. They've been using LLMs to generate multilingual content from scratch instead of translating the original copy into multiple languages and then passing it on to human editors for quality assurance and fine-tuning."[2]

- **Personalization:** It can produce highly individualized content, product recommendations, and customer experiences at scale. An example from Amazon involves shopping assistance:

  Rufus is now available to all US customers in the Amazon Shopping app. (See Figure 3.1.)

  August 27, 2024: Rufus is currently rolling out to US customers on desktop.

  Earlier this year, we introduced Rufus, our new generative AI-powered conversational shopping assistant. Rufus is designed to help customers save time and make more informed purchase decisions by answering questions on a variety of shopping needs and products right in the Amazon Shopping app—it's like having a shopping assistant with you any time you're in our store. We're pleased to share that Rufus is now available to all US customers in the Amazon Shopping app, and is currently rolling out on desktop.[3]

- **Customer service:** GenAI can do complex query handling and proactive issue resolution. Octopus Energy is using generative AI to draft customer emails, seeing an 18% boost in customer happiness scores compared to human-only responses. GenAI is reportedly handling a third of all their inquiry emails, freeing up their human agents to tackle more nuanced topics.[4]

---

[2] https://phrase.com/blog/posts/chatgpt-translation.

[3] https://www.aboutamazon.com/news/retail/how-to-use-amazon-rufus.

[4] https://www.bcg.com/publications/2023/how-generative-ai-transforms-customer-service.

Figure 3.1 Amazon's Rufus is a GenAI shopping assistant.

- **Marketing:** It enables hyper-personalized marketing messaging. Arts and crafts retailer Michaels implemented a personalization strategy across SMS, Facebook, and email channels. Their AI platform generates personalized content by analyzing Michaels' brand voice and customer data, predicting which messages would resonate best with individual "makers" (Michaels' customers).[5]
- **Sales:** Need automated lead nurturing? ICICI Bank in India is using generative AI to personalize email marketing and boost sales. They're not just solving low engagement and poor conversion rates. Their GenAI can understand and solve problems, powered by machine

---

[5] https://www.mckinsey.com/capabilities/growth-marketing-and-sales/our-insights/how-generative-ai-can-boost-consumer-marketing.

learning and natural language processing to tailor content, predict customer behavior, and even learn from each interaction. As a result, they're offering real-time customer support at scale, rising sales, and happier customers.[6]

The food service distributor Sysco maintains nearly 2 million SKUs, about 200,000 of which are in high demand among customers. The firm has been leveraging traditional AI and analytics to make product recommendations, but generative AI can incorporate unstructured data, such as images or social media data, to capture additional signals. "This will help us be even more creative feeding the shopping cart for our customers," Peck said. "We are starting to see bigger shopping carts and higher margins by turning traditional AI into more generative AI."[7]

- **Sentiment analysis:** GenAI produces adaptive responses that cater to the emotional state of the customer, enhancing empathy in interactions. Airbnb leverages generative AI for sentiment analysis to monitor guest-host interactions, gaining real-time insights into customer experiences and identifying areas for improvement. This allows the company to continuously refine its services based on attitude trends to deliver tailored, high-quality experiences.[8]

GenAI is poised to revolutionize customer contact by applying one or more specific capabilities of which the technology is capable:

- **Voice and video interactions:** It allows more natural and human-like interactions, automating customer service. As generative AI advances, we're seeing more natural and human-like interactions in voice and video formats. AI-powered virtual assistants can engage in fluid conversations, understanding context and nuance far better than their predecessors. In video interactions, AI can generate realistic avatars or even entire video content, opening up new possibilities for personalized video marketing or customer support. These

---

[6] https://landbot.io/blog/top-examples-generative-ai-in-sales-processes.

[7] https://mitsloan.mit.edu/ideas-made-to-matter/incorporating-generative-ai-your-companys-technology-strategy.

[8] https://www.netscribes.com/artificial-intelligence-ai-in-sentiment-analysis-and-industry-use-cases.

technologies are making automated customer interactions feel more genuine and engaging.

- **Predictive insights:** It can handle proactive management of potential issues or offers of relevant solutions. GenAI can anticipate customer needs, identify potential issues before they arise, and suggest relevant solutions or offers proactively. This capability allows businesses to stay one step ahead, whether it's predicting when a customer might churn, identifying cross-sell opportunities, or forecasting emerging trends in customer preferences. By leveraging these insights, companies can create more proactive and value-added customer experiences.

- **Dynamic FAQs:** It makes possible dynamic, personalized knowledge bases based on evolving customer inquiries and trends. One-size-fits-all FAQs don't fit anybody. Dynamic, personalized knowledge bases that evolve based on customer inquiries and trends feels inevitable. Smart FAQs can understand the context of a customer's journey, their past interactions, and current needs to provide highly relevant information. They can also identify gaps in the existing knowledge base and suggest new content, ensuring that the FAQ system continuously improves and remains up-to-date.

- **Co-creation of products:** With GenAI companies can tailor products and services more closely to individual desires. Customer-centricity can include involving customers in product development. By analyzing customer feedback, usage data, and market trends, AI can suggest product improvements or entirely new features. It can even generate product concepts based on customer preferences. This collaborative approach, where customer input is actively integrated into the design process, can result in products that more closely align with individual desires and market needs.

In short, GenAI fundamentally changes how businesses connect with consumers. The potential for creating more meaningful, emotionally resonant brand-consumer relationships is significant. Companies have only just begun to explore the possibilities for increased personalization and engagement from the technology.

However, it also has its share of challenges like maintaining brand authenticity, ensuring the ethical use of customer data, balancing efficiency with true human interaction, and mitigating the potential for these systems to hallucinate. These are not unsurmountable problems but need to be kept in mind when plunging forward with our latest, shiny new object.

To fully understand the astonishing potential and the potential hazards, it's important for businesspeople who focus on customers to have a basic understanding of what generative AI actually is under the covers.

How Did We Get Here?

In the early 1990s Jim Sterne spent his time explaining packet switching to corporate leaders. They understood communication over the phone and the fax machine, and broadcast over radio and TV. But this Internet thing was a different animal, and it was necessary that they made the conceptual shift from one-to-one and one-to-many to many-to-many. Otherwise, they couldn't wrap their heads around what an interactive World Wide Web with ecommerce and social media might look like.

In the same vein, generative AI is a completely different kind of computing than what we've come to know.

Deterministic Computing

For more than 80 years, traditional computing followed a clear set of rules—much like ENIAC, the first general-purpose computer created in 1945. ENIAC wasn't just a calculator; it could compute. Computers are programmable. They have memory. Computers can make decisions based on the results of their calculations. They have if/then statements, branching, and looping in programs so they can solve complex problems that require different actions based on various conditions.

Unfortunately, these computers did not speak English, but rather talked in code. We had to learn assembly language, FORTRAN, COBOL, SQL, C++, Python, and so forth to get them to do our bidding. Excruciatingly specific instructions, typed into the machine in the most precise manner, produce programs that do exactly what we want. The slightest typo results in an error message while bigger blunders result in the dreaded Blue Screen of Death.

At the start, anybody with a personal computer had to know how to write some code to get it to be useful. Using business computers back in the day required a healthy knowledge of the command-line interface. Once commercial software packages showed up, the industry boomed and never looked back. Specific programs for specific applications solved all sorts of problems but were still made by typing excruciatingly specific instructions in the most precise manner. Even when point-and-click interfaces came along, you still could make mistakes by pointing or clicking in the wrong place. And every application has its bugs.

But the result was generations of people coming to expect the computer to do what it was told—exactly—and nothing else. These machines were great for recording, storing, sorting, indexing, tabulating, calculating, quantifying, and measuring.

In the 1980s and 1990s, even AI was deterministic. "Expert systems" were based on deterministic rules. Many companies still use them, but they are difficult to scale and change, and they rely on expert judgment (abstracted into computer-based rules) to make decisions.

Probabilistic Models

In the 1970s, statisticians came along looking for ways to use computers for analysis. It turned out that they were very good at it. Statisticians shifted the goalposts from the heretofore deterministic to the probabilistic. They construct predictive analytics models that forecast what might be based on what has been.

Start with a year's worth of data and build a statistical model that accurately describes the outcome variable for the first 9 months (because you know the outcomes), setting the last 3 months of data aside. Run the 9-month model and see how well it predicts the following three (for which you also know the outcomes). If it doesn't do well, it's time to tweak it (trying out different variables, data transformations, and algorithm types) until it does. When you've finished, you have a magical tool that lets you predict the future, assuming that it continues to be like the past. Eventually, you get a model that is better than a coin flip and, if it's good, better than a team of highly educated experts prophesying based on years of experience and gut feel. We call this *predictive analytics*, but it's also the simplest form of machine learning.

However, these simple models typically use relatively simple algorithm types (such as regression) and are full of deliberate and unintentional assumptions—we're only human. Statistician George Box is frequently quoted as having said, "All models are wrong. Some models are useful." As we've hinted, all models have a limited life span. Assumptions do not age well because the only thing you can count on is change. With myriad variables embedded in a model, all it takes is a change in the weather, the stock market, the economy, the competition, etc., and you need to start over to train your models again. Use the same process as described and employ the resulting model until it too is no longer good at predicting.

It is possible to automatically retrain models from new data but not very common—it generally requires automated monitoring to see how well a model is predicting (called *machine learning operations*, or MLOps), as well as a human to decide that the model should be retired, find new data, etc.[9] And most machine learning models typically employ more complex model types than regression analysis. Algorithms like decision trees, neural networks, and support vector machines are used to create supervised, unsupervised, and reinforcement learning models, all of which play a part in the eventual creation of generative AI. It's important to remember, however, that the same statistical logic applies in every type of machine learning, including generative AI. We're still trying to train models on past data and using the result to predict future data.

Supervised learning identifies patterns after being given lots of examples with known and labeled outcomes. It can predict whether there is a cat in the picture (when trained on many labeled cat and not-cat images) or whether certain behaviors look like a fraudulent transaction (when trained on many labeled fraud and not-fraud transactions). The supervision refers to the outcomes data being known and labeled in advance.

Unsupervised learning identifies correlations or other relationships in data on its own by finding the attributes that appear to be associated. It might reveal that people who live further from a retail location purchase more expensive things online from that company, or that people who visit a website in the afternoon are more likely to respond to a free shipping offer than those who visit in the evening. The machine can find statistical relationships of all kinds, even ones that are true but not useful. It is true that 70-year-old smokers live longer than 70-year-old nonsmokers, but that's only because the handful of smokers who made it to 70 are healthier in general. It's also good for identifying clusters of similar things—including customers.

Reinforcement learning helps find better answers where there is no "right" answer—as in trying to win a chess or video game, where it has

---

[9] https://www.iguazio.com/glossary/model-retraining.

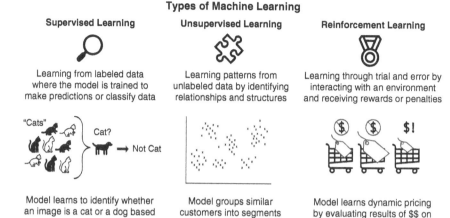

Figure 3.2   Types of machine learning.

been widely used. It is designed to take action and change its mind on the fly based on the results of its efforts. Marketers are forever trying to put the right message in front of the right person at the right time, but there is no definitive answer. Gone are the days of getting a seemingly brilliant idea from Madison Avenue and testing it in focus groups for months before committing to a large purchase of television time. Instead, a reinforcement learning system can try sending hundreds of messages to thousands of people to see which message at which time works better for which kinds of people. (See Figure 3.2.)

In a recent article with Peter High, Tom has referred to these types of machine learning as "analytical AI."[10] They argue that the purpose of such methods is to analyze data and predict future outcomes based on past data. They contrast it with generative AI, which of course uses analytics but has the primary purpose of content creation.

Historical Downsides

The approaches described earlier face different challenges. Deterministic (typically rule-based) AI models are rigid, executing instructions with no tolerance for error, which often led to system failures if anything

---

[10] Thomas H. Davenport and Peter High, "How GenAI and Analytical AI Differ—and When to Use Each," *Harvard Business Review*, 13 December 2024, https://hbr.org/2024/12/how-gen-ai-and-analytical-ai-differ-and-when-to-use-each.

went wrong and were based on expert knowledge instead of data. Probabilistic models add flexibility and data-driven precision, but they sometimes make bad predictions (known as *hallucinations* in generative AI) and sometimes struggle with overfitting (models that are too closely designed for specific training data), making them sometimes unreliable in the wild.

Supervised learning models are dependent on labeled data. That makes them expensive and labor-intensive to train when already labeled data isn't available. When they rely on human-labeled examples, they can fall victim to human error. Unsupervised learning finds correlations that may be true but not useful, or even misleading, due to the lack of clear guidance on what constitutes relevance. Reinforcement learning, with its trial-and-error approach, can be inefficient and time-consuming.

Generative AI can work with unstructured data—text, images, video, etc.—in addition to rows and columns of numbers. Unlike deterministic models that follow predefined rules, generative AI can create and predict new content based on patterns on which it is trained, allowing for greater adaptability. It is self-supervised, finding patterns in text or image content without requiring labeling. Being trained on massive datasets lets GenAI generalize across different contexts and shine in innovation. Generative AI models can learn iteratively through user interaction and feedback like reinforcement learning but with direct adjustments by subject-matter experts instead of interpreted by programmers. But they also have their challenges; it's hard to assemble the massive amounts of data and computing power to train them, and they have that well-known hallucination problem.

So how are generative AI models built, and how do they work?

Generative AI

Generative artificial intelligence can generate a wide variety of output types based on its training, including forms that are obviously related to customer relationships:

- Text
- Images
- Videos
- Music

- 3D models
- Personalized product recommendations
- Financial forecasts
- Product designs

and others that are tangential but reveal the scope of GenAI's capabilities:

- Game characters and storylines
- Computer code
- Artificial datasets (synthetic data)
- Financial forecasts
- Protein sequences (to create new drugs)
- And more every day

OpenAI's ChatGPT 3.5 took the world by storm when it was released on 30 November 2022, reaching more than one million users within a few days and more than 100 million users by January 2023. The "3.5" is an indication that this weird technology had been in the works for a while. But this version was the one that captured the public's hearts and minds. As of this writing, we're at GPT4 and various intermediate versions of it, with GPT5 rumored to be on the way.

Generative Pretrained Transformer (GPT)

Generative AI has several key components, which we'll discuss one letter (G, then P, then T) at a time.

- **Generative:** Instead of finding things online like a search engine, storing and retrieving information like a database, or finding correlations like unsupervised machine learning, GPTs are designed to create—to generate.

  Diffusion models generate quality images from text. They work by gradually denoising random noise into a coherent image, reversing a process that adds noise to training images. Think of them like sculptors, removing that which does not look like the thing the artist is trying to represent. They are a leap forward from generative adversarial networks and are trained on huge datasets of labeled pictures—of cats, for example. Diffusion models are good for generating video as well.

Our focus is going to be on large language models (LLMs), because they are very useful in creating content for customers to consume.

- **Pre-trained:** LLMs are pre-trained on text rather than pictures. Lots of text. Massive amounts of data. While OpenAI do not disclose how much data it uses to train ChatGPT, so much text is needed for advanced capabilities, we might run out. Even at the rate the amount of scrapable text on the Internet is growing—on top of hundreds of thousands of books—textual data available for training may eventually become exhausted. This concern has reached a point where data scientists are training LLMs to generate synthetic data. Whether that's the solution or more sustainable AI practices like transfer learning and continual learning will win out, the point is that these LLMs are given vast amounts of text to read.

  But they don't read it. They measure the statistical frequency of distances between words. In the preamble to the US Constitution, the words *people* and *United States* in "We the people of the United States" are right next to each other while *people* and *constitution* are farther apart. That's where it starts.

  The purpose is to guess what the statistically most likely next word will be. If, on one page, you read "you could knock me over with a…" and the sentence continued on the next page, you might well assume that the next word is *feather*. It could be *wet noodle* or *slight breeze*. But the *most likely* word is *feather*.

  An LLM takes in all the text and builds a mathematical model of the language. *Cat* has a relationship to *dog*, and *dog* has a relationship with *bone*. But *cat* and *bone* are much, much farther apart.

- **Transformer:** With this pre-trained model to work from, the transformer's job is to "pay attention" (hence the important Google paper that kicked off generative AI, "Attention Is All You Need"[11]) to different parts of a sentence or text all at once, rather than reading it in order like we do. The goal is to grasp context and meaning. "We need a tie" can mean a lot of different things depending on the

---

[11] A. Vaswani et al. "Attention Is All You Need," paper presented at *NIPS' 17: Proceedings of the 31st International Conference on Neural Information Processing Systems,* 2017, https://dl.acm.org/doi/10.5555/3295222.3295349.

context. By paying attention to previous sentences, it can calculate that *tie* refers to formal neckwear, a tennis game, or something to secure one's long hair from getting caught in a machine. Transformers capture long-range dependencies and can generate new sequences (sentences) based on the patterns they've learned.

A generative pre-trained transformer is then fine-tuned with rules to make it well-behaved. OpenAI published their model spec in May 2024,[12] which addresses the model's "tone, personality, response length, and more... Shaping this behavior is a still nascent science, as models are not explicitly programmed but instead learn from a broad range of data."

OpenAI's rules are "Instructions that address complexity and help ensure safety and legality," including the following:

- Follow the chain of command.
- Comply with applicable laws.
- Don't provide information hazards.
- Respect creators and their rights.
- Protect people's privacy.
- Don't respond with not safe for work (NSFW) content.

Next come the guidelines that drive the GPT's day-to-day interaction with users:

- Assume best intentions from the user or developer.
- Ask clarifying questions when necessary.
- Be as helpful as possible without overstepping.
- Support the different needs of interactive chat and programmatic use.
- Assume an objective point of view.
- Encourage fairness and kindness, and discourage hate.
- Don't try to change anyone's mind.
- Express uncertainty.
- Use the right tool for the job.
- Be thorough but efficient, while respecting length limits.

---

[12] https://openai.com/index/introducing-the-model-spec.

These rules and guidelines are followed by OpenAI's safety and alignment efforts:[13]

- **Training with human feedback:** We incorporated more human feedback, including feedback submitted by ChatGPT users, to improve GPT-4's behavior. We also worked with more than 50 experts for early feedback in domains including AI safety and security.
- **Continuous improvement from real-world use:** We've applied lessons from real-world use of our previous models into GPT-4's safety research and monitoring system. Like ChatGPT, we'll be updating and improving GPT-4 at a regular cadence as more people use it.
- **GPT-4-assisted safety research:** GPT-4's advanced reasoning and instruction-following capabilities expedited our safety work. We used GPT-4 to help create training data for model fine-tuning and iterate on classifiers across training, evaluations, and monitoring.

Because we're now calculating words instead of numbers, computing has shifted from deterministic through probabilistic to linguistic (Figure 3.3). To be clear, generative AI is applying probabilistic machine learning, but the effect of predicting words rather than numbers is that we've made a step-change from learning to speak computer to the computer learning to speak English.

This is a new form of computing, and it will take some getting used to. We need to acclimate to the idea that the output is generally valuable but cannot be trusted without double-checking. We need the creators of foundation LLM models to train them how to behave in general, and then marketers need to teach them how to interact with customers.

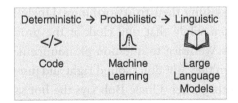

Figure 3.3 The evolution of computer interaction.

---

[13] https://openai.com/index/introducing-the-model-spec.

The analogy of generative AI as an intern holds. We need parents to train their offspring to be courteous, curious, and kind while we teach them what it means to work in a given industry at a given company.

Linguistic Computing

Instead of instructing the computer to do what we say and expecting specific, accurate, and precise responses, we communicate with it as we would an intern. Just tell it what you want…and then shake your head in despondency when you see that—smart as it is—it doesn't know what it needs to know in order to be truly helpful.

Ask interns to write a report and they will, but without any knowledge of corporate formats, standards, or expectations. The interns may have graduated from the best school in the world but have no practical knowledge of the world.

That's where prompt engineering comes in. Give the LLM context—lots of context—and eventually a well-crafted prompt will generate output more like what you're after. In fact, the output is surprisingly good and disarming. After all, ChatGPT was told to, "Be as helpful as possible without overstepping."

However, it's important not to be fooled. Do not think LLMs have feelings or understand how the world works. Humans have feelings and try to find the right words. LLMs have all the words but no concept of feeling or meaning. They are making predictions based on what other people have written—no more, no less. In other words, like analytical AI, they are probabilistic—but make predictions of words, not numbers.

Despite their heavy statistical orientation, LLMs have all of the ambiguities that humans do. When meeting a person, you spend a fair amount of effort assessing their trustworthiness. Uncle Bob is full of solid, down-home wisdom while that one clerk at the grocery store is full of conspiracy theories. We learn to question pronouncements from our most trusted friends when they just don't sound right and just don't pass the smell test. We also learn that when Uncle Bob says the hot sauce is not too bad, we know to avoid it at all costs.

Therefore, it's vital to be suspicious of everything an LLM tells you. The biggest argument against generative AI is that it's not trustworthy. It hallucinates and therefore isn't reliable or always useful. A hallucination is the result of the algorithm guessing the next most likely word or concept without regard to the truth—because it doesn't know truth, it only knows statistical likelihood. The more sophisticated your expertise, the more capable you are of evaluating the output to see if it passes the smell test.

Junior sales and marketing people will be able to crank out a great number of emails, landing pages, and podcast scripts, but without an educated, talented human-in-the-loop, the quality will be average at best. Critical thinking and domain expertise are the most important human skills to combine with the use of GenAI.

Data scientists are working overtime to get their LLMs to be more accurate, and they're making progress. In the meantime, we can embrace the creativity. If you *don't* expect LLMs to tell the truth, the whole truth, and nothing but the truth and if you *don't* expect them to be good at math and if you *don't* expect them to be free from bias, then you can become comfortable with the idea that they are an amazing brainstorming partner rather than an encyclopedia. The trick is to ask them for opinions rather than facts.

Asking for Opinions, Not Facts

One of Jim's first interactions with ChatGPT (after mistaking it for a search engine and being terrifically disappointed) was getting help writing a blog post. He had written 12 paragraphs and asked ChatGPT to write a 1-paragraph introduction. The result was horrendous. After an hour-and-a-half of "prompt engineering" trying to bend the machine to his will, Jim spent 5 minutes writing the introductory paragraph and realizing his mistake. He then asked ChatGPT to review the article for structure and flow. It responded that he should move paragraph 7 up below paragraph 4. This was extremely unexpected—yet amazingly powerful. While the transitions between paragraphs had to be rewritten, the logical flow of the article was vastly improved.

Generative AI turns a computer that can only record, remember, repeat, report, reanalyze, etc., into a device that can strategize, brainstorm, collaborate, synthesize, and innovate. Not only can it spit out a calculation of how many people had positive, negative, or neutral things to say on social media; it can now parse those comments for linguistic nuance.

This changes our relationship with machines:

- Instead of just asking our computers to correlate, we can ask them to consider causation.
- Instead of just quantifying, we can ask them to qualify.
- Instead of just classifying, we can ask them to contextualize.
- Instead of just sorting, we can ask them to synthesize.
- Instead of just translating languages, we can ask them to interpret meaning.
- Instead of just categorizing, we can ask them to contextualize.
- Instead of just organizing, we can ask them to prioritize.

The types of questions we can ask are significantly different:

- What innovative principles from the public sector might be applied to this problem?
- How can I prepare for potential future scenarios of my situation?
- What are some unintended consequences?
- How can the principles of Ju-Jitsu be applied to this problem?
- What are some out-of-the-box-thinking solutions that might work here?
- What if we did the opposite of what's expected?
- How could we turn this problem into an opportunity?
- What does a pre-mortem review of this potential project look like?
- What would our competitors never see coming?
- How can I deconstruct this problem into smaller tasks?
- How are these disparate concepts connected?
- What are some alternative perspectives?
- What does it look like from a different angle?
- How can I expand on this idea?
- How can it help me think clearly using first principles?
- What seems to be missing?
- What does a more creative solution look like?
- What else might I have asked?

In the realm of customer relationships, it can bring forth the wisdom of the ages. We can ask GenAI for advice about customer relationships from these eminent thinkers on the topic (or to tell you who they are if you don't know):

- David Ogilvy
- Bill Bernbach
- Leo Burnett
- Philip Kotler
- Jack Trout and Al Ries
- Steve Jobs
- Seth Godin
- Gary Vaynerchuk
- Ann Handley
- Andy Crestodina
- Rand Fishkin
- Jay Baer
- My boss or my boss's boss (okay, it might not know anything about them)

This is not the computing we grew up with—and we've only just started learning how to leverage this new technology. If we can all program computers in English, we all become programmers, especially since 6 November 2023, when OpenAI released a new capability.

Creating GPTs and Projects: The End of Prompt Engineering

In November 2023, OpenAI introduced GPTs and described them this way:[14]

You can now create custom versions of ChatGPT that combine instructions, extra knowledge, and any combination of skills.

We're rolling out custom versions of ChatGPT that you can create for a specific purpose—called GPTs. GPTs are a new way for anyone to create a tailored version of ChatGPT to be more helpful in

---

[14] https://openai.com/index/introducing-gpts.

their daily life, at specific tasks, at work, or at home—and then share that creation with others. For example, GPTs can help you learn the rules to any board game, help teach your kids math, or design stickers.

Anyone can easily build their own GPT—no coding is required. You can make them for yourself, just for your company's internal use, or for everyone. Creating one is as easy as starting a conversation, giving it instructions and extra knowledge, and picking what it can do, like searching the web, making images or analyzing data.

The user interface for GPTs feels very much the same as asking ChatGPT a question or giving it an instruction. The difference is that it remembers specific instructions—as well as files uploaded for it to consider—for a given use case.

This conversational interface means you can always go back and tweak it as needed. This is closer to working with a smart intern than ever. Once it's got the hang of the type of report or format or tone that you're after, it never forgets.

One GPT is created to understand the product manual and the product FAQ inside-out. The next is well trained in interacting with customers. Another is adept at asking customer satisfaction survey questions. Yet another is tuned to produce reports on customer temperament. Bonus: they can interact with each other.

The customer interaction GPT can call on the product knowledge GPT just as a customer service rep might call on their internal product marketing manager. The reporting GPT periodically emails out how customer attitudes have changed and alerts others to spikes and drops in satisfaction, feature requests, and competitive comparisons.

This essentially allows nonprogrammers to write software. GPTs are the earliest and simplest versions of AI agents, which we'll describe in greater detail in Chapter 7, "Better Task Automation with AI Agents."

Is It Cheating?

Publishing companies have issued edicts that AI must not be used in generating books. That's understandable given that the US Copyright Office currently only recognizes copyright for works "created by a human being." [15] It has also recently recognized that human changes to AI-generated content can also be copyrighted.

Our feeling is that humans are a tool-building species and generative AI is a tool. Tools evolve from basic to sophisticated across different domains. Is the food better if you used a spoon as opposed to a whisk? Is it cheating to have used a blender? Does the use of a food processor disqualify the meal from consideration?

We've moved from hands-on, labor-intensive processes to tools that do more of the heavy lifting. The value we get out of these tools still depends on how well we use them. A food processor might save you time, but it's your skill in the kitchen that turns ingredients into a meal. Can you tell the difference between corn on the cob boiled in water or zapped in the microwave? A spreadsheet might crunch numbers faster than a calculator, but it's your understanding of accounting that drives real insights.

The time and effort that something takes should not be a factor in the quality and value of the result (see Figure 3.4 on the disconnect between effort and value).

The value of the result is dependent on knowledge, experience, and talent. A beautiful, carved sideboard is still beautiful regardless of whether power tools were used in the process. On the other hand, a beautiful, carved

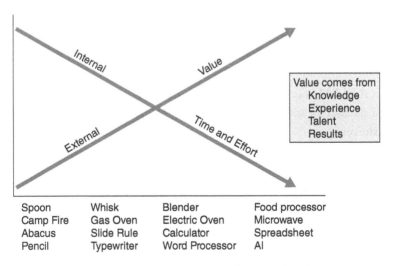

Figure 3.4 The disconnect between effort and value.

---

cabinet is obviously more beautiful—soulful if you will—and longer lasting than an IKEA BESTÅ,[16] which is "made of chipboard, fiberboard or solid wood, while the inside is a honeycomb filling structure made of mostly recycled paper, which is extra durable thanks to its special construction. The board is then covered with a protective paint, foil or veneer depending on the style wanted."

IKEA furniture is ideal for a student where longevity expectations are measured in semesters, but nobody thinks of a BESTÅ as a potential heirloom.

Granted, there are important issues involving copyright violation when LLMs or image creation models use copyrighted information to train the models. It's not a clear-cut case, since model outputs are almost never exactly the same as the content used to train them. However, this issue is making its way through the courts at the moment, and no one knows exactly how it will turn out. In the meantime we feel that you can use GenAI models without fear of prosecution.

Pro Tip: Flip the Script

Are we spending too much time learning how to communicate at the command-line interface by calling it "prompt engineering"? What if we're approaching LLMs from a legacy mindset wrought from conventional thinking and a traditional perspective? What if, instead of engaging in prompt engineering, we asked the computer to prompt us?

Providing a prompt and getting the LLM's response often feels constrained and linear, limiting the depth of the exchange. So flip the script and let the LLM take the lead. Let it guide you to be even more creative. Let it be a partner in ideation and innovation—about customer-facing topics or whatever.

As with all prompt engineering, you'll need to frame interaction judiciously, providing enough context without being overly restrictive. Encourage the LLM to ask open-ended questions where you are continually challenged to think beyond initial assumptions. Clearly define the role of the LLM as a catalyst for creative exploration, ensuring that the final decisions remain yours.

---

[16] https://www.ikea.com/us/en/p/besta-storage-combination-with-doors-white-stained-oak-effect-lappviken-stubbarp-white-stained-oak-effect-s49139722/.

Maintain an active role in steering the conversation. You want the machine to be a guide and a coach, not a teacher. Leverage LLMs to enhance customer engagement strategies, streamline innovation processes, and inject fresh perspectives in all decision-making.

Flipped Script Uses

- Brainstorm new product features by having the LLM ask about user pain points, market trends, and technical feasibility.
- Generate ad concepts by considering different customer personas, brand voice, and calls-to-action.
- Explore growth opportunities by surfacing relevant industry data, suggesting analogous cases, and stress-testing ideas with scenario planning.
- Refine customer service approaches by simulating interactions, evaluating potential responses, and identifying areas for improvement in communication tone and empathy.
- Create content marketing strategies by analyzing competitor approaches, uncovering niche topics, and generating a content calendar with diverse formats and channels.
- Optimize pricing models by exploring different pricing strategies, analyzing competitor pricing, and considering consumer behavior insights and economic trends.
- Enhance team collaboration by generating icebreakers, brainstorming session topics, and conflict resolution strategies tailored to team dynamics.
- Conduct market segmentation analysis by identifying key demographics, evaluating purchasing behaviors, and suggesting targeted marketing approaches for each segment.

Tips for Flipping the Script

The effectiveness of LLMs in solving your marketing or customer interaction problems can be greatly enhanced by applying prompt-based tips like these:

- Prime the LLM with context about your goals, but allow space for it to explore.
- Encourage the LLM to ask "what-if" and "how might we" questions to prompt divergent thinking.

- Ask the LLM to reflect what it's heard and synthesize key themes periodically.
- Prompt the LLM to bring in outside inspiration—from data, examples, and lateral domains.
- Give positive reinforcement for insightful questions and novel idea combinations. (We don't know why this works but "Good job! Can you do better?" does, indeed, improve the output.)
- Ask the LLM to identify potential blind spots by questioning assumptions and challenging conventional wisdom in your approach.
- Encourage the LLM to offer alternative perspectives by asking it to consider the problem from the viewpoint of different stakeholders or cultural contexts.
- Instruct the LLM to simulate a debate between opposing viewpoints, encouraging you to weigh the pros and cons of each side.
- Request the LLM to suggest incremental steps for testing ideas in low-risk environments before scaling them up.
- Have the LLM create analogies or metaphors to reframe your thinking and help you see the problem or opportunity in a new light.

Knowing how generative AI works and keeping in mind how it is a fundamentally different form of computing is necessary for understanding the impact it can have in customer communication and relationship-building.

Preparing for Change

Like most data-related technologies, generative AI is not a plug-and-play tool that can be fired up and put to use immediately. It is not a kitchen appliance. It needs some serious attention to technical infrastructure, workflow analysis, and a commitment to an aggressive change management process to leverage this new tech.

Integrating AI systems with existing customer relationship management tools is not a cakewalk. Your data engineers will have to validate the seamless data flow between AI and CRM systems. Creating unified customer views across AI and traditional platforms is a forever endeavor.

Generative AI is not going to take over whole jobs or even giant swaths of functions. But it will aid in the speed and quality of specific customer-related tasks. The swift proof-of-concept application of generative

AI to your customer-centered processes is a matter of identifying those tasks that are the most automatable, with the least effort, garnering the best results in the lowest amount of time.

Employees will need training, starting with well-crafted policies and guidelines. Your staff will need to know what is forbidden, allowed, required, encouraged, and celebrated. Specific tools, use cases, technical requirements, and legal edicts all come into play. Data literacy and AI literacy will be the order of the day.

Training programs must be tailored to each department to ensure they have the proper instructions, knowledge, and skills. Upskilling will get a lot more accomplished with the staff you have while the prospect of reducing headcount will set you behind the curve. Humans are still critical to the best use of AI. After all, trusting the machine to adhere to your soon-to-be-published ethical standards is a very risky business.

Generative AI in the Present and Future

Generative AI represents an actual paradigm shift in how businesses can engage with customers. It offers unprecedented capabilities for personalization, creativity, and efficiency across marketing, sales, and customer service. It also brings significant challenges that need thoughtful navigation. By itself it's not the key to great customer science, but it's a big step forward.

The key lies in understanding the shift in mindset from deterministic, rule-based systems to probabilistic, language-based interactions followed by a commitment to investment in technical infrastructure, data management practices, and employee training. Layer on robust ethical guidelines and governance structures to ensure responsible use and a solid change management plan and you'll be ahead of the competition.

> We are absolutely at a place where, if AI development completely stopped, we would still have 5–10 years of rapid change absorbing the capabilities of current models and integrating them into organizations and social systems. I don't think development is going to stop, though.
>
> *Ethan Mollick, associate professor, The Wharton School*[17]

---

[17] https://www.linkedin.com/posts/emollick_we-are-absolutely-at-a-place-where-if-ai-activity-7237649948341669888-VQ0x.

Looking ahead, generative AI will challenge existing business models, redefine customer relationships, and push companies to reconsider how they measure success. This technology is a tool, but it's also a catalyst for the future we'll create. The decisions we make today will shape what's to come. The philosophical question is, what kind of future do you want to build with it? The immediate question is what steps to take now.

In the next chapter, we will explore the fuel of both analytical and generative AI—also known as data. You simply can't have good AI models—or customer science in general—without it.

4

Better Data

For the last several decades, the amount and variety of customer data has been increasing dramatically. In general, more data makes it possible to personalize offerings and communications to customers more accurately and effectively. Peter Norvig, one of the earliest and most distinguished data scientists at Google, once commented that "More data beats clever algorithms." However, the second part of his comment is often forgotten: "but better data beats more data." Organizations wanting to build a better relationship with their customers must wrestle with the question of gathering more data on them versus improving the data that they already have. That issue has both algorithmic and ethical implications.

The general situation in the customer data domain is that there is an increasing amount of it, and companies aren't doing enough with it. As one (Spanish) customer intelligence vendor put it in a blog post with which we agree (emphasis theirs, and sources available in the footnoted original):

Organizations **have more customer data today than ever before**. In fact, enterprise data assets are growing at 40% every year. Therefore, for most corporations—especially medium and large enterprises—the amount of consumer data is not the issue.

The surprise comes when we look at recent studies on the relationship between customers and companies:

- 62% of consumers believe that companies do not understand their needs.
- Only 15% of CMOs think their company is on the right track when it comes to personalization.
- According to the latest 2022 data, 86% of organizations have not achieved a 360-degree view of their customers.

The dichotomy is crystal clear: **despite companies now having more data about their customers**, most are still **unable to transform it into better decisions, customer intelligence and customer strategies as well as better digital marketing results…the reason why companies are not taking advantage of customer data is not the quantity of data, but the quality of their data…** .

The big problem with leveraging customer data is not quantity. The **more customer data we have, the more complex it is to manage**. Instead, the real difficulty for companies is in **transforming data into marketing insights** in data management and the difficulties involved in validating its quality, getting rid of unnecessary or erroneous data, and processing it to make it actionable.[1]

We'll discuss this quality versus quantity trade-off at various points throughout this chapter. We'll also describe some of the reasons why this customer data thing is so challenging.

Demographic Data

Customer data management has become much more difficult given the amazing amount of data that it's possible to obtain on customers. The most basic form of data is demographic: Who is the customer, and what are their personal attributes independent of our company? If you sell to businesses,

---

[1] "How Much Data Do I Need to Know My Customers?" Bismart blog post, https://blog.bismart.com/en/kale/how-much-data-do-i-need-to-know-my-customers, accessed 26 August 2024.

the similar data is sometimes called *firmographic*. Details of the technology used by the customer are called *technographic*.

Early users of database marketing were happy to have accurate names and addresses for customers, but the world has become much more complex, as the following list of demographic/technographic customer data illustrates. We now have the possibility of acquiring and using many different demographic or technographic data elements that didn't exist or were not possible to obtain before.

- Name (and variations used online and in social media)
- Address (postal and email)
- Telephone (mobile and yes, even fixed line) numbers
- Key ID numbers, such as Social Security
- Gender
- Age
- Race/ethnicity
- Religion
- Marital status
- Number of children
- Occupation—current and previous
- Income
- Wealth
- IP address
- Type of computing or mobile device used

Some of this demographic and technographic data can be obtained from customer transactions with a company. Other data in the previous list can be sourced from external data brokers for a fee, sometimes known as *data enrichment*. Obviously, companies should think carefully about what data they actually need about customers before spending money to obtain demographic details that they are unlikely to need or use. Even if you plan to extract demographic data directly from the customer—e.g. from a warranty card—you may be surprised at how difficult it is to persuade them to supply it and how much money it takes to gather it effectively.

Even for "free" customer transaction data, however, substantial effort may be required to determine the true identity of a customer. This issue is known as *identity resolution*. Co-author Tom Davenport, for example, might be known variously as Thomas Davenport, Thomas Hayes Davenport, Thomas H. Davenport, T.H. Davenport, even Tommy Davenport (as a child), and most accurately Thomas Hayes Davenport Jr. He has employed all of those names in purchasing products and services from vendors at one time or another and swears that his purpose has never been to commit fraud.

Identity resolution is critical if you want to know the sum total of what a customer is actually purchasing from you, how they respond to marketing initiatives, and the lifetime value of the relationship. If the customer happens to call with a service issue, knowing their identity in all its combined formats is also extremely helpful in knowing how to resolve it without having to ask too many questions.

The process of identity resolution has come a long way over the past several years (see Figure 4.1), and you can thank progress in artificial intelligence for that. It used to be accomplished through the use of decision rules (in something called *master data management*, which we'll describe further later in this chapter), but the number of rules sometimes approached the number of names to be combined. As we'll discuss later in this chapter, most identity resolution vendors—it's rare for companies to do it without external help—employ machine learning models. They might suggest, for

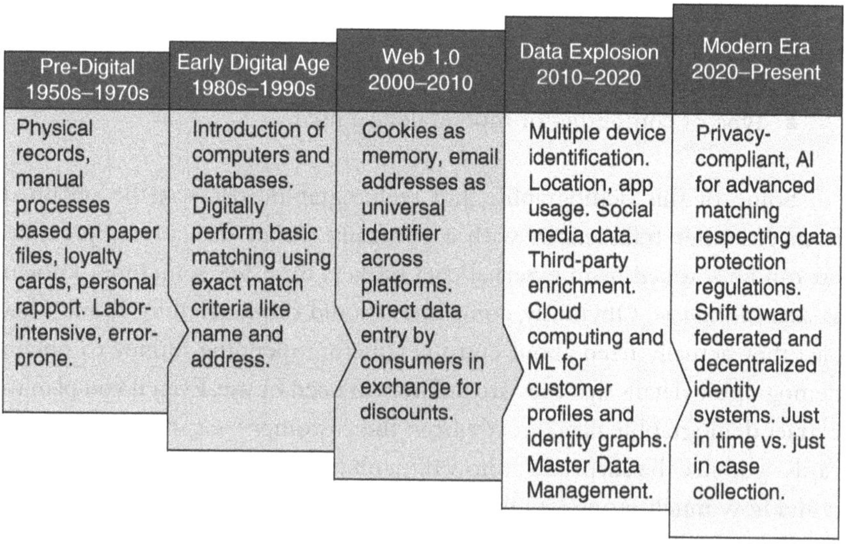

Pre-Digital 1950s–1970s	Early Digital Age 1980s–1990s	Web 1.0 2000–2010	Data Explosion 2010–2020	Modern Era 2020–Present
Physical records, manual processes based on paper files, loyalty cards, personal rapport. Labor-intensive, error-prone.	Introduction of computers and databases. Digitally perform basic matching using exact match criteria like name and address.	Cookies as memory, email addresses as universal identifier across platforms. Direct data entry by consumers in exchange for discounts.	Multiple device identification. Location, app usage. Social media data. Third-party enrichment. Cloud computing and ML for customer profiles and identity graphs. Master Data Management.	Privacy-compliant, AI for advanced matching respecting data protection regulations. Shift toward federated and decentralized identity systems. Just in time vs. just in case collection.

Figure 4.1   **Progress of identity resolution approaches over time.**

example, that all those names for Tom (particularly if they reside at the same address) have a high probability of being the same person. So it merges them into one "master record" or "golden record."

Of course, all demographic data is not as easily available as a customer name. But there are often ways to enrich or augment the demographic data that a company can easily get from customer transactions. Take wealth, for example. Banks and other providers of financial services would prefer to offer their wealth management services to potential customers who are wealthy. But how do we find out who's got a lot of dough? An individual bank only knows to some degree how wealthy its own customers are—they may have a relatively low "share of wallet" for the customer—and it has no idea of the wealth levels of potential customers.

There are, of course, some pretty good proxies for wealth, including whether someone owns a home, their ZIP or postal code, and whether they have a mortgage—all matters of public record. But a home is only one financial asset. How does a bank marketer find out who has a lot of cabbage to invest?

One approach would be to join the IXI "data sharing club," now owned by Equifax. Tom wrote about this organization in 2013:

> We may also see the further rise of "data clubs" in which companies who furnish data to a cooperative can get some back in exchange. IXI Services, a division of Equifax, is one of these. Banks supply information (at the zip code level) on their customers' assets to IXI Services, and they can get back data on noncustomers' assets.[2]

IXI is still going, and 95 large banks participate in customer wealth data sharing. According to Equifax, that represents almost half of US-invested assets by customers.[3] In other words, it will provide a pretty good idea of how wealthy a potential customer is.

---

[2] Thomas H. Davenport, "Turning Our Data Sights Outward," *The Wall Street Journal*, 8 January 2013, https://www.wsj.com/articles/BL-CIOB-1394.

[3] "The Foundation of IXI Data," Equifax, https://assets.equifax.com/marketing/US/assets/the-foundation-of-IXI-data.pdf.

Customer Engagement Data

But there are many other types of data from which companies can better understand their customers. One important one is customer engagement data—how the customer has engaged with your company and its products and services. It is widely argued that the best predictor of future customer activity is past customer activity, particularly purchases. Like demographic or firmographic data, engagement data is often available from a company's business transactions and go-to-market channels. The following are some attributes:

- All past purchases and returns
- Transactions by channel
- Web/mobile clicks, page views, cookies, conversions
- Abandoned shopping carts
- Responses to paid search ads and terms
- Sweepstake and contest entries
- Product usage information (if online connection)
- Visits to customer portals and support sites
- Responses to marketing offers
- Store visits (from credit or loyalty cards)
- Referrals to other potential customers

Customer engagement data is also subject to the entity resolution problem, and that needs to be resolved before engagement data is correctly recorded or aggregated from a customer. But even the "all past purchases" data element can be difficult to aggregate. If, for example, changes in corporate structure, such as acquisitions, divestitures, or discontinued businesses or product lines, have taken place since a purchase, would or should purchases be recorded accurately? Perhaps the purchases were recorded on information systems—or even paper records—that are no longer in use. And should they be recorded in the original price paid or inflation-adjusted dollars? And is there a point at which past purchases from a customer no longer matter? Perhaps when the customer is no longer a resident of this vale of tears (i.e. dead)?

Software-as-a-service (SaaS) companies have taken the lead in monitoring some aspects of customer engagement. They can do so because they have access to exactly what the customer is doing with the software.

If they're not using it at all, or using it ineffectively, chances are good that the customer is not engaged with the product and is a strong candidate for attrition or nonrenewal of the software license. This type of monitoring is a major focus of the "customer success" departments that have been created in many SaaS companies. As more types of products become connected to the Internet, we are likely to see more of this type of customer engagement analysis.

Subjective and Attitudinal Customer Data

There is a final type of data that is most likely to come directly to a company or organization from its customers. It is based on customer feedback—the subjective opinions and satisfaction of customers. Despite its subjectivity, it can be a good indicator of the likelihood of continued purchases from that customer. In other words, it's definitely worth capturing and analyzing. This type of data has become more common and important since the rise of social media over the last decade or so.

Some customer feedback is easy to elicit, capture, and use as inputs to predictive models. One popular 10-point measure of customer satisfaction proposed by Tom's friend Fred Reichheld and consultants Bain & Co., the Net Promoter Score (NPS), has been tied to company-level shareholder return growth through repeat and referred sales revenues.[4] Fred Reichheld conceived of the score as a relatively simple means of assessing what customers really think about a company with which they have done business. While academic studies have not always found strong correlations between NPS and consumer sales, many companies believe ardently in the value of NPS.[5] It's perhaps the easiest and most straightforward input to a company's understanding of customer satisfaction.

However, some feedback requires considerable analysis to become useful. Customer opinions can involve multiple topics and can be difficult for machines to decipher and summarize. That was historically a barrier to

---

[4] The Net Promoter Score is described in Frederick F. Reichheld, "The One Number You Need to Grow," *Harvard Business Review*, December 2003; the newer research on "earned growth," is described in Frederick F. Reichheld, Darci Darnell, and Maureen Burns, "Net Promoter 3.0," *Harvard Business Review*, November–December 2021.

[5] Sven Baehre et al. "The Use of Net Promoter Score (NPS) to Predict Sales Growth: Insights from an Empirical Presentation," *Journal of the Academy of Marketing Science* 50: 67–84 (2022). doi: 10.1007/s11747-021-00790-2.

the effective use of this type of data. Fortunately, there is now generative AI, which can do an excellent job of summarizing comments, disentangling multiple subjects, and even making sense of irony and sarcasm.[6]

The following are different subjective feedback types from customer data:

- Social media posts and video engagement, including likes, comments, and shares
- Comments to sales or service representatives ("Your call may be recorded")
- Emails or letters to the company
- Responses to surveys
- Scores on satisfaction measures, e.g. net promoter scores
- Focus group observations
- Referral behavior (Fred Reichheld believes this is a significant driver of revenue)

Other Types of Data from Third Parties

If all that internal data weren't enough—and in many cases it isn't—there is a world of external data from which companies can draw to enrich their internal customer profiles. Of course, integrating it with internal data can be challenging because of the identity resolution issues we discussed earlier. Some of the data available from external providers is described in the following list; the limits of these external data resources are really limited only by your imagination. If there is something you want, it is probably available from someone.

- Hobbies (from purchases, subscriptions, memberships)
- Real-time location at home or in car (Google Nest, GM OnStar)
- Past locations (from mobile phone providers)
- Internet search queries
- Voting registration, political contributions
- Credit scores and histories
- Bankruptcies
- Arrests, convictions

---

[6] Thomas H. Davenport, Jim Sterne, and Michael E. Thompson, "GenAI Can Help Companies Do More with Customer Feedback," *Harvard Business Review*, 29 April 2024, https://hbr.org/2024/04/genai-can-help-companies-do-more-with-customer-feedback.

- Divorces
- Drug prescriptions
- Driving habits, accidents, or traffic tickets

Given such a panoply of available external data, how does an organization decide what data to acquire? Assuming that your organization has decided that having the data would advance your business goals, there are financial, technical, and ethical dimensions to the decision. On the financial side, how likely is it that the extra information will provide enough "lift" (increased conversions) to your predictive models that you will pay back the cost of the data and of integrating it with your own? Are there less expensive ways to obtain similar insights on your customers?

Technically, how feasible and expensive will it be to integrate the data with your existing customer profiles? Does your organization have the technology infrastructure to acquire, merge, and use the data? Are there data security issues involved in acquiring or storing the data?

Ethically, does your planned use of the external data violate any regulations? Will your customers feel that your company has their permission to use the data to market or sell to them or to use it in your operations? Will you feel comfortable telling your customers that you have the data and the purpose for which you intend to use it?

We'll discuss other ethical issues around customer data and technology in Chapter 10. However, one example of poor ethical policy relative to external data involves driving data. Several insurance companies bought data from Lexis Nexis Risk Solutions on customers' detailed driving behaviors, including all trips taken, start and end times for them, and any speeding or "excessive" acceleration or deceleration during them.[7] Manufacturers of Internet-connected cars sell the data to Lexis Nexis, which sells it to insurers. Customers who are judged to be more dangerous drivers are charged higher rates—even though in most cases they were not aware that their driving data was being sold or even aggregated. Had they known it seems likely that some customers would no longer buy from that car manufacturer or would disable data collection if possible.

---

[7] Kashmir Hill, "Automakers Are Sharing Consumers' Driving Behavior with Insurance Companies," *The New York Times*, 11 March 2024, https://www.nytimes.com/2024/03/11/technology/carmakers-driver-tracking-insurance.html.

Data Quality for Internal and External Data

We have always thought of data quality as not the most fascinating subject but a very important one. Poor data quality disables many attempts to build relationships with customers. We've all seen it—emails that are addressed to the wrong person, ads that make no sense based on our interests or past purchases, even salespeople who address us with the wrong name.

During the recent political campaign for US president, Tom received a request for a contribution from one of the candidates (that candidate did not win, unfortunately). Usually there is no acknowledgment of contributions already made, but this time there was a mention and the amount of previous contributions to this candidate in the first line. The problem is that it dramatically overstated the contribution amount. Even so, of course, the candidate wanted more money. There are plenty of online sources about political contributions, and of course the candidate should have good internal records on that issue. But like many organizations, it had data quality problems that hindered the effectiveness of the communications.

Even companies that specialize in identity resolution are not immune from data mangling. Melissa Data Corporation ("a leading provider of global contact data quality and identity verification solutions"[8]) once sent Jim 17 copies of their brochure touting that they could "combat fraud, ensure compliance, and build trust with online identity verification." (See Figure 4.2.)

Tom's friend and co-author Tom Redman has been writing about data quality for decades and dealt with the issue himself at AT&T for many years. Many companies are overwhelmed by the poor data quality issues they face, but Redman advocates commonsense assessments of current data quality and activities to improve it.[9] For example, his "Friday Afternoon Measurement" activity measures data quality for the last 100 records created—e.g. the last 100 customers put into the customer database. Most companies have less than 50% completely accurate records.

Redman also argues for fixing data quality problems at the source, where "regular people" gather data on customers and other business entities

---

[8] https://www.linkedin.com/company/melissa-data-uk/about/.
[9] For example, see Thomas C. Redman, "Assess Whether You Have a Data Quality Problem," *Harvard Business Review*, 28 July 2016, https://hbr.org/2016/07/assess-whether-you-have-a-data-quality-problem.

Figure 4.2 Melissa's identity resolution prowess in doubt.

and enter them into systems of record. This idea was first quantified by George Labovitz and Yu Sang Chang in 1992 (the specific reference is unclear despite wide mentions of the creators and date), who argued that the cost of poor data quality is multiplied by a factor of 10 as it moves through an organization:

- Preventing poor data quality at the source costs $1 per record.
- Fixing a data quality problem after it is identified costs $10 per record.
- The cost to the business of doing nothing about the problem is $100 per record.

With inflation and much more extensive usage of information systems in organizations, Matillion (a data quality software vendor) argues that the costs have risen to $10/$100/$1000.[10] Redman, however, argues in

---

[10] Mark Balkenende, "The 1:10:100 Rule of Data Quality: A Critical Review for Data Professionals," Matillion website blog post, 01 July 2024, https://www.matillion.com/blog/the-1-10-100-rule-of-data-quality-a-critical-review-for-data-professionals.

discussions with Tom that fixing management, not software, is the best solution to these problems.

Data quality problems are particularly pronounced for externally sourced data, and it is often difficult or impossible to correct them. Not only may basic facts be wrong, but external data brokers often make inferences about consumers that are inaccurate.[11] There are several semi-anecdotal reports of poor quality data from data brokers, though no systematic studies that we could find—perhaps because most brokers only respond to individual data quality issues at most.[12] Several articles describe the poor data accuracy in data broker Acxiom's "About the Data" portal for consumers, though this service is no longer available. Given the quality problems that often come with third-party data about customers, it's vital to "try before you buy" to learn whether data quality problems are manageable.

What If Your Customers Aren't Consumers?

As we noted briefly earlier in this chapter, business-to-business (B2B) organizations usually have a different set of issues with customer data than business-to-consumer (B2C) companies, and business-to-business-to-consumer (B2B2C) companies yet another set.

Business-to-Business Companies

B2B companies usually have a much smaller number of business customers than consumer-oriented companies do. The good news about that is that B2B companies can more easily keep track of their customers and their relationship with them. The bad news is that each customer company can be a very complex entity, with multiple subsidiaries, departments, and individual executives who might be involved in a purchase. Connecting all of them isn't easy, so many companies use the external numbering system called Data Universal Numbering System (D-U-N-S) that assigns a number to each location of a company that allows keeping track of how smaller

---

[11] Suzanne Smalley, "'Junk Inferences' by Data Brokers Are a Problem for Consumers and the Industry Itself," Recorded future website blog post, 12 June 2024, https://therecord.media/junk-inferences-data-brokers.

[12] See, for example, John Lucker, "Predictably Inaccurate: Big Data Brokers," LinkedIn blog post, 18 November 2014, https://www.linkedin.com/pulse/20141118145642-24928192-predictably-inaccurate-big-data-brokers.

groups aggregate into a larger firm. It's the equivalent of "entity resolution" for a big company.

For a particular company or business unit, the type of data collected and employed isn't that different from B2C companies. It should include detailed information on what the company has purchased in the past, what marketing information company executives received, any inbound communication from the company, and salespeople's assessments of who the key buyers are and their feelings about the supplier's products and services. Because B2B purchases often involve high monetary value, leads are another critical data element to capture and exploit. This information can be held in CRM systems or customer data platforms, though they are likely to be smaller in volume and somewhat less structured than in B2C firms. Management of B2B customer data and relationships is sometimes referred to as *account-based marketing.*

Personalization of offers and marketing approaches would seem to be irrelevant in B2B situations. But the most sophisticated B2B companies don't just keep track of their customer company organization structures; they also keep track of individual buyer executives (sometimes called *stakeholders*) within them. Tom studied this area several years ago and wrote an article about it.[13] Two large tech companies excelled at this practice. One, IBM, had at the time more than 5 million businesses as customers, with 50 major product and service categories it was selling. Each of its customer organizations had on average four key buyers. The company needed to target sales and marketing approaches to each company and potential buyer. To do this, it created a score for each customer executive, reflecting their propensity and ability to buy the company's offerings, so that sales and marketing approaches could be more effective.

This approach, called *propensity modeling,* is increasingly automated with automated machine learning techniques. Using traditional human-crafted modeling, the company once employed 35 offshore statisticians to generate 150 propensity models a year. Then IBM hired a company called Modern Analytics that specializes in automated machine learning, or what it calls the Model Factory. Machine learning approaches quickly bumped the number

---

[13] Thomas H. Davenport, "Move Your Analytics Operation from Artisanal to Autonomous," *Harvard Business Review,* 02 December 2016, https://hbr.org/2016/12/move-your-analytics-operation-from-artisanal-to-autonomous.

of models up to more than 5000 models. The models use 5 trillion pieces of information to generate more than 11 billion scores a month predicting a particular customer executive's propensity to buy particular products or respond to particular marketing approaches. Eighty thousand different tactics are recommended to help persuade customers to buy. Using nonautomated approaches to propensity modeling to yield this level of granularity would require thousands of human analysts if it were possible at all.

At IBM 95% of the models are produced without human intervention, but in the remaining cases humans need to intervene to fix something. The company also employs several people to explain and evangelize for the models to sales and marketing people, but far fewer than the 35 statisticians it previously used.

Cisco Systems uses a similar approach. It went from doing tens of artisanal propensity models to tens of thousands of automated ones. A small group of analysts and data scientists in a group called Global Customer Insights generates these models each quarter. Cisco assessed the analytics efforts to be worth more than $1 billion in sales uplifts, and the company won an award from the American Marketing Association.

But in addition to this form of personalization, there are a variety of other customer science approaches that B2B companies can adopt to better appeal to customers. They can certainly practice search engine optimization (SEO), using testing different forms of online content to see which is most likely to yield a high search ranking. They can employ A/B and multivariate testing on their web pages to optimize data such as click-throughs, time spent, and conversions through their websites. These types of activities typically involve web and mobile data. B2B companies can employ marketing automation programs to reduce the human labor involved in email and online marketing campaigns, and if they do so, they should track campaign response by the customer company overall and by the company's stakeholders.

Business-to-Business-to-Consumer Companies

Business-to-business-to-consumer (B2B2C) companies, which are generally manufacturers of consumer products, have historically been in an unenviable position. They sold their product to distributors or retailers, who then sold it to consumers. As a result, they had very little information on which specific consumers were buying their product or the attributes of those customers.

In many such situations, the only information they typically received was aggregated and anonymized data from data collection firms. In grocery manufacturing, for example, Nielsen (now called NielsenIQ) and Information Resources (recently renamed Circana) gathered scanner data from grocery stores and provided it—usually after a delay of weeks—to grocery manufacturers. Both the delay and the inability to establish a relationship with specific consumers was frustrating for these companies.

B2B2C companies are trying to do an end run around their intermediaries, particularly retailers. We saw this in the Nestle example in Chapter 1; the company is using ecommerce to go direct-to-consumer as much as possible—not only to eliminate the costs of retail intermediaries but to get possession of their end customer's data. Other large consumer goods manufacturers, such as Procter & Gamble and Unilever, are also moving to direct-to-consumer (DTC) sales and even employing direct delivery services to get products to consumers. In doing so, of course, they are able to establish a direct relationship with consumers, know more about what makes them buy particular products, and learn more about the effectiveness of their marketing efforts.

At the same time, retailers have realized that they have a valuable resource in their data and are selling customer information to manufacturers (in addition to the data aggregators, whom they have sold to for decades). 84.51°, a data analytics company, and its parent company Kroger, the largest grocery-only chain in the United States, describe their data and insights offering this way:

> 84.51° Insights brings together first-party customer data, shopper science and strategy to give brands, agencies and grocery-affiliated partners unparalleled business knowledge and customer intelligence to drive a variety of business objectives. We help brands better understand the shopper's path to purchase.[14]

Similarly, Walmart has begun to make its own data available to suppliers through a business unit called Walmart Data Ventures. Some consumer

---

[14] "84.51° Insights," 84.51° website, https://www.8451.com/industries/consumer-packaged-goods.

insights (anonymized) are for sale; others are provided free to suppliers. Mark Hardy, the head of the unit, described some of the benefits to suppliers:

> Already today, our suppliers and our merchants are gaining insights about what customer behaviors and preferences are. We are then able to use that data to drive more personalized, targeted messages to the customers themselves so that we are relevant to them, rather than just being spam.[15]

In other words, the position of B2B2C companies relative to customer data is brightening, and there are new options for learning about customers and improving the relationship with them. However, B2B2C companies don't want to alienate retailers and other intermediary distribution channels, so they are stepping cautiously into the world of direct-to-consumer and first-party data.

AI and Customer Data

What can AI do for customer data? Most people would focus on the analysis benefits of AI, which are considerable: predictions, recommendations, personalization, and the like. But in this chapter focused on customer data, we'll focus on the benefits of AI for managing customer data—specifically, integrating it across an organization.

We've already described many of the challenges large organizations have with customer data. It is inaccurate, duplicated, incomplete, and overlapping, and the same customer is often described in different ways. What can be done about this? A brief historical discussion may be helpful. Before roughly a decade or so, the only way to integrate customer data was with an approach called *master data management* (MDM), which involved the use of decision rules to decide what to do with each customer record. MDM projects were typically very labor-intensive and time-consuming, and many of them were never finished. The objective of integrating the data was a valid one, but the means of accomplishing it—a series of decision rules—were often not up to the task.

---

[15] Nicole Silberstein, "Walmart Is Sharing More and More of Its Data with Its Suppliers: Here's Why," Retail TouchPoints website, 25 January 2024, https://www.retailtouchpoints.com/topics/data-analytics/business-intelligence/walmart-is-sharing-more-and-more-of-its-data-with-its-suppliers-heres-why.

More recently, companies have begun to integrate diverse data records with AI—not generative AI but old-fashioned machine learning. It "scores" data records to assess the degree to which they are consistent with other records. If the score is high enough (say, 95%), the two records are merged. If the score is lower than the automatic merge level, the record is sent to a human expert to try to reconcile the differing data.

This approach to integrating data has already proven to be much more successful and less difficult than MDM. Tom is an advisor to one company that provides this capability called Tamr. Many companies have used Tamr to integrate their customer (or supplier or product or financial) data. One that did so was Western Union, which is primarily in the business of money transfer.[16] Western Union is attempting to move to providing its services digitally, but it still has many retail agents. The customer data for online and retail customers has been in different formats, but Western Union is trying to integrate them and to achieve a 360-degree view. The integration, however, was challenging, with 1.2 billion customers sending and receiving money in the last decade and 200 million in the past 2 years, all across retail, website, and mobile channels.

Harveer Singh, the company's chief data architect, said that they had used MDM to integrate 80–90% of the data. But that wasn't enough to really provide value. "You make a real difference in that 10–20% zone. That's when you can reduce fraud or increase revenue. Our product has remained the same so to have a business result, we have to look at how much money we can make from those customers or how much risk we can reduce," he said. He concluded, "To master 200 million records using the traditional way of writing rules, we'd be doing it for 10 years and probably still wouldn't be able to do it."

Using AI from Tamr, Western Union was able to create an additional set of master records for 3–5% of their customers with little human intervention. Singh commented, "For an active customer base of 200 million people, this is huge. I now know a lot more about that three to five percent of customers. I know these are my real customers. I spend less on marketing because I'm not reaching out to the same person over and over again. These could be the ones committing fraud or spending the most money. This makes a very big difference between our top-line revenue and bottom-line growth."

---

[16] "Know Your Customers, Drive Your Growth," Tamr Customer Case Study, https://www.tamr.com/western-union-customer-story, last accessed 02 September 2024.

The task of customer integration for organizations like Western Union is never really finished, but it's important to do as much as possible and put solutions in place that yield progress. As with other forms of AI, it's likely that the data integration technology will get better in the future.

The Ethics of Customer Data

How much data on customer attributes should a company acquire, and what should it do with it? This is as much an ethical question as a technical one. Customers are often conflicted about their answers; on the one hand, they are nervous about companies having so much information about them. On the other hand, they want personalization of ads and offers. This tension is an important issue in the ethics of consumer data, and we'll try to address it further in Chapter 10 on the ethics of these technologies and data sources more broadly. But we want to point out some of the issues here.

Consumers generally say they want personalization. A 2021 survey, for example, found that 71% of consumers say they expect businesses to recognize them and personalize to their interests, and 76% are frustrated by the absence of personalization. In addition, companies that say they personalize report higher levels of revenue growth than those who do not.[17] Other less recent surveys also show a strong consumer preference for personalization.

On the other hand, two surveys from 2021, one of businesses and one of consumers, depict the challenge companies face with regard to data collection on consumers, which is necessary for effective personalization. Among 250 business executives, 70% reported that they expanded their collection of personal consumer data during the previous year. However, 86% of consumers said they have growing concerns about data privacy, and 30% said there are no circumstances under which they'd share data with businesses. Only 12% said they'd share data to personalize ads, and 17% would do so to help companies improve their products and services.[18]

---

[17] Nidhi Ahora et al. "The Value of Getting Personalization Right—or Wrong—Is Multiplying," McKinsey & Co., 2021, https://www.mckinsey.com/capabilities/growth-marketing-and-sales/our-insights/the-value-of-getting-personalization-right-or-wrong-is-multiplying.

[18] "Corporate Data Responsibility," KPMG, August 2021, www.visit.kpmg.us/CDR2021.

From a policy standpoint, consumers generally feel that things are getting out of hand with their data. According to a 2022 Ipsos poll, 70% of Americans think that, over time, limiting who can and can't access their data has become tougher.[19] This poll also found that only 34% of Americans think that companies adequately safeguard consumer data.

This might imply that consumers safeguard their own data, but that raises another contradiction. Ipsos also asked the poll's 1005 respondents about how they protect their data. Only 16% of respondents took all six data security measures about which Ipsos asked. Another 49% of respondents took three or fewer of these measures.

In the same survey, 78% of respondents said they wanted to require companies to obtain their consent before accessing and using their data. Similarly, 71% wanted to stay anonymous online, and 70% wanted the ability to scrub their data from the Internet. Taken as a whole, the results suggest that the average consumer is both worried about their online data and unsure of how to protect it.

For organizations pursuing data for better customer relationships, then, there is a challenging minefield of opinions to negotiate. The minefield is increasingly becoming more difficult because of regulatory constraints, which are always changing—at least outside the United States. For now it should be clear that unlimited gathering, usage, and monetization of customer data is a risk to an organization's reputation and its customers' goodwill. Leaders can go astray both by not gathering enough and doing enough with customer data and by gathering and doing too much.

We've discussed both better data and an exciting new technology thus far, as well as given examples of how they are combined. Now it's time to delve more deeply into specific objectives of these tools in the context of customer relationships. Personalization, the subject of the next chapter, is one of the most important uses of data and technology to achieve the objectives of customer science and improve customer relationships.

---

[19] Neil Lloyd and Chris Jackson, "Most Americans Say It Is Increasingly Difficult to Control Who Can Access Their Online Data," Ipsos, 9 January 2022, https://www.ipsos.com/en-us/news-polls/data-privacy-2022.

5 | Better Personalization and Hyper-Personalization

Personalization is one of the most important ways to use customer science and technologies to increase customer engagement. It suggests to potential customers that the advertised or offered product or service is particularly suited to their specific needs and desires. It promises to preserve customers' attention and time, making them aware only of offerings in which they would be interested. At least theoretically—as we'll argue, there's not much data on the topic—those time and attention savings and targeted offerings will increase customer engagement and purchases.

Personalization—also known as *one-to-one marketing*—is hardly new. The concept has its roots in the idea of segmentation, which treats different groups differently from a marketing perspective. Personalization is ostensibly about appealing to specific individuals, but they are often addressed on the basis of different group memberships—a customer's gender, sociodemographic status, geographical residence, age, etc. Generally speaking, the more attributes used to segment customers, the closer segmentation comes to personalization.

As we've discussed, one-to-one marketing was a popular concept in the late 1980s and 1990s. However, few firms had the data or modeling ability to create a differentiated offer for each consumer of their product or service. Thus, full personalization was more a concept than a reality in the first decade or two of its existence; in practice, it was not distinguished from segmentation.

Over the last decade, with the rise of electronic commerce and online marketing, personalization has been used in marketing as a means of targeting digital advertising, offers, and other customer-oriented content. The vast amount of data involved in digital customer relationships, and advances in AI methods, make it increasingly possible to approach the ideal of a unique offer for each customer.

However, most approaches to personalization have not been very sophisticated or effective. They have usually fallen well short of the one-to-one ideal, either because they lacked accurate and detailed data on which to base the personalization or because they used relatively primitive methodological approaches and algorithms. Today, when sufficient data is available, there are more sophisticated approaches that can help to realize the true promise of personalization. We'll refer to these precision approaches as enabling *hyper-personalization* to differentiate them from the previous approaches.

Many managers, however, lack a good means of characterizing the technology and sophistication of alternative personalization approaches. Vendors tout their own approaches without mentioning limitations. Each approach has its own data requirements and technical underpinnings.

We'll also discuss the privacy trade-offs involved in personalization. The potential value of personalization is highly appealing to marketers and product/service designers, and even to start-up CEOs designing new business models. As we suggested in the previous chapter on data, however, there are important issues around customer privacy and perceptions of invasiveness to be addressed, and personalization based on data should generally be conducted with transparency and customer permission. The appeal of personalization is also in flux due to privacy concerns, so those who plan to adopt it need to be aware of current opinion and regulation.

What to Personalize?

Personalization is applicable to a wide variety of marketing approaches. Perhaps the most common is personalized advertising, either for digital or—less commonly today—"analog" (direct mail, television, etc.) ads. Offers and discounts on particular products and services can also be personalized. Channels for reaching the customer can be personalized based on their channel preferences. In online commerce, search rankings and other aspects of web and mobile sites can be personalized. Personalization initiatives are sometimes known as "next best offers" or "next best actions."

Specific offers of products and services typically have the objective of increasing conversions; next best actions sometimes include relationship-building communications that may build overall customer engagement. Next best actions may include content on how the customer can improve their experience with the product or service, how the product or service can be used most effectively, or simply how to live a better life. Whenever possible, the actions should be personalized not only with regard to the product or service purchased, but on other customer attributes that increase the likelihood of their relevance.

Morgan Stanley's wealth management practice, for example, has created a next-best action system that provides machine learning–based personalized investment recommendations to its customers (mediated through investment advisors, who send the recommendations to customers). It also incorporates the ability for advisors to send messages that don't involve investments, such as birthday wishes, advice on family health and wellness matters, and even sports team results. The company has found that investment advisors who use the system significantly outperform those who do not in growing assets under management, and have higher productivity and frequency of engagement with customers.[1]

Digital content, whether in marketing messages, web pages, or other forms of expression, is easily personalized today with generative AI and might be assumed to build customer engagement more than transaction-oriented digital advertising. Digital products, such as music recommendations, are

---

[1] Thomas H. Davenport, "The Future of Work Now: Morgan Stanley's Financial Advisors and the Next Best Action System," *Forbes*, 16 May 2020, https://www.forbes.com/sites/tom davenport/2020/05/16/the-future-of-work-now-morgan-stanleys-financial-advisors-and-the-next-best-offer-system/?sh=7fd496fb7027.

heavily personalized by companies like Spotify. Political campaigns are increasingly personalized, although most campaign emails and text messages don't get the details right. Personalized content increasingly includes news feeds, leading to the "filter bubble" concern that people see content only from sources with which they agree.

In addition to marketing materials, the detailed attributes of products and services can also be personalized. Financial services firms like Morgan Stanley personalize investment portfolios with "robo-advice." Clothing companies allow shoes and other goods to be personalized at the time of manufacture. Even medical services and treatments—known as *precision medicine* or *personalized medicine*—are increasingly targeted to an individual's genome or other biological makeup.

Personalization is increasingly coming to recommendations as well, not just for products or services but also for life behaviors. These approaches employ the behavioral economics idea of the "nudge" to influence behavior. Start-ups are employing the concept of "precision nudges" to influence weight loss, economic habits, and overall health and nutrition.[2] To the degree that these personalized services benefit customers beyond encouraging the purchase of an individual product or service, they would seem to advance customer engagement.

Benefits of Personalization

There are many potential benefits of personalization. Some of the reputed benefits are based on survey research, while others are based on online consumer behavior. Most involve increased sales or conversion rates rather than broader metrics of customer engagement. A McKinsey 2021 survey, for example, found that 71% of consumers say they expect businesses to recognize them and personalize to their interests, and 76% are frustrated by the absence of personalization. In addition, companies surveyed that say they personalize report higher levels of revenue growth than those who do not.[3] Several other less recent surveys show a strong consumer preference for personalization.

---

[2] Thomas H. Davenport, James Guszcza, and Greg Swartz, "Using Behavioral Nudges to Treat Diabetes," *Harvard Business Review*, 10 October 2018, https://hbr.org/2018/10/using-behavioral-nudges-to-treat-diabetes.

[3] Nidhi Ahora et al., "The Value of Getting Personalization Right—or Wrong—Is Multiplying," McKinsey & Co., 2021, https://www.mckinsey.com/capabilities/growth-marketing-and-sales/our-insights/the-value-of-getting-personalization-right-or-wrong-is-multiplying.

As customers become more sensitive to privacy issues with their data, they may be less interested in personalization, or at least may require a higher degree of accuracy in targeting their personal preferences in order to justify the trade-off. However, the exact frontier at which the desirability of personalization is outweighed by the desire for personal privacy is difficult to establish, in part because the two traits are poorly connected in the minds of many consumers.

Previous Approaches to Personalization

AI enables the most effective hyper-personalization strategies, but there are previous approaches that have been used to personalize offers or actions for many years. These were typically based on single or a few factors, resulting in less accurate personalization for customers. For example, a popular simple approach to personalization involves "retargeting" based only upon a previous expression of customer interest: a purchase, a click on a website, an opened email, a downloaded whitepaper, or an inbound call to a call center. It assumes that past interest is an indicator of ongoing interest in a related product, category, or company.

Retargeting vendors often claim a much higher level of click-throughs for retargeted ads than those seen for the first time—the usual numbers mentioned are 0.7% for first-time view versus 7% for retargeted.[4] However, click-throughs do not in themselves comprise either conversions or engagement.

Companies may also use single or a few data-based attributes of the customer to create personas that are known or assumed to be associated with increased purchase behavior. Such attributes may include location, demographic factor (gender, age, ethnicity, etc.), associational or institutional membership (affinity marketing), or collaborative filtering (making recommendations for one customer based on expressed interest or purchases by others with similar tastes). Data for this approach to personalization is often purchased from third-party data aggregators; however, such attribute

---

[4] See, for example, this (undated) compilation of retargeting statistics at the Wishpond.com site: https://blog.wishpond.com/post/97225536354/infographic-7-incredible-retargeting-ad-stats. Original sources of these statistics are not clear, however.

data are often inaccurate.[5] Attribute-based persona approaches may be combined with retargeting and are usually more effective than retargeting alone. One or a few data-based attributes can also be achieved through A/B type experimentation, i.e. a click on one version of a web page versus another.

An older, relatively simple form of AI that is common in marketing automation and campaign management systems uses rules to make simple personalized offers. It allows differential treatment (offers, content, etc.) of different groups based on a few rules involving such factors as demographics, previous purchases, or geographic residence. This approach is particularly common in marketing automation software, such as Salesforce's Pardot or HubSpot's Marketing Hub. The use of rules allows for the use of multiple customer attributes at once (using "and" or "or" logic) for personalization. A set of segmentation rules, for example, might specify sending a particular marketing message to males over 30 in age and living in the Southeastern states. However, beyond a small number of rules, they can begin to conflict or become confusing.

Rules are employed because they seem logical to a human marketer, not because they have been statistically determined to yield an optimum result in either short-term conversions or longer-term engagement. In other words, they are not data-driven. Rules have the benefit of being easily understood by marketers and their stakeholders. Each rule, of course, also requires a specific data variable on customers to be able to apply the rule. One can't personalize an offer based on an age rule if age is not a variable present in the data.

Contemporary AI-Based Approaches to Personalization

The most sophisticated, precise, and difficult form of personalization—in other words, hyper-personalization—involves machine learning models. Unlike rule-based personalization, machine learning can employ multiple

---

[5] Nico Neumann, Catherine E. Tucker, and Timothy Whitfield, "Frontiers: How Effective Is Third-Party Consumer Profiling? Evidence from Field Studies," *Marketing Science* 38(6): 918–926, 2019, https://pubsonline.informs.org/doi/pdf/10.1287/mksc.2019.1188. See also Elizabeth Dwoskin, "Data Broker Discloses What It Knows," *The Wall Street Journal*, 04 September 2013, https://www.wsj.com/articles/BL-DGB-29054; and Tom Bergin, "How a Data Mining Giant Got Me Wrong," Reuters, 29 March 2018, https://www.reuters.com/article/us-data-privacy-acxiom-insight/how-a-data-mining-giant-got-me-wrong-idUS KBN1H513K.

different customer, product, or contextual attributes with few complications and tends to have much more precision than rule-based approaches. It allows a company to have many different groupings or segments—millions of unique offers in principle. Machine learning–based personalization can even approach the elusive one-to-one segmentation to which marketers have long aspired. This approach has been possible for several decades if the needed data are available. For example, the UK-based supermarket chain Tesco pioneered such hyper-personalization using its Clubcard loyalty program data in the late 1990s and early 2000s, generating 12 million unique offers for grocery promotions.[6] More recently, in the inflationary economy of 2022, Tesco is focusing on personalizing discounts to Clubcard holders.[7]

Hyper-personalization approaches using machine learning can be product-centric, customer-centric, or a combination of the two. Product-centric approaches such as "collaborative filtering" rely on the "people who bought this product also bought this other product" approach, generating coefficients of product relatedness based on purchase data. All a company needs to know about its customers using this approach is what products they have bought or expressed interest in.

Some companies go deeper into the product-centric approach by classifying attributes of the products. Netflix's well-known recommendation engine, for example, classifies each movie and TV show along multiple product attributes, such as subject, stars, directors, and the like. It can then recommend content with the same attributes of purchased content to customers. Attribute classification is useful, but it can be labor-intensive. Creators or manufacturers of products often don't supply attribute information.

In addition to information about titles, Netflix's personalized recommendations are based on self-reported customer entertainment preferences, viewing history and ratings of watched titles, other members with similar tastes and preferences (it categorizes more than 2000 different "taste communities"), and situational factors such as time of day, device type, and length of a typical viewing session. The information is used to

---

[6] Thomas H. Davenport and Jeanne G. Harris, *Competing on Analytics* (Boston: Harvard Business Review Press, second edition, 2017), pp. 138–139.

[7] James Davey, "Loyalty Pays Off for Tesco as Britons Feel the Pinch," Reuters, 23 February 2022, https://www.reuters.com/business/retail-consumer/loyalty-pays-off-tesco-britons-feel-pinch-2022-02-23.

present a personalized set of titles to each viewer on their screens.[8] Netflix's personalization has clearly contributed to a better customer experience and contributed to high subscriber growth for many years (it declined somewhat in 2022 due to economic and post-pandemic contraction but grew again in 2023) and to higher combined usage than cable and satellite viewing combined.[9]

An example of the customer-centric approach to personalization might employ not only past purchases but such variables or features as customer demographic data, recent life events, estimated income levels, communications channel preferences, and any responses to previous offers. It would combine these variables to develop a predictive model of how a customer might respond to the personalized offer. Each potential customer would then be scored using the model in terms of the likelihood of purchasing a product or category. Only those with a high score would receive an offer or action related to that product. With many different models in production deployment, a company could approach a different offer for each customer.

The grocery store chain Kroger, for example, has 60 million customers in its loyalty programs, and it delivered 1.9 billion personalized offers to its customers in 2021. It employs a large-scale machine learning model development and deployment capability in its 84.51° data and analysis subsidiary.[10]

These offers are primarily focused on encouraging sales transactions rather than customer engagement. Yet 84.51° and Kroger are also beginning to focus on personalized nutritional information and recommendations that may boost engagement over time. The retailer's OptUP program calculates a nutrition score based on a customer's recent purchases using Kroger loyalty card data. Shoppers can also browse an app while shopping to see

---

[8] Netflix website, "How Netflix's Recommendation System Works," https://help.netflix.com/en/node/100639.

[9] "The Netflix Effect: How Netflix's Commitment to Extreme Personalization Is Impacting Customer Expectations," WBR Insights, no date, https://nextgencx.wbresearch.com/blog/netflix-effect-commitment-extreme-personalization-customer-expectations.

[10] The company is named after the longitude of Cincinnati, where it is based. See Thomas H. Davenport, "84.51° Builds a Machine Learning Machine for Kroger," Forbes, 02 April 2018, https://www.forbes.com/sites/tomdavenport/2018/04/02/84-51-builds-a-machine-learning-machine-for-kroger/?sh=3bd47a0c64e1.

nutrition scores of individual products and can receive "Better for You" recommendations of healthier but related products.

While Kroger has a high volume of data on shopper behavior, what usually makes customer-centric models difficult is obtaining the necessary data. To employ them, a company needs extensive data on customer attributes and labeled outcome data, for example, purchase of the product or category or response to an offer. Loyalty programs are particularly useful for this purpose, because many aspects of customer behavior can be tracked over time. In digital ad placement models, cookies have historically been an excellent source of data about websites that customers have visited, which can be used to predict customer interest in ads. However, consumers are beginning to be wary of cookies, and some companies like Google keep threatening to phase them out of their web browsers.

Third-party data aggregators and brokers, however, are increasingly providing personalization attributes using data from multiple sources.[11] They might combine, for example, a consumer's web browsing history with credit card purchases, social media activity, the email domain name, the type of device used to access the Internet, and other characteristics. The widespread availability of these types of data make it easier to create sophisticated machine learning–based personalization models, but they probably will hasten the backlash to personalization as well.

In addition to the availability of more data, another traditional constraint on marketers seeking to personalize for greater customer engagement is being eased. Machine learning model creation (called *automated machine learning* [AutoML]) and ongoing maintenance (called *machine learning operations* [MLOps]) are becoming more automated, making the machine learning activities more accessible to nondata scientists. This means business or marketing analysts with some quantitative orientation and who understand customers and markets are in many cases able to create personalization and other types of models using machine learning. They can also ensure that the models do not "drift" and continue to effectively predict customer behavior over time using MLOps systems. At Kroger and 84.51°,

---

[11] For an excellent description of the types of data available from third-party providers and how it is used, see Stuart A. Thompson, "These Ads Think They Know You," *The New York Times*, 30 April 2019, https://www.nytimes.com/interactive/2019/04/30/opinion/privacy-targeted-advertising.html.

for example, "insights specialists" work alongside professional data scientists to create machine learning models, and their greater level of business insights sometimes make their models more useful than those of data scientists.[12]

Personalization Model Types

Many model types in machine learning can be used for personalization (Table 5.1). The most sophisticated AI companies typically employ multiple types in combination or for different circumstances. The most

Table 5.1   Types of AI models used in personalization

Type of model	Definition	Strengths	Weaknesses
Supervised learning	Training models	Prediction	Requires labeled data
Unsupervised learning	Requires little or no model training	Clustering like customers	Segmentation only; not better than other methods
Deep learning	Supervised multilayer neural network models	Adds precision to predictions	High volume of data required; low interpretability
Reinforcement learning	Maximizes longer-term objective with rewards	Prediction over time	Requires data on sequence of actions
A/B and multivariate testing	Compares two or more online alternatives	Causal outcomes	Becomes complex with multiple arms and when combined with ML

[12] Thomas H. Davenport, "The Future of Work Now: AutoML at 84.51° and Kroger," *Forbes*, 21 October 2020, https://www.forbes.com/sites/tomdavenport/2020/10/21/the-future-of-work-now-automl-at-8451and-kroger/?sh=6839782f4b0e.

common type is supervised learning models, in which models are trained on labeled data and then used to make predictions. A common labeled outcome is whether the customer bought a particular type of product. The model makes a prediction of how likely the customer is to buy it in the future and what factors are statistically associated with that buying behavior. Traditional supervised ML models, without a set of deep layers, have been used for many years in personalization. Among the companies using supervised learning for personalization among other methods are Disney Parks and Resorts (using Magic Band data worn on customer wrists for personalized itineraries), Netflix, Nike, Instagram, and Starbucks.

Some companies have begun to employ multilayer or deep learning neural network models for personalization.[13] Among the early adopters of this approach was Dynamic Yield, which was acquired by McDonald's to support its personalization efforts (and those of other companies as well) in 2019 and then sold to Mastercard in 2021. These models require more data and are less interpretable than traditional ML models but can often supply more accurate predictions. In addition to McDonald's, companies using the Dynamic Yield personalization technology include Lands' End, PacSun, Sephora, and Forever 21. Netflix has developed some of its own approaches and models using deep learning for personalization.

Unsupervised machine learning models can also be used to identify segments or clusters of like customers on several features or variables and thus can also support personalization.[14] Segments, however, are not a highly precise form of personalization. In addition, these models also require extensive data, and they don't necessarily provide higher value than other less advanced approaches to data-based segmentation such as factor analysis or K-means clustering. There are many discussions of unsupervised learning for customer segmentation in the academic literature, but these methods are not widely used in business personalization. Some start-ups have approaches, however. Twik.io is an 8-year-old start-up that personalizes a website visitor's experience in real time. It uses unsupervised

---

[13] Deep learning models are neural networks (themselves a form of machine learning) that use nodes based on features or variables to convert data inputs to outputs such as predictions; they are "deep" with several or many layers of intermediate nodes.

[14] Unsupervised learning attempts to find clusters, patterns, or anomalies in a collection of data with unlabeled outcomes.

learning to segment website visitors based on their computer fingerprint and real-time behavioral analysis, even at the moment of initial visit. Twik handles the entire process, from data collection through analysis to real-time customization.

Twik identifies and tags important events (like add-to-cart, checkouts) and adapts to each visitor in real time through client-side browser modifications, rendering changes through browser/DOM manipulation. It automatically identifies business goals and then subtly adjusts the experience based on both "lookalike" profiles and actual user behavior. These adjustments can include reorganizing product catalogs, restructuring navigation menus, localizing currencies, and even generating AI-powered content variations—all while maintaining a coherent experience through a weighted algorithm that prevents jarring changes for frequent visitors.

To employ multiple model types and choose among them, some leading companies are using reinforcement learning (sometimes in combination with deep learning models) to find the best models at optimizing a longer-term reward function such as a set of clicks or conversions over time.[15] Different reinforcement learning models can be automatically evaluated and compared. Netflix, for example, uses reinforcement learning to try to optimize customers' long-term satisfaction with its entertainment content.

Finally, many companies combine experimental results with other types of models. A/B and multivariate testing approaches can be used to understand customer preferences, particularly for personalizing online content. The outcomes of such experiments are causal rather than correlational, which often provides a higher degree of certainty about outcomes. Stitch Fix, for example, has built a "centralized experimentation platform" using a variety of experimental designs to optimize the effectiveness of clothing recommendations for customers.[16]

---

[15] Reinforcement learning is a form of unsupervised learning in which a program attempts to maximize a reward in a particular sequence of situations over time. It can employ a variety of algorithm types. It is most commonly used in games, including autonomous chess, Go, and Atari video games.

[16] Aaron Bradley, "Building Our Centralized Experimentation Platform," Stitch Fix website, 30 July 2019, https://multithreaded.stitchfix.com/blog/2019/07/30/building-centralized-experimental-platform/.

Contextual Factors in Personalization

In addition to customer and product/service attributes, successful personalization models also often include contextual factors about the transaction or offer. They may, for example, include the season, time of day, or specific customer location (if revealed through an app, for example), which can influence the nature of the offer. Companies may also decide to make offers only on products that are in stock at a local store or through ecommerce purchases.

Contextual factors may also address the channel through which the personalized offer or action is made. A large bank, for example, experimented with mortgage loan discount offers for high-balance customers that were presented through its automated teller machines. However, that led to longer customer waits at the ATMs, and the bank decided to only employ such offers in a mobile app or web channel.

When adding contextual factors to other types of data, personalization based on multi-attribute machine learning is likely to become the dominant type in the future. As data becomes increasingly available, it can be used to make accurate predictions of the marketing offers and purchase/relationship contexts to which customers will respond. Only traditional supervised or deep learning models allow for very granular segments using multiple contextual and offer-oriented features to make predictions—so many factors that no human could keep them all straight. Models can also be monitored and retrained over time to ensure their ongoing accuracy.

A Successful Personalization Example at Starbucks

One highly successful personalization approach is embodied in Starbucks' AI platform called "Deep Brew." Starbucks had historically relied on its baristas in physical stores to personalize offers and actions to customers and thereby increase customer engagement, but this became increasingly difficult as customers began to order in advance through the company's smartphone app and was impossible when stores were closed during the COVID pandemic except for drive-thru orders or drink pickup. Deep Brew, which was initially focused on English-speaking markets in the United States, Canada, and United Kingdom, was launched in 2019. It not only included personalization functions for the Starbucks app but also assisted with administrative activities in the stores, such as reorder points for supplies and labor scheduling.

DeepBrew was Starbucks' first major foray into machine learning, and the company formed a small, dedicated team of data scientists to prototype the recommendation engine and other models. Starbucks had massive amounts of data on past customer purchase patterns to employ in personalization, which it applied to emailed promotions, in-app featured products and discounts, and games and prizes.

The team concluded that deep reinforcement learning would create the most powerful models for recommendations, so it ultimately adopted that approach. Alternative models are tested against each other using an A/B testing approach. The criteria being optimized are total revenue from a sale and the likelihood of the customer buying additional items beyond their normal purchase. The team's goal was to personalize across all touchpoints and channels. Starbucks now uses the models to create more than 10 billion "hyper-personalized" recommendations per year. The models learn rapidly and continuously from new data.

Now data and customer behavior-based recommendations take into account likely customer preferences like vegetarian food, price sensitivity, tea versus coffee, baked good preferences, etc. Recommendations are also used within the drive-thru experience but are not based on customer identity. In that channel the focus is on contextual factors such as location, time of day, and weather. During the pandemic when drive-thru lanes were the only way customers could get Starbucks products from stores, data scientists added a feature assessing the length of the drive-thru line. When lines were uncomfortably long, customers at the drive-thru screen received recommendations for drinks that are easy and quick to prepare.

DeepBrew is viewed as successful within Starbucks not only for personalization but for its other administrative functions and as an enabler of customer engagement as customers increasingly order through the mobile app; about a quarter of all orders go through that channel. Kevin Johnson, Starbucks' CEO in 2021, credited DeepBrew in part with Starbucks' ability to grow same store sales, mobile app sales, and drive-thru sales throughout the COVID pandemic period.[17]

---

[17] Emma Liem Beckett, "Starbucks' Digital Success Partially Driven by AI Engine, CEO Kevin Johnson Says," RestaurantDive website, 28 April 2021, https://www.restaurantdive.com/news/starbucks-digital-success-partially-driven-by-ai-engine-ceo-kevin-johnson/599182.

However, the AI project wasn't easy to accomplish. Some managers used to an intuitive and consensus-based decision culture were not initially receptive to a personalization approach based on machine learning models that they did not understand. Knowing this, the data science team employed agile development approaches with frequent prototype reviews and carefully tracked the costs and benefits of adopting the models. They maintained a dashboard of key performance indicators during the development of the new model and process behind DeepBrew. There was a major focus on preventing a security breach or hack. And senior executives calmed Starbucks frontline associates by stating often that DeepBrew would not replace human workers but rather free them up to develop closer personal ties to customers.[18] From our own experience and employment data, it would appear that neither of these has happened.

The Models Are the Easy Part

AI executives at Starbucks often point out that developing the needed machine learning models for personalization was the relatively easy part of the project. Persuading stakeholders, ensuring security, and demonstrating value were important management tasks that were perhaps more difficult than the actual modeling.

The AI managers also emphasize that the model development process was only a small part of the technology development for DeepBrew. The systems or processes necessary to surround DeepBrew's ML models included configuration, data collection, feature extraction, data verification, machine resource management, analysis tools, process management tools, serving infrastructure, and performance monitoring. Together these infrastructure activities required much more time, effort, and investment than the modeling activities.

This isn't only true at Starbucks. Deploying a machine learning system into "production mode" is typically a complex effort involving substantial human, cultural, and technical change. This is also the case with less advanced technical solutions than machine learning. When Tom researched personalized "next best offer" systems several years ago, it became apparent

---

[18] Jennifer Warnick, "AI for Humanity: How Starbucks Plans to Use Technology to Nurture the Human Spirit," Starbucks website, 10 January 2020, https://stories.starbucks.com/stories/2020/how-starbucks-plans-to-use-technology-to-nurture-the-human-spirit.

that the "analyzing and executing" stage for offers had to be preceded by substantial efforts to define objectives and gather multiple types of data and succeeded on a continuous basis by "learning and evolving" activities.[19]

Generative AI and Personalization

With its ease of content creation, generative AI can create personalized ads and offers with relative ease. It can create personalized text or images, and in some cases even videos, based on demographic and previous purchase information about the customer. Many technology start-ups have the capability to generate personalized offers.

Nutella, for example, has even created seven million different jar wrappers using generative AI, although they don't seem to be tied to customer data. The used car retailer Carvana created 1.3 million personalized videos for its customers, recounting the day they purchased their vehicle. Cadbury has used generative AI to create personalized birthday songs for customers. It would seem that the only barrier to personalized content is the creativity of marketers.

How Much Personalization Is Too Much?

The rapid growth in digital media and tools for personalizing ads and offers has led to a growing consumer backlash on grounds of consumer privacy, although it has not yet had a substantial effect on personalization or customer engagement related to it in the United States. Common approaches used for personalization, including capturing and analyzing customer online behaviors and purchases, have been criticized as amounting to "surveillance capitalism."[20] While most consumers seem to still appreciate some degree of personalization, they may react negatively to personalized offers that seem to be too personal—based on attributes or activities viewed as private. Or they may require a higher level of personalization—more accurately attuned to their needs and desires—for the amount of privacy they believe they are giving up.

The fact is that we don't really yet know the limits of personalization. For better or worse, surveillance capitalism is in its early stages and has

---

[19] Thomas H. Davenport, Leandro DalleMule, and John Lucker, "Know What Your Customers Want Before They Do," *Harvard Business Review*, December 2011, https://hbr.org/2011/12/know-what-your-customers-want-before-they-do.

[20] Shoshana Zuboff, *The Age of Surveillance Capitalism* (Public Affairs, 2020).

thus far been hindered by poor quality data, insufficient volumes of data, challenges in establishing a persistent customer identity, and lack of methodological sophistication among many marketers. Most consumers, it seems fair to surmise, would not view advertising and marketing offers as attacks on their privacy if they are closely targeted to the products and services they really desire.

In addition, the appropriate balance of privacy versus personalization is likely to vary across individual consumers. Some will perceive any loss of privacy as a fair value exchange if their shopping is made more efficient and enjoyable by personalization. Others will be placated by companies being transparent about what they do with data about consumers, and even explanations of why they may have seen a particular personalized ad or offer. Facebook, for example, has offered a "Why Am I Seeing This Ad?" feature since 2014, and in 2019 Facebook added details behind personalization approaches such as the interests or categories the advertiser was attempting to appeal to, and the source of the data used for personalization.[21] Still other consumers may want no data-based personalization at all.

Personalization of ads and news on mobile devices has been affected over the past few years by changes in vendor policies. Apple, for example, announced in 2022 its device identifier for advertisers (IDFA) would require opt-in from iOS device users. IDFA previously allowed apps to personalize ads, offers, and content based on third-party app iPhone activity, but that was no longer possible. Prominent app providers like Facebook and YouTube estimated that the "app tracking transparency" move cost them billions of dollars in advertising revenue.[22]

The ability to personalize marketing is also governed in part by particular regulatory constraints. The European General Data Protection Regulation (GDPR) does restrict the ability to use data for personalization, although it has limited utility in this regard because of individual consumers' lack of understanding of the implications of their consent for

---

[21] Iris Hearn, "Facebook Expands "Why Am I Seeing This Ad" Feature to Provide More Detailed Insights to Users," *Impact*, 15 July 2019, https://www.impactplus.com/blog/facebook-expands-why-am-i-seeing-this-ad-feature-to-provide-more-detailed-insights-to-users.

[22] Matthew Fox, "$315 Billion in Market Value Erased After Apple IDFA Privacy Changes," Business Insider Markets, 03 February 2022, https://markets.businessinsider.com/news/stocks/facebook-meta-stock-apple-idfa-ios-privacy-change-social-media-2022-2.

personalization, as well as limited enforcement mechanisms for violations.[23] The California Consumer Privacy Act (CCPA), the state-level data privacy legislation that took effect in 2020, allows consumers to opt out of having their data be sold to another user. However, CCPA has also had little impact on personalization of advertising thus far, in part because of low opt-out rates by consumers.[24]

Personalization is thus a continuously evolving concept based on increasing levels of digitization and data, advancing methods for artificial intelligence, and changing perceptions of customers and regulators about privacy/personalization trade-offs. Astute marketers can make increasingly effective use of sophisticated personalization approaches, but they should be aware that the value of and reaction to any particular approach is likely to be limited in time. In addition, because of the difficulties of defining and measuring customer engagement accurately, marketers should take a broad perspective on how personalization affects long-term customer behavior and measure multiple aspects of it. It seems likely that well-executed hyper-personalization enabled by artificial intelligence can help in preserving customers' time and attention amid an overwhelming flow of information and hence increase customer engagement over time. But this expectation is based on logic and only limited and narrow empirical findings, and both research and practice need to be pursued over a longer time and greater breadth than they have thus far.

The next chapter addresses another common objective in customer relationships: hearing and understanding the voice of the market. We'll describe how organizations can use AI and other technologies to make sense of the customer voice and take action on it.

---

[23] Michèle, Finck, "The Limits of the GDPR in the Personalisation Context" in U. Kohl, J. Eisler (eds), *Data-Driven Personalisation in Markets, Politics and Law* (Cambridge University Press, 2021). https://ssrn.com/abstract=3830304.

[24] Kate Kaye, "CCPA Hasn't Affected Ad Revenues, but Indirect Effects Could Hurt," Digiday website, 25 February 2021, https://digiday.com/media/ccpa-early-impact/.

6

Better Customer
Voice Analysis
and Action

The voice of the customer (VoC) is music to the ears of product teams, marketing mavens, sales representatives, and customer service professionals. These departments spend an enormous amount of energy trying to imagine what potential buyers might want, what messaging they might respond to, and what solutions will best address their problems. If you get enough people talking, you'll learn what they love and hate about your offerings, spot problems you need to fix, and understand what the real customer experience is like out in the world rather than in brainstorming meetings.

It's common knowledge that it costs more to win a new customer than to keep an old one. Making and keeping customers happy cuts down on churn, lowers acquisition costs, and ultimately boosts the lifetime value of each customer. The key to improving satisfaction is spotting what might turn a customer off and mitigating friction.

Every product manager knows why their product is good. They know the value it provides. They know the best use cases for it. They are also surprised when faced with real customers who do not share their clear

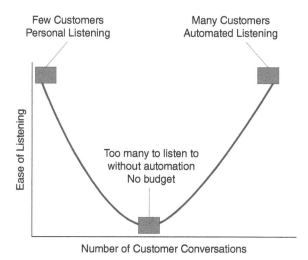

Figure 6.1   **Understanding customers is challenging in the middle.**

vision of the product. That's because the product manager is not the target audience. The intuitive insights every company has about their offerings' value propositions fall flat when real people try to use their "ideal solution" in the real world. As customer expectations rise, it's imperative to really get inside their heads and understand what makes them tick.

At first, this seems a straightforward task. A small company may talk to each and every customer on a daily basis. Large companies can programmatically calculate what gives customers joy and what frustrates them through (pre-GenAI) natural language processing (NLP). If the volume of contacts falls in between large and small volume, all a company could do is sample a fraction of comments and hope they were getting to the truth. (See Figure 6.1.)

Generative AI to the Rescue

Today, GenAI gives companies of all sizes a new tool for parsing customer feelings. While this technology often grabs headlines for its customer-facing applications like personalization and chatbots, it has untapped potential in decoding customer sentiment and top-of-mind topics. By leveraging

GenAI to enhance our understanding of the customer, we can uncover insights that might otherwise remain hidden. This enhanced VoC data can drive meaningful improvements across the board—from boosting customer satisfaction to refining product features and elevating the overall customer experience.

Large language models (LLMs) have the ability to help in many ways:

- **Intelligent call/email triage:** LLMs can analyze the full context of customer communications to accurately route and prioritize issues, moving beyond simple keyword matching.
- **Adaptive categorization:** As customer needs and company offerings evolve, LLMs can dynamically update their categorization schemes without requiring manual reconfiguration.
- **Sentiment analysis:** LLMs can detect nuanced emotional tones in customer communications to flag urgent or sensitive issues for human intervention.
- **Intent prediction:** By understanding the context and history, LLMs can anticipate likely next steps or follow-up questions, allowing for more proactive customer service.
- **Personalized routing:** LLMs can factor in individual customer history and preferences to route issues to the most appropriate agent or department.
- **Multilingual support:** LLMs' language understanding capabilities enable seamless routing and categorization across multiple languages without separate systems.
- **Continuous improvement:** With reinforcement learning, the system becomes more accurate and nuanced over time based on feedback and outcomes.
- **Compliance adherence:** LLMs can be trained to recognize and flag communications that may have regulatory or compliance implications.
- **Insight generation:** Beyond routing, LLMs can aggregate and analyze communications to surface emerging trends or systemic issues.
- **Human-AI collaboration:** While automating routine triage, LLMs can also enhance human agent capabilities by providing relevant context and suggestions.

Boosting Customer Satisfaction

The customer voice has historically been difficult for computers to understand. For example, the ability to understand sarcasm is a tough nut to crack. Take, for example, this social media post: "Loved the extra leg room in economy—my knees only touched my chin!" Any traditional NLP system would immediately classify that as positive feedback. GenAI, however, can discern the underlying frustration in such comments, accurately categorize the sentiment, and even suggest appropriate responses. This capability allows an airline to better understand passengers' true experiences, address specific pain points, and, ideally, add a couple of inches between seats (though that seems a bit unlikely).

GenAI far outpaces traditional surveys or single metrics (such as Net Promoter Scores) in identifying and tagging issues. The ability to understand the context—even multiple contexts—of a complaint is new. "Our server was great, but the lobster bisque was too salty" is easily understood by a human, but scored unevenly by a traditional NLP system, which would struggle to label it positive or negative and so will settle on neutral. GenAI can parse the statement and route the appropriate portion of it to the attention of the right people. The waiter is issued an "Attaboy," and the chef earns a demerit.

It's not just tabulating loves and hates. It's truly hearing the customer in a way that assures them that they have been heard. Often, the act of complaining is enough and a refund or a replacement isn't necessary. Just the fact that the individual knows they were heard is enough. "Your comment is very important to us; thank you for taking the time" is rote. "We're sorry for the inconvenience" is insulting. "We're sorry the lobster wasn't properly seasoned and appreciate your kind words about your server" is a strong signal that the voice of the customer actually *is* important to the company.

Improving Customer Experience with Automated Message Routing

Customer experience is a holistic topic that is often misunderstood by large companies due to the fragmentation of the organization. For example, Jim was once asked to conduct a workshop on behalf of the newly appointed Director of Customer Experience at a large British telecom company. The meeting got off to a rocky start. When Jim asked about the customer journey starting with the first touchpoint, advertising, he was met with blank stares. Jim asked about the last touchpoint, the installation of the telco equipment. How were they monitoring the timeliness of the technicians' arrivals and the condition of their vans? Blank stares came from the workshop audience. The director of customer experience and team reporting to them were responsible only for the call center.

Even with high satisfaction and product loyalty, overall customer experience is undermined by mistargeted marketing, faulty packaging, broken processes, and untrained personnel. The ability to accurately gauge customer sentiment during interactions plays a crucial role in shaping perception and fostering loyalty.

Generative AI accelerates problem identification, classification, and prioritization, streamlining issue resolution. Moreover, it can craft targeted communications to relevant stakeholders about specific customer experiences and recommend actions. By leveraging AI's capabilities, organizations can more rapidly pinpoint areas for improvement, address concerns proactively, and maintain a consistent, high-quality customer experience across all channels. This approach not only enhances customer satisfaction but also contributes to long-term loyalty and brand advocacy.

The primary challenge in managing complex customer inquiries is directing the inquirer to the most appropriate service channel. Back in the day, it started with the switchboard: "How may I direct your call?"

"I'd like to know the price of your furniture." Transfer to sales.

"This item arrived broken." Transfer to customer service.

"I don't understand how to make this work." Transfer to technical support.

"Could you make a customized version for me?" Transfer to product management.

"You double billed me." Transfer to accounting.

We tried, and most would say failed, at using touch-tone telephone menus. "For sales, press 1. For customer service, press 2...." Even more frustrating? Interactive voice response (IVR). The inability to properly understand the spoken word mostly results in the caller angrily shouting, "Agent! Representative! Human!" due to the limitations of understanding situational context and generally poor speech recognition with IVR.

Generative AI offers a more sophisticated approach to inquiry categorization and routing. By analyzing the nuance of customer language and context, GenAI can more accurately determine the nature of the inquiry and direct it to the most qualified agent or resource, even multiple resources. This not only enhances efficiency but also significantly improves the customer experience by reducing unnecessary transfers and shortening resolution times.

The customer remains oblivious to the intricate web of internal data processing systems and policies that require seamless integration to address what they perceive as a straightforward inquiry. Of course, a great many inquiries are anything but straightforward, as is this hypothetical one:

> There was a pop-up for a special discount, and I entered the code, but you charged me full price anyway. And then, you sent the wrong color. Then, the replacement you sent didn't work when it got here. And you charged my credit card for both of them! Now, I'm getting dunning emails and it's driving me nuts! And two days ago, my bank said my credit card was compromised and so I need to update that. The new card now has my married name.

Large call centers are primarily staffed by younger employees with high turnover rates.[1] The likelihood of a twenty-something knowing how to even start to mollify the client and address their issues is slim. A highly skilled and well-trained rep will recognize the frustration in the customer's tone, provide reassurances, and then focus on resolving marketing discrepancies, addressing product defect issues, and updating the customer's record. An exceptional customer service representative (CSR) will meticulously document all aspects of the interaction to boost management's efforts to monitor customer satisfaction trends, product quality, and process improvement initiatives.

This comprehensive approach serves multiple purposes. It immediately addresses the customer's concerns, works toward a long-term solution, and contributes valuable data for organizational improvement. By accurately capturing the nuances of each interaction, top-tier CSRs provide a goldmine of information that can drive strategic decisions, enhance product development, and refine customer service protocols.

---

[1] https://www.avoxi.com/blog/call-center-attrition-turnover-rates/.

However, given the average tenure of call center workers, that outcome is not the norm. Enter GenAI with its ability to successfully automate interactions. GenAI can recognize the context in a convoluted call or email and hand off the automated routing to internal systems with all of the proper labeling, categorization, and severity attributes. Additionally, through reinforcement learning from human feedback (RLHF), these systems continuously improve.

RLHF happens when the subject-matter expert reviews output from a GenAI system and corrects it a variety of ways. Corrections can be general ("be more conciliatory"), detailed ("when the wrong color or size of a product is shipped, offer a replacement before offering a refund"), or highly informative ("read the attached product user guide, learn what questions to ask when a customer says the product doesn't work to determine if the problem is a product defect or a misunderstanding of the product functionality").

The use of GenAI to parse complex customer messages and refer them to the appropriate office is shown in the following example (written by this book's authors and published in *Applied Marketing Analytics*):[2]

> In recent conversations with Michael Thompson of First Analytics, he explained how he utilized an LLM and LangChain (a framework to construct LLM-powered apps) to help a regional grocery store automate email communications and operational responses. For instance, an example email might read: "My rotisserie chicken was expired by two days, and I could not use my rewards card. My personal shopper was great though. She was very responsive when I called to ask questions and quick to bring my groceries out. On top of that, she had my order ready three hours early, which was AMAZING."

Traditional natural language models would have had significant trouble categorizing this message, as they typically identify only one topic per message and label them as positive, negative, or neutral. The mix of sentiments and variety of issues in the email would mean it would traditionally require

---

[2] *Applied Marketing Analytics*, Volume 10-1 (2024–2025), https://www.henrystewartpublicat ions.com/ama/v10.

manual handling. However, the system First Analytics created is capable of parsing the entire message, identifying the different issues, and generating a response draft for human review:

"Dear (Name), Thank you for taking the time to share your experience with us. We're truly sorry to hear about the inconvenience you faced with the expired rotisserie chicken and the issue with your rewards card. Your feedback is invaluable, and we want to assure you that we are taking immediate steps to address these concerns. We're delighted to hear that your personal shopper was able to provide positive and efficient service. It's great to know that your order was ready ahead of schedule and that she was responsive to your needs. We'll certainly pass along your praise to her, as we know how important it is to offer exemplary customer service. We greatly appreciate your patronage and will strive to make your future visits nothing short of excellent. Warm regards, (Customer Service)."

This is an excellent example of a well-tuned LLM that works within strict guidelines. The model goes a step further by recognizing which departments are involved, the extent of their responsibility, and the likelihood they can take action.

In this case, the comment highlights a mixed experience at the grocery store, where the customer had issues with a product's freshness (expired rotisserie chicken) and the inability to use their rewards card but praised their personal shopper for being responsive and efficient. The relevant departments to notify include:

1. Store Operations: This department must be informed about the expired rotisserie chicken as it poses a significant food safety issue requiring immediate attention.
1.1 Fact: Store operations manage the stores. Likelihood: 100%.
1.2 Assumption: They can take immediate corrective action on food safety and product quality. Likelihood: 90%.
2. IT: The inability to use a rewards card could indicate a system issue needing resolution.

2.1 Fact: IT manages the company's IT capabilities. Likelihood: 100%.

2.2 Assumption: IT is the likely department to address rewards card issues. Likelihood: 85%.

3. Human Resources (HR): The positive feedback about the personal shopper could be used for employee recognition. While not directly related to the problems, acknowledging good work helps maintain high standards.

3.1 Fact: HR is responsible for managing HR needs. Likelihood: 100%.

3.2 Assumption: HR will be interested in positive employee feedback for recognition. Likelihood: 80%.

4. Supply Chain: Although not directly mentioned, expired products may signal an issue with inventory turnover that the supply chain department could investigate.

4.1 Fact: The supply chain is responsible for getting merchandise to stores. Likelihood: 100%.

4.2 Assumption: They may have insights into why an expired product was on the shelf. Likelihood: 60%.

5. Purchasing: This department, while least relevant to the specific issues raised, should be informed that a product they sourced was found expired.

5.1 Fact: Purchasing is responsible for procuring products. Likelihood: 100%.

5.2 Assumption: They have less direct control over in-store issues like product expiration but should still be informed. Likelihood: 50%.

In summary, store operations and IT should be prioritized to address immediate issues of food safety and system glitches, respectively. HR should be notified for employee recognition, while supply chain and purchasing may need to look into the broader issue of product quality.

As this example illustrates, having GenAI help out in customer service will decrease wait times, optimize agent utilization, and enhance first-call resolution rates. A predictable ripple effect is an uptick in calls from customers who recognize that your organization is more responsive than ever and more likely to assist them with reduced on-hold time and less need for repeated storytelling, thereby minimizing frustration.

Real-World Examples

The poster child for using GenAI for customer service has been Klarna, the "buy now, pay later" ecommerce financing company, which leveraged AI to elevate their customer support. Klarna reported using GenAI assistants to take over the work of 700 employees and reducing resolution times from 11 minutes to just 2 minutes while maintaining high customer satisfaction levels. Klarna's CEO insists that the 700 employees will not lose their jobs but will not be replaced with attrition.

Klarna's self-reported success in customer service caught a lot of attention as far back as February 2024.[3]

New York, NY—27 February 2024—Klarna today announced its AI assistant powered by OpenAI. Now live globally for 1 month, the numbers speak for themselves:

The AI assistant has had 2.3 million conversations, two-thirds of Klarna's customer service chats

It is doing the equivalent work of 700 full-time agents [though, as we noted, most are still employed there]

It is on par with human agents in regard to customer satisfaction score

It is more accurate in errand resolution, leading to a 25% drop in repeat inquiries

Customers now resolve their errands in less than 2 minutes compared to 11 minutes previously

It's available in 23 markets, 24/7 and communicates in more than 35 languages

It's estimated to drive a $40 million USD in profit improvement to Klarna in 2024

There are many vendors who are attempting to replicate this kind of success. Covin, an AI customer experience start-up, reported[4] that Salesforce Sales Cloud leverages generative AI to enhance the efficiency and effectiveness of call center operations in several key ways:

---

[3] https://www.klarna.com/international/press/klarna-ai-assistant-handles-two-thirds-of-cu
stomer-service-chats-in-its-first-month.

[4] https://convin.ai/blog/generative-ai-for-customer-service.

- **Personalized customer communication:** Uses AI to analyze customer history and behavior, enabling personalized service that anticipates customer needs.

    Example: Predicting customer issues and suggesting solutions before the customer fully articulates the problem.

- **Automation of routine tasks:** AI automates data entry, scheduling, and follow-ups, freeing customer service agent to focus on complex customer conversations.

    Example: Automatically updating customer records post-interaction, ensuring all information is current and accurate.

- **Improved agent training and performance monitoring:** AI monitors calls and provides feedback, helping to train contact center agents and improve their performance over time.

    Example: Identify patterns in customer service agent interactions that lead to successful resolutions and use these insights to train other team members.

Agent Support

Automating customer inquiries takes a concerted effort to implement. That takes time. And no matter how sophisticated a system one creates, there are always weird situations that defy logic and imagination. Completely unexpected occurrences will not be found in the customer service handbook, in the rules-based database of coded instructions, or in a GenAI system trained on that which came before. A door flying off a Boeing airplane or a French phone bill for €12 quadrillion due to a printing error is not an anticipated situation.

Customers themselves are not the most trustworthy when it comes to delivering complete or coherent information, but GenAI systems can be (see Table 6.1).

These factors call for a hybrid approach combining automation where feasible with humans where needed. As natural language processing and machine learning capabilities advance, the proportion of inquiries that can be reliably automated is certain to increase over time. At USAA, for example, the initial approach was to use GenAI to help call center agents answer questions more rapidly and accurately. The longer-term goal is to

Table 6.1   How GenAI might assist customer service agents[5]

Generative AI capability	Description
Real-time suggestions	Offers contextually relevant responses and prompts during interactions
Sentiment analysis	Identifies the emotional state of customers in real-time for tailored responses
Troubleshooting steps	Provides step-by-step guidance for resolving common issues
Personalized responses	Generates responses based on customer history and preferences
Knowledge base navigation	Retrieves and summarizes information from the organization's knowledge base
Language translation	Offers real-time translation for multilingual support
Summarization of complex issues	Condenses lengthy queries into concise summaries for quicker understanding
Predictive support	Anticipates issues based on past interactions and trends
Escalation guidance	Advises on when to escalate issues based on complexity and urgency
Compliance and policy adherence	Reminds agents of policies and compliance requirements during interactions
Training and onboarding	Provides simulated scenarios and feedback for agent training
Emotionally intelligent responses	Generates responses that are emotionally attuned to the customer's sentiment
Data analysis and insights	Analyzes interaction data to identify trends and inform improvements

[5] Ibid.

Generative AI capability	Description
Automation of routine tasks	Handles repetitive enquiries, allowing agents to focus on complex interactions
Enhanced follow-up	Suggests or automates follow-up actions based on customer interaction history

Source: Adapted from [5]

provide customers with direct access to the GenAI system, but always with an easy way to contact a human agent.[6]

While USAA used an existing LLM model with custom content (we'll describe how that works below), another option is to use an outside vendor's product that is specifically focused on customer service. Several companies have been at the forefront of developing AI and machine learning solutions to enhance call center operations and customer experiences, including Invoca and Replicant. Their pioneering AI-powered systems can provide automated responses to common customer inquiries, suggest appropriate actions to appease dissatisfied callers, recommend troubleshooting steps for technical issues, and expand agents' options for processing returns and refunds.

A demo video on the Replicant website shows the following conversation between a distressed driver and an automated car insurance claims representative:[7]

"Thank you for calling Countryside Insurance. I'm a thinking machine on a recorded line. I was able to locate a policy linked to this phone number. Am I speaking with Benjamin?"

"That's me."

"Perfect. I have your policy right in front of me. How can I help you today?"

---

[6] Thomas H. Davenport and Randy Bean, "How GenAI Helps USAA Innovate," *MIT Sloan Management Review*, 23 October 2024, https://sloanreview.mit.edu/article/how-genai-helps-usaa-innovate.

[7] https://www.replicant.com/demo/contact-center-ai.

What follows is a master class in AI-driven customer service. The agent learns about a hit-and-run accident on the highway, first confirming the caller's safety and location. After establishing there were no injuries, the AI systematically collects essential information, demonstrating its ability to adapt and correct misunderstandings—particularly during the license plate documentation of the car that caused the accident.

"Are you able to send me photos of the damage to assist with your claim?"
"I'm happy to."
"I'll text you a link. Please open it and attach photos of the front, back and sides of the vehicle. I'll be here if you have questions."

After receiving the photos, the AI seamlessly transitions to practical solutions, offering two local repair options and confirming the caller's platinum membership benefits, including rental car coverage. Most notably, when handling sensitive payment information, the AI shows appropriate security awareness:

"Just so you know, we won't be recording this next part of the call while I take your payment details..."

The interaction concludes with the AI recognizing human emotional needs. When the caller admits to feeling shaken and requests human assistance regarding police reports, the AI smoothly transitions to a human representative, ensuring continuity by noting, "They will have a full record of this call." The entire claim process, from initial contact to repair scheduling and emotional support handoff, takes less than 4 minutes—exactly as the AI had promised.

Another AI agent company, Forethought, claims to be able to reduce trouble ticket volume by 87%, reduce costs per ticket for common inquiries like password resets, and resolve issues autonomously, learning from natural language and tickets.

Financial institutions are not allowing clients to interact directly with automated agents due to the regulated nature of investment advice. As at USAA, they offer real-time AI coaching for human advisors. The agent has access to the client's full account, investment history, and risk tolerance. The advisor readily accepts input from the AI agent but is on the hook for the actual advice given.

Unregulated industries can use this approach where the automated agent acts as a real-time call coach serving up just-in-time data and offering advice on handling upset customers or on how to increase the likelihood of the desired action (such as a purchase conversion or scheduling a demo). This allows human agents to focus on building rapport and addressing complex issues while AI handles routine tasks and information retrieval.

A utility company utilizing outbound calling for customers in arrears benefited from an AI system that not only evaluated the agent's tone for empathy but also monitored for adherence to state and federal regulations regarding debt collection practices. This dual-function AI capability helps organizations balance regulatory compliance with customer-centric service delivery.

The application of generative AI to support customer service representatives can be applied to virtual agents. Mukherjee and Kamath explore this concept in their paper "Intelligent Auto-Learning Generative Knowledge Finder for Proactively Aiding a Virtual Agent."[8] In their view, virtual agents learn directly from human customer service interactions, dramatically improving their capabilities without constant manual updates to knowledge bases. Rather than relying solely on preprogrammed responses, these AI assistants analyze conversations between customers and human agents to expand their understanding and responses.

This self-improving system means virtual agents become more competent over time, learning not just from their own interactions but from observing how human agents handle complex situations. They pick up new solutions, explanations, and approaches, reducing the need for human intervention while providing faster, more accurate responses. This would be a significant shift from traditional knowledge management, where virtual agents were limited by their initial training and manual updates. The result is a virtual agent that continually gets smarter, responds more quickly, and

---

[8] Mukherjee, A. and Kamath, N. P. (17 July 2023), "Intelligent Auto-learning Generative Knowledge Finder for Proactively Aiding a Virtual Agent," Technical Disclosure Commons, available at https://www.tdcommons.org/dpubsseries/6059.

requires less human backup—all while maintaining consistency with how your best customer service representatives handle similar situations.

Some companies bypass vendors and build their own customized models for customer support. Training a foundational model like OpenAI's ChatGPT or Anthropic's Claude is a time-consuming and expensive task. Financial software, data, and media company Bloomberg introduced its own large language model—BloombergGPT—in March 2023,[9] "drawing on the company's existing data creation, collection, and curation resources." It's been estimated to have cost somewhere between $1 million[10] and $10 million.[11]

The model's effectiveness was rigorously evaluated using standard language model benchmarks, financial-specific tests, and internal assessments aligned with Bloomberg's intended use cases. Results indicated that BloombergGPT significantly outperformed other models in financial tasks, while also demonstrating robust capabilities in general language processing.

It turns out they were just a little too far ahead of themselves. According to the often-quoted generative AI expert Ethan Mollick,[12]

This remains one of the most consequential experiments in AI: Bloomberg spent over $10M training a GPT-3.5 class AI on their own financial data last year…only to find that GPT-4 8k, the AI available to billions of people around the world, and without specialized finance training, beat it on almost all finance tasks! There was a moment that we thought proprietary data would let organizations train specialized AIs but the largest frontier models are just much better at most complex tasks.

This does not mean, however, that one can rely on the latest foundational model to do all the heavy lifting. Instead, companies are starting with the foundational models and adding their own proprietary content with an approach called *retrieval augmented generation* (RAG) to enhance their customer service capabilities.

[9] https://www.bloomberg.com/company/press/bloomberggpt-50-billion-parameter-llm-tuned-finance.

[10] https://www.linkedin.com/posts/rajistics_what-it-takes-to-build-bloomberggpt-and-activity-7089609531961348096-iIAs.

[11] https://www.threads.net/@ethan_mollick/post/C46AfItO8RS?hl=en.

[12] Ibid.

RAG adds well-curated internal documents about products, services, and protocols for addressing customer concerns and instructing these fit-for-purpose models to only answer questions about the narrowly defined topics they were created for. They are to use their foundational knowledge to parse context and manage linguistic response, but stick only to relevant information from rigorously curated document repositories to ensure quality and accuracy. The RAG approach tends to minimize hallucinations and also usually allows the model to cite what documents it used in its answer so that users can consult them for additional information.

From Translation to Interpretation

Another task generative AI seems to excel at is interpretation of colloquial language.

The following is the original (British) English:

> The marketing team was over the moon when their campaign went viral, but it wasn't all sunshine and roses. Some keyboard warriors got their knickers in a twist over a subtle Easter egg, claiming it was tone-deaf. The higher-ups were not amused and read the riot act to the creatives. In the end, they had to bite the bullet and pull the ad, leaving the team with egg on their face. It was a real dog's breakfast, and they knew they'd have to go back to the drawing board if they wanted to avoid another cock-up.

From there, it was translated into German, the German into Greek, and the Greek back into English by Google Translate into German. All fine for the most part, but the final translation included:

> The higher ups didn't think it was funny and gave the creatives a pass.

The creatives were definitely not given a pass. They were read the riot act. The same task given to ChatGPT 4o produced a version much more faithful to the original meaning:

> The marketing team was excited when their campaign went viral, but it wasn't all rosy. Some online critics were upset due to a subtle Easter egg, claiming it was inappropriate. The higher-ups were not

pleased and **reprimanded the creatives**. In the end, they had to bite the bullet and withdraw the ad, leaving the team in a tough spot. It was a real mess, and they knew they'd have to start from scratch if they wanted to avoid another mistake.

Translation over interpretation can be a big deal for global organizations trying to provide global customer support. Companies need more than word-for-word translations. This opens up a world of marketplaces when it comes to supporting customers and is useful across communication channels (e.g. chat, email, phone, video) because it can account for cultural nuances and idiomatic expressions that would otherwise be lost in direct translation.

Global organizations can now achieve far more nuanced understanding and engagement with their customers worldwide. Beyond simple translation, AI systems can identify emerging market trends, shape products to match local preferences, and craft communications that resonate with cultural expectations. Companies can spot potential issues before they become problems and engage in sophisticated analysis of customer sentiment, tone, and intent across multiple languages and regions. This enables organizations to engage with customers in a more natural and culturally appropriate way while maintaining brand consistency across markets.

How Do You Feel?

Sentiment analysis is a messy business. It's fine to ask somebody how they are feeling. They'll say, "Fine, thank you," and, if pressed, will reveal some murky approximation of their attitude at the moment. After all, humans have feelings and struggle to find the words, and LLMs have all the words with no concept of feeling.

But as soon as you ask 20 people how they're doing, it becomes a nearly impossible task to summarize. The solution for large quantities of respondents was picking a number between 1 and 10 much like a doctor will ask you about your pain level. With thousands of customer interactions daily through calls, emails, and open-ended text responses, most companies adopted the expedient approach of categorizing feedback as positive, negative, or neutral, thus giving up any hope of nuance.

Enter the Net Promoter Score (NPS) that brought back the 1–10 scale measuring the likelihood that an individual would recommend a company, product, or service to a friend or relative. Scoring a 7 or 8 is tolerable, but those scoring 6 or less are deemed detractors. The NPS metric became widely adopted by many companies with consumers as customers. While easy to measure and aggregate, these methods still lacked the depth needed to truly understand customer sentiments and motivations.

Since traditional NLP can't deal with sarcasm, irony, or subtle linguistic cues, we turn to GenAI. By processing both text and voice, GenAI can judge a customer's emotional state with remarkable accuracy. That output becomes part of the prompt for tailored responses or for escalating to human agents when necessary. The result is a more empathetic approach to customer communication, enhancing the overall experience. We're beyond simple sentiment analysis and into a deeper understanding of customer needs and frustrations, which in turn enables more effective problem-solving and emulates empathy.[13]

GenAI can enhance the analysis of customer feedback. For example, ChatGPT was given the prompt: "How would you rate the sentiment of this review? 'The material used is cheap and flimsy. The product broke within a week of use. Not worth the price.'" The LLM responded: "The sentiment of the review is clearly negative. The reviewer expresses dissatisfaction with the material quality, durability, and value of the product, indicating a poor overall experience."

This analysis extracts specific pain points mentioned by the customer: material quality, durability, and perceived value. This granular understanding can inform product improvements, customer service responses, and marketing strategies—at scale. So much more than positive/negative/neutral, GenAI identifies trends and recurring issues and can prioritize which customer concerns require immediate attention, improving response times and overall customer satisfaction.

When prompted to "Rate it on a scale of -10 to 10," ChatGPT offered a more precise assessment: "Given the strongly negative tone of the review, with complaints about the material quality, durability, and value, I would rate the sentiment towards the lower end of the scale. It might be around

---

[13] Aattouri, I., Mouncif, H. and Rida, M. (2023). "Call Center Customer Sentiment Analysis Using ML and NLP," in *14th International Conference on Intelligent Systems: Theories and Applications (SITA)*, pp. 370–6.5. Mehta, R. and Chili.

−8 to −9, as the review expresses significant dissatisfaction without any noted positive aspects."

A scale of −10 to +10 is way too complex for human interpretation when faced with lots of responses. GenAI can therefore be given a list of adjectives to imbue it with significant nuance (see Table 6.2).

When using sentiment analysis to look at public opinion on social media, the overwhelming quantity of input becomes even more problematic. GenAI can identify recurring themes, hashtags, and keywords; detect sudden spikes in conversations around specific topics or competitors; recognize patterns in user behavior and engagement; and even predict which topics may go viral.

One study demonstrates that an analysis of Instagram reviews achieved 77.77% accuracy in identifying user sentiments,[14] and another identified sentiment trends from Twitter data with impressive accuracy of 98.72%[15] showing the effectiveness of combining multiple neural network layers for precise analysis and models like GPT for fine-tuning sentiment detection.

Table 6.2 GenAI can explore a wider and more nuanced range of feelings

−10	Extremely negative	Outraged, betrayed, infuriated
−8	Very negative	Disappointed, frustrated, angry
−6	Moderately negative	Annoyed, dissatisfied, upset
−4	Somewhat negative	Concerned, displeased, skeptical
−2	Slightly negative	Unsettled, hesitant, mildly irked
0	Neutral	Indifferent, detached, unemotional
+2	Slightly positive	Curious, hopeful, mildly pleased
+4	Somewhat positive	Content, satisfied, relieved
+6	Moderately positive	Happy, enthusiastic, grateful
+8	Very positive	Delighted, excited, elated
+10	Extremely positive	Ecstatic, overjoyed, thrilled

[14] Eliviani, R., & Wazaumi, D. D. (2024). "Exploring Sentiment Trends: Deep Learning Analysis of Social Media Reviews on Google Play Store by Netizens," *International Journal of Advances in Data and Information Systems*, 5(1): 62–70. doi: 10.59395/ijadis.v5i1.1318.

[15] Ati, Modafar & Khan, Muhammad Usman & Kiran, Isha. (2022). "Social Media Trends Analysis Using the Bi-LSTM with Multi-Head Attention," pp. 295–299. doi: 10.1109/ICECTA57148.2022.9990328.

This allows businesses to make data-driven decisions based on real-time social media feedback.[16]

Sentiment to the Rescue

Starbucks' mobile app team wanted to know if their product investments were actually improving customer satisfaction and loyalty. Over their multiyear partnership, the consultancy Monks helped Starbucks gain deeper customer understanding to optimize the user experience of their loyalty app.

At a Marketing Analytics Summit in London in 2024, Juliana Jackson described[17] how the Monks' data science and experimentation teams developed a *small* language model for an AI Customer Voice Analysis solution. This two-fold effort was aimed at improving search navigation and subsequent page content.

Large vs. Small Language Models

Large language models process hundreds of billions or even trillions of parameters having been trained on expansive datasets including books, articles, code, and websites. They recognize intricate patterns in language, follow complex reasoning chains, and generate human-like text across an array of topics and styles.

Small language models, constrained by more limited parameters and training data, excel at specialized tasks within narrow domains. While lacking the broad capabilities of their larger cousins, these focused models offer key advantages: they run faster, cost less to operate, require minimal computing resources, and can often match or exceed the performance of large language models within their specialty area.

The first step was identifying and classifying searches into informational intent, navigational intent, and transactional intent. Analyzing the voice of the customer with natural language processing and employing *textual*

---

[16] R. Catherin Ida Shylu, S. Selvarani, "Aquila Optimization Algorithm with Advanced Learning Model-Based Sentiment Analysis on Social Media Environment," *SSRG International Journal of Electronics and Communication Engineering*, 10(2): 25–32, 2023. doi: 10.14445/23488549/IJECE-V10I12P103.

[17] https://www.monks.com/case-studies/ai-customer-voice-analysis.

entailment,[18] they were also able to connect search and page intent. They analyzed typical data sources like Google Analytics and native app metrics, and combined those signals with conversion data, mobile order and pay adoption and retention information, and customer voice feedback.

With this holistic view, Monks surfaced user frustrations and features that were disrupting the customer experience and holding users back in mobile ordering and payment. The resulting experimentation mapped out a user-centric approach that also supported business objectives. Over 9 years, they optimized and refined the user interface (UI) and user journeys for online ordering, in-store transactions, digital receipts, tipping, and more. Password reset and the mobile ordering flow were flagged as needing urgent attention.

By setting up an AI engine to continuously analyze app store reviews across markets, Starbucks now proactively experiments and iterates to boost customer lifetime value and mobile app adoption. Data and experimentation, paired with deep user empathy, is a powerful combination.

Recommendation Conversation

It is increasingly apparent that interactions with customers in digital commerce will increasingly be conversational. For example, Amazon has rolled out a talking dog named Rufus (see Figure 6.2). Well, the feature was *named* after a dog. Here's what Amazon had to share in their post called "How customers are making more informed shopping decisions with Rufus, Amazon's generative AI-powered shopping assistant."[19]

> Rufus is designed to help customers save time and make more informed purchase decisions by answering questions on a variety of shopping needs and products right in the Amazon Shopping app—it's like having a shopping assistant with you any time you're in our store.
>
> Since introducing Rufus, we've been thrilled to hear directly from customers how Rufus has helped them with broad-range and specific shopping questions, and everything in between. Customers

---

[18] Ibid. Textual entailment refers to the relationship between two pieces of text, where one (the hypothesis) can logically be inferred or understood from the other (the premise). In simpler terms, if the premise is true, the hypothesis is also likely true.

[19] https://www.aboutamazon.com/news/retail/how-to-use-amazon-rufus.

have already asked Rufus tens of millions of questions, and we've appreciated their feedback so far. Using Rufus, customers are:

- Understanding product details and hearing what other customers say
- Getting product recommendations
- Comparing options
- Getting the latest product updates
- Accessing current and past orders
- Answering questions not obviously related to shopping

We believe this represents a step change in the human–machine–interface. Instead of searching with Boolean expressions that use logical operators to limit or broaden search results (AND, OR, NOT, etc.), the

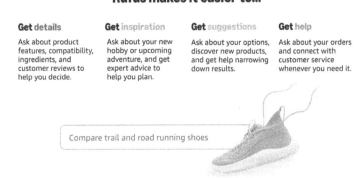

Figure 6.2 Amazon's GenAI shopping aide.

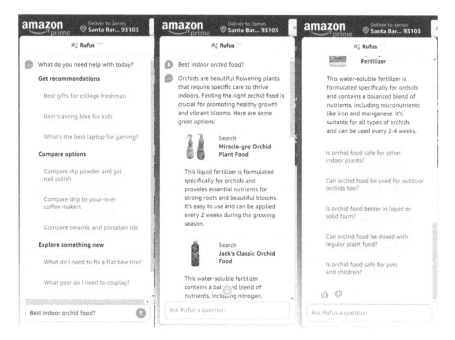

Figure 6.3   Amazon's Rufus shopping assistant in action.

conversational interface is a great deal more like asking a shopkeeper for a recommendation by stating the problem or desire rather than trying to decide from a hundred options (see Figure 6.3).

Automated Data Collection and Support

In addition to analyzing customer feedback, GenAI can lend a hand in collecting it. Coupled with reinforcement learning, GenAI can create a survey and learn what combination of questions given to what types of customers in what sequence and cadence yields the most valuable responses.[20,21] A survey system could engage customers in a dialogue about their experience, ask about their likes and dislikes, and address frustrations and concerns all in one session. The output from these conversations could then be fed into

[20] Cao, Y., Sheng, Q. Z., McAuley, J. and Yao, L. (2023). "Reinforcement Learning for Generative AI: A Survey," *Arxiv*, available at https://arxiv.org/ abs/2308.14328.

[21] Franceschelli, G. and Musolesi, M. (2024). "Reinforcement Learning for Generative AI: State of the Art, Opportunities and Open Research Challenges," *Journal of Artificial Intelligence Research*, 79: 417–446, available at https://jair.org/index.php/jair/article/view/15278.

reports that would identify weaknesses and opportunities, anticipating needs and preferences. This information would be vital to advertising, marketing, customer service, and product development professionals (see Table 6.3).

Table 6.3 Limitations of traditional VoC analysis methods vs. GenAI[22]

Feature	Traditional VoC analysis methods	GenAI capabilities
Feedback timeliness	Slow: often involves manual collection and processing	Real-time analysis and insights
Data scope	Limited by sample size, response rates, and question design	Vast: can process large datasets from multiple sources
Analysis depth	Generally surface-level; constrained by pre-defined questions	Deep: capable of nuanced sentiment analysis and uncovering underlying themes
Predictive insights	Limited: mostly retrospective analyses	Advanced: can forecast trends and customer behaviors
Customization	Restricted by survey design and focus group structure	Highly flexible; adaptable to various data types and questions
Operational efficiency	Labor-intensive: requires significant manual effort	Automated: minimizes the need for manual intervention
Scalability	Challenging to scale due to logistical constraints	Easily scalable to accommodate growing data volumes
Multilingual support	Limited: dependent on translation resources	Robust: can analyze and understand multiple languages

(continued)

[22] *Applied Marketing Analytics*, Volume 10-1 (2024–2025), https://www.henrystewartpublications.com/ama/v10.

Table 6.3   (Continued)

Feature	Traditional VoC analysis methods	GenAI capabilities
Data integration	Often isolated: difficult to integrate with other data streams	Seamless: can integrate with a wide range of data sources
Customer experience	Passive; relies on customer initiative to provide feedback	Proactive: can actively analyze customer interactions across platforms

Source: Adapted from [22]

Warp Speed Change Management

It is widely known that GenAI "hallucinates," a moniker we feel has done more harm than good. The outputs are usually plausible but sometimes factually incorrect or nonsensical. It would be clearer to say that it "fabricates." To repeat from Chapter 3:

> The biggest argument against generative AI is that it's not trustworthy. It hallucinates and therefore isn't reliable or always useful. A hallucination is the result of the algorithm guessing the next most likely word or concept without regard to the truth—because it doesn't know truth, it only knows statistical likelihood. The more sophisticated your expertise, the more capable you are of evaluating the output to see if it passes the smell test.

This is counter to what we expect a computer to do (although oddly, not counter to what we expect from humans) and that creates a risk-rich environment. As a research article noted:

> Non-deterministic behavior introduces new technical, legal and financial risks into every aspect of concept, design, manufacture and use. Three critical questions are raised from a technologist's perspective: what is the

relevant legal framework; how to model nondeterministic behavior; and how actions are authorized.[23]

In most companies, the IT infrastructure is complex and fragile. Integrating legacy systems, new systems, and acquired systems is hard enough without everybody in the organization suddenly having access to this new, constantly changing generative AI capability that is impossible to pin down and stabilize. Successful adoption and business transformation requires a balance of the drive for innovation with the need to comply with regulations and ethical principles, and the precariousness of the tech stack already in place.

AI fabrication is particularly concerning for voice of customer programs. Accuracy is paramount, and a made-up insight can send product development, customer service training, and marketing messages in entirely wrong directions. While AI excels at processing massive amounts of customer feedback data, the most popular foundational models have been fine-tuned to generate plausible-sounding conclusions.

If you're analyzing thousands of customer service transcripts, an LLM might identify a pattern of customer dissatisfaction that seems logical and compelling but might be conflating unrelated issues or inferring causation where none exists. If product teams or service managers act on these fabricated insights, they could waste resources solving nonexistent problems while ignoring real issues.

AI could formulate trends or correlations in open-ended survey responses that confirm stakeholder biases rather than reflect customer sentiment. When analyzing brand mentions and customer conversations on social media, AI could hallucinate context or misinterpret sarcasm and cultural references. AI might create plausible but incorrect connections between customer journey touchpoints, leading to misguided journey optimization efforts.

The solution lies in applying AI as an assistant rather than an oracle. Until the technology matures further, maintaining human oversight and control over AI systems will remain a top priority. This "human-in-the-loop"

---

[23] Gillespie, T. (2021). "Risk Reduction for Autonomous Systems," in Lawless, W. F., Llinas, J., Sofge, D. A., Mittu, R. (eds.), *Engineering Artificially Intelligent Systems. Lecture Notes in Computer Science.* Springer, Cham, available at https://link.springer.com/chapter/10.1007/978-3-030- 89385-9_11.

method structure is not just to ensure alignment (ensuring AI systems behave in ways that are consistent with human values, goals, and intentions) but to include the knowledge, talent, and experience of subject matter experts.

As with all change management efforts, the biggest challenge is managing people and processes. GenAI is such a novel technology that most employees haven't had a chance to form an opinion about it or understand its potential. If your organization has an AI policy beyond "Do Not Touch," you're in the lead. And then there's the fear that GenAI will replace their roles with machines—a concern that may be justified in some cases. Success comes to those who have or can create a culture of experimentation and a willingness to learn by doing—and sometimes failing.

Listen Up, Listen Well, Listen Soon

The voice of the customer has always been a critical input for businesses to understand their market, identify opportunities, and address issues. Deploying AI-powered conversational agents on websites, mobile apps, and messaging platforms, companies can engage customers in personalized, contextual dialogues that are a more natural interface than traditional surveys or feedback forms. Bots can get customers to share deeper insights and more heartfelt opinions.

Generative AI can also be used to analyze unstructured data like open-ended survey responses, product reviews, and social media posts. This allows businesses to gain a more comprehensive view of the customer voice.

As generative AI matures, we expect to see these technologies close the loop—not just collecting and analyzing customer feedback, but using those insights to automatically generate personalized content, product recommendations, and proactive customer service. This virtuous cycle has the potential to dramatically elevate the customer experience while providing businesses with a continuous flow of actionable intelligence.

The next breakthrough in customer-facing technologies is likely to be AI agents. That's the subject of our next chapter.

7

Better Task Automation with AI Agents

Task automation in marketing and other customer-facing functions was typically done by either robotic process automation (RPA) systems or marketing automation tools, both of which employed rule-based decision-making approaches and were limited and inflexible. AI agents—autonomous systems capable of making decisions about and then performing complex tasks—are taking center stage and for good reason. From automating data-intensive workflows and deriving actionable insights from vast data repositories to providing personalized customer experiences, AI agents are becoming indispensable allies. Agents are, or will soon become, the new software applications.

As Amir Hajian, the vice president of data science at Canadian start-up Arteria, which specializes in managing document-based information, put it to us in a recent interview:

> "LLM-based agentic workflows can significantly streamline the process of extracting and processing information from complex documents. By breaking down tasks into specialized components handled by different

143

agents, the system can efficiently navigate intricate processes, from data extraction to calculation and verification. This approach not only enhances accuracy but also reduces the need for extensive programming, making it easier to adapt to various document types and information requirements. It's much easier to do even more complex tasks with the same system. Agentic systems are going to be one of the most exciting things of our time, and how we build software and intelligent systems is changing dramatically."

Self-Reflective Tool Users

Generative AI LLMs develop a deep understanding of language and can generate human-like responses. As a result, they have generated a cascade of new capabilities and advances in productivity. However, LLMs alone are not sufficient for an AI agent to perform complex tasks.

This is where tool handling comes in. AI agents have the ability to interact with external tools and application programming interfaces (APIs), allowing them to access up-to-date information, perform calculations, and execute actions in the real world. By integrating LLMs with tool-calling capabilities, AI agents become agentic and highly versatile.

The process of an AI agent completing a task can be broken down into three main stages (see Figure 7.1):

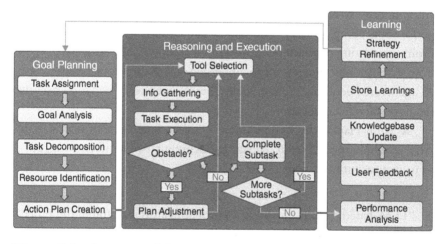

Figure 7.1 Agent workflow.

1. **Goal initialization and planning:** When a user assigns a task to an AI agent, the agent first analyzes the goal and breaks it down into smaller, manageable subtasks. It identifies the tools and information required to complete each subtask and creates a plan of action.
2. **Reasoning using available tools:** As the AI agent progresses through the subtasks, it leverages its available tools to gather the necessary information and perform the required actions. If the agent encounters gaps in its knowledge or faces obstacles, it can dynamically adjust its plan and seek additional resources.
3. **Learning and reflection:** Once the task is completed, the AI agent reflects on its performance and incorporates any feedback received from the user or other agents. It updates its knowledge base and refines its strategies for future tasks. This continuous learning process allows AI agents to improve over time and adapt to evolving user needs.

One of the key advantages of AI agents over traditional analytical AI models is their ability to provide explanations for their actions. By maintaining a record of the tools used and the reasoning behind each decision, AI agents can act with transparency and accountability. At least at a macro level, users can examine the agent's thought process and understand how it arrived at a particular conclusion, recommendation, or action. Since agents will often invoke LLMs, there may still be some lack of transparency in how the LLM chose a particular word or phrase.

Benefits of AI Agents for Task Automation

AI agents are still evolving, but we anticipate that they will bring a boatload of benefits to task automation, particularly in the context of customer data management. To name a few:

- **Increased efficiency:** AI agents can process vast amounts of data and perform complex tasks much faster than humans. They can work tirelessly around the clock, eliminating the need for breaks or downtime. By automating repetitive and time-consuming tasks, AI agents free up human workers to focus on higher-value activities.
- **Enhanced accuracy:** AI agents are not susceptible to human errors caused by fatigue, distractions, or biases. They can consistently apply predefined rules and algorithms to ensure accurate and reliable

results. This is particularly important in data-intensive tasks where even small errors can have significant consequences. Again, LLMs may "hallucinate" in some tasks they perform as agents, but we can ask other agents to check on their responses.

- **Personalized experiences:** AI agents can leverage customer data to provide personalized experiences at scale. By analyzing individual preferences, past interactions, and contextual information, AI agents can tailor recommendations, offers, and support to each customer's unique needs. This level of personalization can greatly enhance customer satisfaction and loyalty.

- **Continuous improvement:** Unlike static systems, well-designed AI agents have the ability to learn and improve over time. Through feedback mechanisms and data analysis, AI agents can identify patterns, optimize their strategies, and adapt to changing customer behavior. This continuous improvement leads to more effective and efficient task automation over time.

- **Cost reduction:** By automating tasks that previously required human intervention, AI agents can significantly reduce labor costs. Some AI agents may still require a human-in-the-loop, but in most cases the tasks performed by agents will reduce human labor. Agents can also handle a high volume of interactions simultaneously, eliminating the need for large customer support teams. Additionally, AI agents can help optimize resource allocation and minimize waste, leading to further cost savings.

- **Scalability:** AI agents can be easily scaled up or down to meet changing business needs. As customer data grows and interactions increase, AI agents can handle the increased workload without the need for additional human resources. This scalability allows businesses to quickly adapt to market demands and maintain a competitive edge.

- **24/7 availability:** AI agents can operate continuously, providing round-the-clock support and services to customers. This is particularly valuable in today's global business environment where customers expect instant access to information and support regardless of time zones or business hours.

While the benefits of AI agents are compelling, it's essential to approach their deployment with a strategic mindset. Businesses must carefully evaluate their specific needs, data quality, and organizational readiness before implementing AI agents. Additionally, human oversight and ethical considerations should be at the forefront of any AI agent initiative to ensure responsible and trustworthy automation.

The Agent Maturity Curve

Let's start by getting our agents in order. At the lowest level we can think of any automated system as an agent. This manuscript is supported by a word processing agent that includes spell-check. The spelling is monitored autonomously in real time, which sounds much more impressive than it feels because we've had so much time to become accustomed to these tools.

OpenAI's leaders shared the following five stages internally to employees in early July during an all-hands meeting:[1]

- **Stage 1:** Chatbots, AI with conversational language
- **Stage 2:** Reasoners, human-level problem solving
- **Stage 3:** Agents, systems that can take actions
- **Stage 4:** Innovators, AI that can aid in invention
- **Stage 5:** Organizations, AI that can do the work of an organization

In his paper "Levels of AI Agents: From Rules to Large Language Models,"[2] Yu Huang proposes five levels of AI agents (Table 7.1).

Starting from Scratch

Levels 0 and 1 are simple reflex agents that can act on fixed rules and respond to recognizable inputs without memory or learning capabilities. They make decisions based solely on the current environment, adhering to preprogrammed "if-then" rules. They can respond only to questions they've been explicitly programmed to recognize.

You know these as the unhelpful, rules-based automatons in the lower-right corner of websites that offer to provide customer service but that everybody loves to hate (see Figure 7.2).

---

[1] https://www.inc.com/ben-sherry/5-steps-that-openai-thinks-will-lead-to-artificial-intelligence-running-a-company.html.
[2] Huang, Y. (2024). "Levels of AI Agents: from Rules to Large Language Models," *arXiv* preprint arXiv:2405.06643.

Table 7.1   Levels of AI agents

AI agent levels	Techniques and capabilities
L0	No AI + Tools (perception + actions)
L1	Rule-based AI + Tools (perception + actions)
L2	IL/RL [imitation learning/reinforcement learning]-based AI + Tools (perception + actions) + Reasoning and decision-making
L3	LLM-based AI + Tools (perception + actions) + Reasoning and decision-making + Memory and reflection
L4	LLM-based AI + Tools (perception + actions) + Reasoning and decision-making + Memory and reflection + Autonomous learning + Generalization
L5	LLM-based AI + Tools (perception + actions) + Reasoning and decision-making + Memory and reflection + Autonomous learning + Generalization + Personality (emotion + character) + Collaborative behavior (multi-agents)

Figure 7.2   Chatbot icon (https://www.flaticon.com/free-icon/chatbot_4616759/Freepik Company S.L).

They are about as helpful as voice response telephone systems: "Your call is important to us. Press 1 to be put on permanent hold. Press 2 to be connected to another recording. Press 3 to be cut off from all means of communication."

Think of Levels 0 and 1 as simple software programs. They do only what they are told. They respond, they suggest, they make rudimentary decisions that are programmed in advance. They might even go as far as to correct spelling mistakes on the fly. But we don't think of them as "having agency." They are brainless or at least very inflexibly-brained tools—classic, unthinking robots.

Level 2 Machine Learning Level 2 agents are reflective. They build and update an internal model of their environment based on new data. This capability goes back decades to "analytical AI" or machine learning. Here is one example:

> Crabtree & Evelyn enlisted Albert [a commercial SaaS offering] to take on their Facebook paid social program and develop a robust strategy that ramped up testing while simultaneously improving cost efficiency. Over time, the marketing team also hoped that the autonomous AI would provide more audience and creative insights. In paid social, Albert gets detailed, machine-level reporting on how interests perform and uses that to optimize audiences, ad sets and lookalikes. Albert expands cautiously, spending budget only after understanding what's working, without limiting campaign reach by just eliminating sources. It is this careful, relentless, multivariate test and learn approach that is the foundation of Albert's unique execution.
>
> In less than two months, Crabtree & Evelyn saw results that had been out of reach when the campaign had been executed manually. Return on ad spend immediately rose 30% while media spend remained flat. In paid social, there is a sensitive relationship between budget/performance/creative fatigue. Albert's ability to analyze real-time data at both micro and macro levels, combined with multivariate testing, enables the system to weigh variables from all areas and find the optimal relationship between all of the above.... Now, with Albert, the machine simultaneously manages prospecting, retargeting and retention all together to deliver the marketing team's KPI. The brand realized this enabled them to be more focused on the KPI itself instead of how they were getting to the KPI. It also meant that now they can learn from Albert about the customer journey

and new personas. Armed with these latest insights, they have a truly customer-led process to develop product, creative and the branding around it.[3]

Level 2 agents gets a bump up to 2.5—at least in our numbering system—with the advent of generative AI. These agents retain limited memory, allowing them to consider past states when making decisions. LLMs respond to prompts and can remember how the conversation began. "Describe a specific cat" can be followed by "Now do another one," and the LLM (usually) understands the context of the conversation. A robotic vacuum can adjust navigation based on obstacles and update its internal model of a room.

These are slightly better than the old answer bot as they understand context. A customer can reach out for help with a new product and ask, "How do I set up my device?" Level 2.5 can respond to the variety of questions a human might ask ("How do I get started?" or "Where do I begin?" or "What's first?") even though it was not programmed to recognize those specific sets of words.

As the conversation progresses, the customer might ask follow-up questions such as "Can I connect it to my home network?" and later "How do I update the software?" The Level 2.5 agent uses its memory of the current session to track the customer's initial setup questions and then builds a coherent flow of responses. This type of limited-memory, context-aware agent also supports customer satisfaction through quick, adaptive responses that follow the conversation's flow naturally.

Level 3 Steps Up to Planning   A Level 3 agent is like creating a simple Custom GTP in ChatGPT, a Project in Claude, or Gem in Gemini. These agents accept additional knowledge and goals and remember them as permanent prompts. They take more cycle time to consider the tasks they are prompted to execute. They respond to inputs and pursue specific objectives. They use basic search and planning techniques to evaluate sequences of actions that can help achieve desired outcomes. For instance, a Global Positioning System (GPS) tool that plans routes based on traffic data exemplifies a goal-based agent in action.

---

[3] https://albert.ai/impact/retail-crabtree-evelyn.

A Level 3 customer service agent adjusts responses based on remembered and perceived customer preferences. It has in-session continuity and can ask clarifying questions. AI agents can be trained to simulate sales calls, allowing sales teams to practice and refine their pitches without the need for human role-players. These agents can capture valuable data from the simulated interactions for analysis and improvement.

For example, the Trevor Project[4] is a crisis intervention organization that had a staffing problem. When it added text communications to their phone bank capabilities, the number of conversations soared. Their target audience, troubled LBGTQ youth, are more at ease texting than actually speaking with a stranger.

Training new counselors in effective, empathetic communication skills was a top-of-the-list problem for the Trevor Project. This is where generative AI can transform the crisis response training. Volunteers engage with AI personas that mimic the diverse range of individuals they may encounter, learning to navigate complex, emotional situations and make critical decisions under pressure. This exposes counselors to a variety of scenarios and acclimates them to crisis intervention without throwing them into the deep end on day one with lives at stake. By generating realistic conversations and providing personalized feedback, these AI systems significantly enhance the effectiveness of training programs.

The customization capabilities of AI personas allow training programs to be tailored to the specific needs and challenges faced by the communities they serve. By replicating the nuances and intricacies of real-world interactions, these AI systems provide volunteers with a more authentic and relevant training experience.

AI helps save lives and provide critical support to those in need by enabling organizations to train more volunteers in a shorter amount of time, while simultaneously improving the quality and depth of the training itself (see Figure 7.3).

As soon as audio capability arrived, the Trevor Project was able to use the same personas and scenarios and create interactive voice sessions. What do you say when the caller gives only one-word answers? How do you

---

[4] John Callery-Coyne, "How Generative AI Is Helping Improve Empathy and Outcomes," presentation at *Marketing Analytics and Data Science Conference* 2024, 21 October 2024, https://schedule.madsconference.com/session/how-generative-ai-is-helping-improve-empathy-and-outcomes/906891.

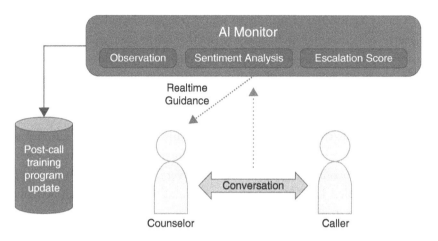

Figure 7.3   Real-time counselor guidance.

mollify a caller who expresses rage at you? How do you comfort somebody who is disassociating?

John Callery-Coyne, who spent nearly 8 years at the Trevor Project as senior vice president of technology, cofounded a company to offer this sort of training to others. ReflexAI provides hyper-realistic role-play simulations that cut training costs in half. It also monitors all interactions for continuous counselor feedback and improvement.

Level 4 Has Agency   With Level 4 agents, we've arrived at the level of Anthropic's Claude's additional capabilities added in October 2024: the ability to see the computer screen, use the mouse and the keyboard, and write *and execute* its own code. This is where the agent has agency, although thus far in relatively limited domains compared to human agency. AI agents are increasingly capable of task decomposition, complex problem-solving, and autonomous action. They can utilize multiple tools, perform reasoning, and create subtasks independently.

From a customer interaction perspective, the Level 4 agent can take action on behalf of the marketer and the customer. It can review past campaign messaging and results data, apply lessons learned across various customer segments and campaign types, and autonomously adapt future marketing content to match the profile of the prospective customer. A Level 4 agent builds knowledge across campaigns, learning patterns to generalize insights, creating proactive, data-informed strategies.

This step takes a great deal more software engineering principles in building agents. Sunil Malya, CTO and co-founder of Flip AI, sees the need to bring formal software engineering architecture to interfaced agents:

"When you build, like really scalable systems …, API Interfaces are well defined. You know the request/response. You know the faulty behaviors. (T)hat part is what's lacking today in most agentic workflows or orchestration systems. Agents are very well-defined input, output structure, right? They'll always reliably give you the output…or…you know how to retry. So the system sort of ends up becoming just like you're calling a library function, etc. So, the developer who's building these workflows…knows exactly the behavior to expect. And underneath, we did all the hard work in terms of (fine tuning) and this is why fine tuning is so important. I'm a strong proponent of that is now you get to control. Your failure chances and cases go really low because you fine-tuned the model."[5]

Level 5 Agents Work Together   Level 5 agents will work in concert with an ecosystem of agents to collaborate on solving problems. In customer interactions, for example, marketing and customer service agents might combine with agents from other business functions like shipping, billing, and tech support to meet all or most of a customer's needs. They can all adapt their tone of voice based on detected customer mood, engaging with memory, agency, and empathy.

As of the end of 2024, as we write, limited Level 5 agents are now possible. Google's NotebookLM can ingest a long document, summarize it, and hand it over to an agent that turns it into a podcast that includes "surprise" and "enthusiasm" in verbal banter between two artificial podcasters. Companies will now have to create detailed persona descriptions for how professional, helpful, cheerful, or authoritative they want their automated systems to sound. These are inherently branding questions.

Level 5 agents also have the ability to improve their performance over time through experience. They can adapt to new situations, discover patterns, and refine their strategies based on feedback. They are particularly valuable in dynamic environments where the optimal course of action may change over time.

---

[5] The TWIML AI Podcast with Sam Charrington, An Agentic Mixture of Experts for DevOps with Sunil Mallya, 04 November 2024, https://twimlai.com/podcast/twimlai.

Mallya and his team at Flip AI came up with a useful framework of a three-tier architecture approach that includes agents, actors, and directors. Agents, in their view:[6]

> "…are the lowest level of abstraction. Then we have actors. And actors are this next level of abstraction, which are sort of cooperative agents (that) are able to take a collection of agents and perform a task. And then you have the director, which is the orchestration layer…to assemble these actors to do something."

(See Figure 7.4 for a given task.)

"The director ends up not being a very complex piece of software," Malya remarks. "It's the latter two that actually become like the real sort of workhorses in the system."

Applied Science

It's a bit mind-bending to consider the possibilities of a breakthrough technology. Just as early users of automobiles couldn't imagine all the places they could drive and early personal and smartphone users couldn't imagine all of the uses of these new tools, people newly exposed

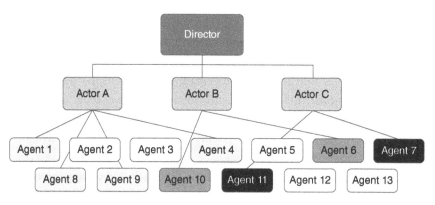

Figure 7.4   Flip AI three-tiered agent framework.

---

[6] Ibid.

to AI agents may have difficulty envisioning the range of possible applications. Here are a variety of customer-facing use cases to spark your imagination:

- **Intelligent chatbots:** AI-powered chatbots understand natural language queries, access customer data, and provide personalized responses. They can answer frequently asked questions, process orders, and mollify upset customers. Intelligent chatbots automate routine inquiries, allowing human agents to focus on more complex and high-value interactions.

- **Personalized recommendations:** AI agents can analyze customer data, including purchase history, browsing behavior, and preferences, to generate personalized product or content recommendations. They can identify patterns and predict customer interests and serve up targeted, relevant suggestions. This enhances the customer experience as well as drives increased sales.

- **Sales assistants:** Virtual sales assistants can guide customers through the purchasing process and provide tailored advice. They can analyze customer needs, budget, and preferences. They can also handle tasks such as lead qualification, appointment scheduling, and follow-up communications.

- **Customer sentiment analysis:** AI agents can analyze customer feedback, reviews, and social media mentions to gauge sentiment and identify trends. These agents can quickly identify sentiment shifts and emerging opportunities. Real-time insights can help businesses proactively address customer concerns, improve products or services, and adapt their strategies accordingly.

- **Fraud detection:** Customer transactions and behavior patterns let agents identify potential fraud or suspicious activities. By leveraging machine learning algorithms, these agents can recognize anomalies and flag them for further investigation. Real-time fraud detection helps protect customers' financial information and minimizes losses.

- **Personalized marketing campaigns:** AI agents can segment customers based on their characteristics, preferences, and behaviors, enabling targeted marketing campaigns. By analyzing customer data, these agents can identify the most effective channels, messaging, and timing for each segment. Personalized marketing not only improves campaign performance but also enhances customer engagement and loyalty.

- **Dynamic pricing:** Customer data, market trends, and competitor pricing analysis agents can consider supply and demand, customer preferences, and historical sales data to recommend the most effective pricing strategies to maximize revenue and profitability.

Directors, Actors, and Agents at Work at a Top 3 Fintech

In a conversation with Jim, a product and AI leader at one of the biggest worldwide fintech, companies shared their approach to creating a single user interface for all of the agents they're building. While most companies deploy separate AI agents for internal and external users, they've deployed a generative AI engine that serves both audiences through a single conversational interface. Customers use this agent for shopping guidance and purchase assistance through an app, while employees consult the same named agent for sales support and product details. Behind the scenes, the agent routes interactions to specialized subsystems, but users experience one consistent personality, tailored to their tone of voice and needs, whether discussing payment options or accessing sales collateral.

The effort to create these agents followed a pragmatic engineering path: 75% focused on core capabilities, 20% on learning mechanisms, and 5% on personality development. This prevents the jarring disconnect when an AI agent attempts sophisticated interactions before mastering basic tasks. That's the path into the "uncanny valley" from which there is no escape.

This product and AI leader echoed Flip AI's Malya call for architectural boundaries and organization of agents similar to how data schemas provide structure. "There are schemas that my group are responsible for, and then there's a universal, top-level data catalog that every agent is tuned to. That way our agents don't answer questions about the business when a customer asks questions."

They have integrated agents directly into existing workflows, embedding them in Slack for the sales and marketing teams rather than introducing yet another interface. In May 2024, the company declared that 90% of their staff were using AI daily, establishing it as an indispensable asset within the company.

Unintended Consequences

AI agents may sometimes take actions or make decisions that have unintended consequences. For example, an AI agent designed to optimize sales may recommend products that are not in the best interest of the customer or may engage in aggressive marketing tactics that damage brand reputation. It's important to carefully define the objectives and constraints for AI agents and regularly monitor their behavior to detect and mitigate any unintended outcomes.

What causes GenAI to potentially go off the rails? A variety of things, starting with its training data. If your AI is learning from biased data, you might end up with a system that's more discriminatory than is good for your brand or your employees. A customer segmentation model, for example, might inadvertently discriminate against certain groups if the training data reflects historical inequities. To keep this from happening, a policy and a process are needed to actively identify and remove biases, regularly audit for fairness, and ensure diverse representation in the teams designing and deploying these solutions.

Next up: privacy. As AI agents become more adept at analyzing vast amounts of customer data, there is an increased risk of privacy breaches or unauthorized use of sensitive information. AI agents may inadvertently reveal personally identifiable information or enable inferences about individuals that violate their privacy rights. Strict data governance policies are called for, including explicit consent for data usage from prospects and customers.

Should somebody take offense and take you to court, your defense will depend on how well you can show your systems are working. The complexity of AI algorithms make it difficult to understand how they arrive at specific decisions or recommendations. This lack of transparency and accountability means organizations should prioritize explainable AI techniques that provide clear insights into the factors influencing AI-generated outcomes. More policies are needed around agent oversight and issue escalation for review of high-stakes decisions.

Employees who create or oversee AI agents or ecosystems of them will also need to be attentive and on the lookout for feedback loops and self-fulfilling prophecies. AI agents that learn from user interactions and outcomes may narrow customer options because they focus on previous behavior. If Amazon only suggested things like the things you bought before, none of us would know they sold anything but books. You'll want to set up some checks and balances to prevent runaway feedback loops, ensure diversity in recommendations, and allow for human intervention when needed.

To guard against these unintended consequences, organizations should prioritize responsible AI practices throughout the development and deployment lifecycle. This includes establishing ethical guidelines, conducting impact assessments, ensuring diverse stakeholder involvement, and fostering a culture of transparency and accountability. Shore up your data quality and data observability skills, don't creep people out by being too familiar, and don't forget to keep humans in the loop.

Keeping humans in the loop will help avoid what we're finding a serious problem: the averaging-out of everything. In a *New York Times* article entitled "I Took a 'Decision Holiday' and Put AI in Charge of My Life,"[7] Amanda Askell, a philosopher and researcher at Anthropic, warned that GenAI can be sycophantic, having been trained on what's been published—mostly positive—and fine-tuned by humans rating their answers. "They can learn to say what they think humans want to hear…(and)…a little bit too guided by what they think you think is good."

One way to combat this fictitious fawning is vigilance. Just like being wary of advice from an obsequious colleague or sales representative, guarding against the wiles of a large language model is good practice. It can be useful to instruct a model like ChatGPT to "Be brutally honest. Pull no punches. Give it to me straight without worrying about my feelings." The results can seem harsh, but far more useful than the flattery it is often prone to.

Google has realized that people want more control over the style and tone of their NotebookLM podcast output. The advanced settings for

---

[7] https://www.nytimes.com/interactive/2024/11/01/technology/generative-ai-decisions-experiment.html.

NotebookLM Plus users now include the ability to choose one of the following conversational styles:

- **Default:** Best for general-purpose research and brainstorming tasks
- **Analyst:** Best for business-oriented strategy and decision-making
- **Guide:** Best for sharing your notebook as a group knowledge base or a help center
- **Custom**[8]

This is a critical step forward as our tacit agreement with happy-clappy output may dull our effort to think things through on our own.

As Tom (along with Julia Kirby) wrote on the importance of human contributions to AI back in 2016:[9]

> People will continue to have advantages over even the smartest machines.... They have the cognitive breadth to simultaneously do a lot of different things well. The judgment and flexibility that come with these basic advantages will continue to be the basis of any enterprise's ability to innovate, delight customers, and prevail in competitive markets—where, soon enough, cognitive technologies will be ubiquitous.

The benefits of agents, however they are defined, are clear. Getting humans to embrace agents will happen differently in different companies and industries. But we're confident that improvements in customer communications and relations will scale rapidly with agents and will be just as important as improvements in internal customer-facing processes and operations—the subject of the next chapter.

---

[8] https://support.google.com/notebooklm/answer/14276569.
[9] https://sloanreview.mit.edu/article/just-how-smart-are-smart-machines.

8

Better Customer-Facing Operations

In addition to generating lots of content, segmenting customers, and personalizing customer experience, GenAI and other technologies can help in a great many ways with customer-facing operations. Most of these operational productivity improvements can be applied across all customer-oriented functions within the organization, but many are unique to the marketing department. Let's start at the top of that organization.

Top-Down Marketing Operations Transformation

When marketing executives rush to implement AI tools for ad copy generation, search keyword optimization, visual content testing, and the like, they end up with a patchwork of point solutions. These are tactics masquerading as strategy. While they deliver quick wins, they miss the transformative potential of AI in marketing operations.

The current marketing technology stack in most organizations is a precarious, unbalanced Jenga tower (see Figure 8.1). Disconnected AI tools handle specific tasks, while humans bridge the gaps between systems.

Figure 8.1 Webcomic dependency.[1]
Source: [1] / xkcd

Data governance varies widely across platforms, making it impossible to measure AI's true effectiveness. So far, most AI deployment (and analytics deployment before that) is reactive rather than calculated. The advent of generative AI is an opportunity to reimagine how marketing operations function in an AI-enabled world.

Executive Vision and Alignment

The transformation begins with senior management. Without clear executive sponsorship and a shared vision of AI's role in marketing operations, strategic implementation fails before it starts. More than budget approvals, this step

---

[1] https://xkcd.com/2347.

requires active engagement from leadership in defining business outcomes, agreeing on success metrics, and committing resources across departments.

If you haven't read Patrick Lencioni's *The Five Dysfunctions of a Team* series of books, guides, and assessments, now is the time. In a nutshell, the five dysfunctions are as follows:

- **Absence of trust:** If the senior team doesn't trust each other, they will not be open or supportive and hide their weaknesses.
- **Fear of conflict:** Without healthy debate, public agreement hides hidden agendas that end up in proxy wars several levels deep in the organization.
- **Lack of commitment:** If the team isn't dedicated to shared goals, their individual objectives will sew conflict and staff discontent.
- **Avoidance of accountability:** Team members must be willing to hold themselves and each other accountable for their performance, which requires clear expectations.
- **Inattention to results:** When teams focus on individual success rather than collective goals, it leads to poor overall performance. Teams must prioritize collective results.

These issues hinder a lot of things in organizations—one reason the book has been a huge bestseller. One of them is using data, analytics, and AI to become more customer-focused. Whether your corporate culture is "move fast and break things" or highly risk averse and highly regulated, all of your senior executives need to be aligned and in sync on their vision of what AI can do for the company.

The Tech and Data Foundation

Building an integrated technology stack means creating an architecture that enables real-time decision-making, automated testing, and continuous performance monitoring. This is the nervous system for your marketing operations.

Is your data house in order? As we discussed in Chapter 4, a unified customer data platform, standardized governance, and automated quality monitoring aren't sexy, but they're essential. Cross-functional data accessibility balanced with privacy and compliance creates the foundation for

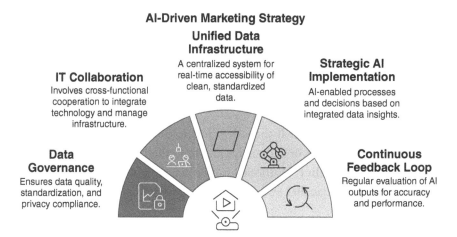

AI-Driven Marketing Strategy

Unified Data Infrastructure
A centralized system for real-time accessibility of clean, standardized data.

IT Collaboration
Involves cross-functional cooperation to integrate technology and manage infrastructure.

Strategic AI Implementation
AI-enabled processes and decisions based on integrated data insights.

Data Governance
Ensures data quality, standardization, and privacy compliance.

Continuous Feedback Loop
Regular evaluation of AI outputs for accuracy and performance.

Figure 8.2   Technical and data foundation.

strategic AI implementation. So, yes, you'll have to get your IT department involved. (See Figure 8.2.)

Process Redesign

The whole "digital transformation" movement started with automating mundane tasks but became transformative when new business processes were created. Instead of simply transferring physical documents, we could collaborate in real time from anywhere and analyze huge datasets. With the advent of the Internet, people were no longer bound by location or traditional methods, opening new avenues for communication, commerce, and innovation.

Now, with generative AI, people are not just using the mouse and keyboard to draft content; we can produce tailored materials for individual customers. Instead of time-consuming prototyping, we can simulate realistic models and scenarios in seconds. Because generative AI can create insights, automate personalized experiences, and generate novel content in a way that's adaptive, scalable, and highly creative, we are faced with the opportunity and need to restructure workflows. This means questioning every assumption about how marketing and other customer-facing operations should work. Rather than automating the current monthly campaign cycle, AI enables continuous optimization of marketing planning based on real-time data. This requires new processes, new metrics, and new ways of working. As Tom and his co-author Tom Redman discuss in a recent article, AI can enable entirely new process designs, as well as helping in the execution of business processes.[2]

New workflows spawn new roles while others become obsolete. Skill requirements shift dramatically. Reporting structures that made sense in a manual world are barriers in an AI-enabled environment. Performance metrics that worked for quarterly campaigns make no sense when real-time optimization is possible.

Strategic AI implementation in marketing operations isn't easy. It requires significant investment in time and resources. It demands leadership courage to fundamentally rethink how marketing operates. It calls for patience as new processes and skills develop. But the alternative—continuing to add tactical AI solutions without strategic integration—leads to increasing complexity, rising costs, and declining effectiveness.

The future belongs to organizations that orchestrate data, analytics, and AI capabilities across their marketing operations, creating seamless, efficient, and effective customer experiences while optimizing resource utilization and improving marketing performance. The question isn't whether to undertake strategic AI implementation, but how soon to begin.

For example, Moderna set out to reinvent customer service through automation and cloud computing. Rather than patching together off-the-shelf solutions, they built their own Omnichannel Cloud Contact Center (OC3) on AWS with customer needs as the foundation.[3] The key innovation was working backwards—starting with the ideal customer interaction and engineering the complete cycle from initial contact through ongoing support across voice, chat, email, web, and text messaging. The platform serves up relevant content to service agents in near real time, putting vital information at their fingertips through an intuitive search interface. This eliminates the traditional scramble to find answers while customers wait.

Self-service capabilities give customers direct access to routine information, while integration with Moderna's CRM provides agents a complete view of each customer's history and context. According to Arpita Bhowmick, senior director, omnichannel contact center products for Moderna, "Everything is integrated, modular, and cloud-based to support

---

[2] Thomas H. Davenport and Tom Redman, "How to Marry Process Management and AI," *Harvard Business Review*, January–February 2025, https://hbr.org/2025/01/how-to-marry-process-management-and-ai.

[3] https://aws.amazon.com/solutions/case-studies/moderna-commercialization-case-study.

scaling and agility. What's unique is that the platform can scale to serve the entire gamut of business functions while following the compliance guardrails." As a result, Moderna is a leader in using AI for faster resolution times, higher customer satisfaction, and a system ready to grow with Moderna's global ambitions.

Creating Competitive Advantage Through AI Adoption

When every company has access to the same AI capabilities, where's the competitive advantage? If everybody can use ChatGPT or analytical machine learning to generate content, analyze customer behavior, and optimize campaigns, what's your edge?

Your first instinct might be to amass as much data as possible. As we have mentioned, that can create better models if the data reveal new insights about customers. But greater volumes of data doesn't necessarily mean better AI performance. Netflix doesn't have more viewer data than Amazon Prime, but it knows exactly which data points matter for predicting viewer behavior and has built systems to capture and analyze them effectively.

Competitive advantage through AI also doesn't come from replacing humans—it comes from augmenting them in unique ways. Klarna is a payment service that offers a variety of ways to pay for purchases, including "buy now, pay later" options. Klarna is available at more than 170,000 online stores and in-store with the Klarna Card. They made a great deal of noise when they announced "Klarna AI assistant handles two-thirds of customer service chats in its first month, and, can do the work of 700 human agents." Klarna didn't fire its 700 agents, but it did begin to give them other tasks and reducing their numbers slowly through attrition. Klarna has also said that it has reduced its marketing spending by 37% (over $10M per year) by using generative AI to replace external agency spending. However, it appears to be using analytical AI less well than generative AI. Between 2023 and 2024 its bad credit percentage doubled. Credit extension is typically a function of analytical AI models.

Klarna turned even more heads when, in an earnings call in August 2024:

Klarna's (KLAR) CEO Sebastian Siemiatkowski said that the company is shutting down its software as a service provider (SaaS) Salesforce

(NYSE:CRM) and within a few weeks will shut down Workday (NASDAQ:WDAY).

"There are large ongoing internal initiatives that are a combination of AI, standardization, and simplification. As an example, we just shut down Salesforce. Within a few weeks, we will shut down Workday. We are shutting down a lot of our SaaS providers, as we are able to consolidate," said Siemiatkowski on a conference call.

Siemiatkowski added that with the help of AI, the company is able to standardize and create a more lightweight tech stack to operate more effectively with higher quality.[4]

The competitive advantage of a smaller, lighter, less expensive tech stack all goes to the bottom line if—a significant *if*—the resulting AI apps/agents can do the heavy lifting that enterprise quality SaaS products were delivering.

Entrepreneur, advisor, and innovative data strategies Love Hudson-Maggio has worked extensively with Salesforce enterprise clients. In a conversation with Jim, she pointed out that like most software products, Salesforce has a great deal of functionality that goes unused. "They started with their flagship CRM offering and they've added a lot, and I'd rather run my campaigns in the CRM than in the marketing cloud, which is a complete marketing platform. Most of the enterprise clients I've seen are only using 30%, and it's the same thing all the time, the same function every day."

This is a viable option for those with a deep technical bench. Alternatively, we have all been on the receiving end of announcements from all the major software companies that they are adding AI capabilities to their systems as fast as possible. The question for you is whether you want to strip down your legacy systems to run lean and mean, or do you want to leverage the experience of the big SaaS companies that are building additional capabilities?

---

[4] Klarna shuts down Salesforce as service provider, Workday to meet same fate amid AI initiatives, https://seekingalpha.com/news/4144652-klarna-shuts-down-salesforce-as-service-provider-workday-to-meet-same-fate-amid-ai-initiatives.

Creating competitive advantage through adoption of AI requires thinking beyond individual tools and tactics. It demands the following:

- Understanding your unique data advantages and focusing AI efforts there
- Rebuilding processes around AI capabilities rather than adding AI to existing processes
- Creating unique combinations of human and machine intelligence
- Building systems to capture and apply learning faster than competitors
- Developing private AI models that leverage your specific knowledge and experience
- Integrating AI across your entire marketing ecosystem

Tom co-authored a 2022 book about companies that have adopted these approaches across their organizations, including in customer-facing processes.[5] The companies profiled in the book that were most focused on customer use cases include Capital One, DBS Bank in Singapore, Ping An in China, Morgan Stanley, Unilever, Kroger, Anthem (now Elevance Health), Scotiabank in Canada, Progressive, CCC Intelligent Solutions, and Well. All of these companies except Well are well-established legacy companies, not digital natives. But the book was largely written before the widespread awareness of generative AI, which may create a new set of "all-in" companies.

The book and our subsequent research suggests that the winners aren't the companies with the most advanced AI tools. They are the companies that use AI to create unique capabilities that align with their business strategy and market position.

Use Case Identification

The best place to start optimizing your workflow with AI is finding use cases on the front line. The people deep inside your company who are doing hands-on work know what processes can be automated or enhanced with this new technical wonder. After all, they have probably been using it for a couple of years already, whether company policy allows it or not. And

---

[5] Thomas H. Davenport and Nitin Mittal, "All In on AI: How Smart Companies Win Big with Artificial Intelligence," Harvard Business Review Press, 2022.

those focused on structured numerical data and improving decision-making have been using analytical AI for many years.

The list of possibilities for both types of AI is practically endless (see Table 8.1).

Table 8.1 Use case examples

Company	Description
Atlassian	Automate support interactions within Slack and Teams.[6]
Cadbury	Scaled and personalized advertising.[7]
DuPont	Sales price optimization.[8]
Estée Lauder	Launch locally relevant ad campaigns.[9]
Heineken	A knowledge management system called "Kim" to improve access to information and decision-making. Also using AI to develop new product concepts.[10]
Instacart	Customer recipes and meal-planning ideas and to generate shopping lists.[11]
Kellogg's	Recipes trend analysis to launch social campaigns.[12]
L'Oréal	Potential product innovation opportunities.[13]
Mars	Ad effectiveness predictions.[14]

(continued)

---

[6] 9+ Use-cases of Generative AI in Marketing, https://www.delve.ai/blog/generative-ai-marketing.

[7] 5 Brands Using Generative AI to Disrupt Advertising, https://hotelemarketer.com/2023/09/10/5-brands-using-generative-ai-to-disrupt-advertising.

[8] https://www.technologyreview.com/2023/07/18/1076423/the-great-acceleration-cio-perspectives-on-generative-ai.

[9] The Estée Lauder Companies and Microsoft Increase Collaboration to Power Prestige Beauty with Generative AI, https://www.elcompanies.com/en/news-and-media/newsroom/press-releases/2024/04-26-2024.

[10] https://www.youtube.com/watch?v=0QrqqorqR1o.

[11] How generative AI can boost consumer marketing, https://www.mckinsey.com/capabilities/growth-marketing-and-sales/our-insights/how-generative-ai-can-boost-consumer-marketing.

[12] Ibid.

[13] Ibid.

[14] How brands like Klarna and Mars are using AI in marketing operations, https://martech.org/how-brands-like-klarna-and-mars-are-using-ai-in-marketing-operations.

Table 8.1   (Continued)

Company	Description
Mattel	Opportunity identification and idea generation.[15]
Walmart	Product catalog improvement.[16] Inventory management.[17]

If you think of use cases as tasks, you can use (or make your own) custom JobsGPT[18] like the one created by Paul Roetzer and SmarterX. JobsGPT uses the O*NET occupational database[19] to break down jobs into tasks and then generates a chart of how AI can be applied. It assesses AI exposure to help with work planning through an Exposure Key ranging from no effect to advanced capabilities. As the levels advance, and AI gains multimodal capabilities—handling images, videos, and audio—it eventually takes on more complex roles, including advanced reasoning, persuasion, and interacting with both digital and physical environments, up to the point of operating as a humanoid robot.

Keep in mind, however, that this type of analysis was done prior to generative AI, and it tended to yield overly aggressive predictions of job loss. For example, in 2013 the Oxford Martin Centre analyzed jobs in this fashion and predicted that 47% of US jobs were at risk of replacement by analytical AI.[20] Twelve years later, very few jobs have been lost to that form of AI. It can be useful to analyze job tasks to determine what AI can do, but most human workers perform multiple tasks, and job elimination from AI has thus far happened slowly if at all.

---

[15] Ibid.

[16] Walmart (WMT) Q2 2025 Earnings Call Transcript, https://www.fool.com/earnings/call-transcripts/2024/08/15/walmart-wmt-q2-2025-earnings-call-transcript.

[17] Decking the aisles with data: How Walmart's AI-powered inventory system brightens the holidays, https://tech.walmart.com/content/walmart-global-tech/en_us/blog/post/walmarts-ai-powered-inventory-system-brightens-the-holidays.html.

[18] https://smarterx.ai/jobsgpt.

[19] https://www.onetonline.org.

[20] Oxford Martin Centre, "The Future of Employment: How Susceptible Are Jobs to Computerisation?" 01 September 2013, https://www.oxfordmartin.ox.ac.uk/publications/the-future-of-employment.

Beyond Cost Reduction

The first wave of AI adoption has companies looking at their biggest cost centers, automating what they can, and celebrating the savings. Content creation? Do it internally instead of giving the work to outside agencies and let the machines do it. Customer service inquiries? Chatbots. Email campaigns? AI-driven automation. Cost per interaction dropped, efficiency metrics improved, and everyone declared victory.

But something interesting happened on the way to cost-optimization nirvana.

Deloitte's Q4, 2024 State of Generative AI in the Enterprise report[21] stated:

- Improved efficiency and productivity and cost reduction are still the top benefits sought by organizations. Those are also cited by 42% of respondents as their most important benefits achieved to date.
- However, 58% reported they realized a more diverse range of most important benefits, such as increased innovation, improved products and services, or enhanced customer relationships.
- Respondents said that embedding generative AI deeply into critical business functions and processes is the top way to drive the most value from their generative AI initiatives.

Organizations reporting the highest ROI from AI were those that had moved beyond automation to focus on revenue growth and customer experience enhancement. We saw similar patterns with analytical AI; a 2022 Deloitte survey found that those getting more value from the technology were more than three times as likely to be pursuing new customer markets and segments, new products and services, and new business models with AI.[22]

Adam Brotman, co-founder and co-CEO of Forum3 and co-author with Andy Sack of *AI First: The Playbook for a Future-Proof Business and*

---

[21] Deloitte's Q4, 2024 State of Generative AI in the Enterprise, https://www2.deloitte.com/content/dam/Deloitte/us/Documents/consulting/us-state-of-gen-ai-q3.pdf.

[22] Deloitte State of AI in the Enterprise 2022 Report, https://www2.deloitte.com/us/en/pages/consulting/articles/state-of-ai-2022.html.

Brand,[23] argues that success will come from adopting a new frame of reference:

> "Our company right now is really focused on leaders getting a system in place, a mindset in place, and a process in place that allows them to run a lot of experimentation and effectively build their own AI lab internally. We're talking about the ability to create and customize software using natural language. We've never seen a situation where nontechnical people can actually be innovative using software on their own."

Brotman agrees that the people doing the actual work are the best positioned to accelerate their efforts. "It's really important for companies to facilitate functional leaders—marketers and sales leads because they know their business better than anybody. And can figure out how to use these frontier AI systems to become really productive and even more innovative."

Those who shifted to value creation saw their return on marketing investment multiply. The difference wasn't in the technology—it was in how they thought about AI's role. (See Figure 8.3.)

Stage 1: Experimentation   Marketing teams dip their toes in the AI waters without a cohesive strategy. They try to optimize pricing, use ChatGPT for email drafts, test Midjourney for social media images, and dabble with basic marketing automation tools. Success metrics are vague—"let's see what

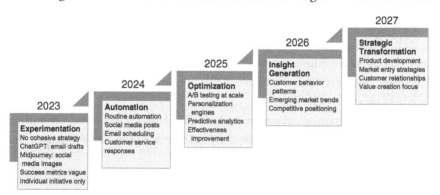

Figure 8.3   Five stages of AI implementation.

---

this can do." Projects start and stop based on individual initiative rather than organizational planning. The focus is on learning and proof of concept rather than business impact. This is where many marketing departments found themselves in 2023—and substantially earlier for analytical AI.

Stage 2: Automation Marketing teams start by automating routine tasks, such as campaign management, social media posting, email scheduling, and basic customer service responses. The focus is purely on cost reduction and efficiency. This is where most companies still operate today.

Stage 3: Optimization Companies begin using AI to optimize existing processes such as A/B testing at scale, personalization engines, predictive analytics for campaign performance. Cost reduction is still important, but the focus shifts to improving effectiveness. Personalization is widespread in terms of both content creation and targeting.

Stage 4: Insight Generation AI moves from executing tasks to generating insights. Marketers employ pattern detection in customer behavior, emerging market trends, competitive positioning opportunities. The technology starts creating value beyond efficiency gains.

Stage 5: Strategic Transformation AI becomes integral to strategic decision-making. It shapes all of the "5Ps" (product, price, place, promotion, people), influences market entry strategies, and transforms customer relationships. Value creation becomes the primary focus, with cost reduction as a secondary benefit.

Impact on Marketing Team Structure and Capabilities

Generative AI and other AI and analytics capabilities represent a fundamental shift in how marketing organizations operate, not merely a new capability to add to the toolset. The technology impacts everything from organizational design to daily workflows to talent requirements.[24]

---

[24] Suzanne Vranica, "Sorry, Mad Men: The Ad Revolution Is Here," *The Wall Street Journal*, 14 December 2024, https://www.wsj.com/business/media/advertising-revolution-artificial-intelligence-data-mad-men-omnicom-interpublic-3c0c056b.

Analytical AI focused on analyzing historical data to surface insights and predictions. It led to changes in marketing organizations, including a partial shift from primarily creative individuals to quantitative analysts. Generative AI creates—it writes copy, designs graphics, composes music, codes applications, and crafts personalized customer communications. This creative capacity means marketing teams must rethink core processes:

- Who ideates and who executes?
- What skills do team members need?
- How do workflows and approvals change?
- Where do humans add the most value?
- What new roles emerge?
- Which old roles evolve or disappear?

As Wharton professor Ethan Mollick put it, "I know this is hard for organizations. And it does involve redoing things, but you cannot have organizations structured the same way. We can't pretend that there isn't another intelligence in the room right now."[25]

The successful marketing department or agency of 2027 will look very different from today's. Creative directors may spend more time training and guiding AI systems than directing human designers. Copywriters might focus on strategy and emotional resonance while AI handles production volume. Analytics teams could shift from running reports to architecting AI models that target personalized offers and ads, and surface real-time recommendations.

This goes far beyond simple task automation. When machines can generate infinite variations of content, customize every interaction, and optimize in real time, the fundamentals of how marketing teams operate must adapt. The organizations that thrive will be those that thoughtfully redesign their teams and processes to capitalize on AI's creative capabilities while maintaining human oversight of strategy, brand, and ethics.

The primary challenge is not implementing the technology; it's reimagining how marketing work gets done when AI is a core team member

[25] Adam Brotman and Andy Sack, *AI First: The Playbook for a Future-Proof Business and Brand*, Harvard Business Review Press (2025).

rather than just a productivity tool. This requires examining every aspect of how marketing teams are structured and operated today.

Collaborative Marketing Operations

The LinkedIn Global Marketing Jobs Outlook report[26] surfaced collaborative problem-solving as a must-have skill for B2B marketers in 2024. "AI is removing so much busywork off our plates we can now focus on more relationship building skills like 'Collaborative Decision-Making,' which we chose as our Skill of the Year."

This makes perfect sense. As AI handles more of the computational and routine aspects of marketing, distinctly human abilities like building relationships, demonstrating emotional intelligence, and working creatively in teams become more crucial. The machine can crunch the numbers, but it takes people working together to determine which questions to ask, which problems to solve, and how to implement solutions in ways that resonate with other humans.

Nearly three-quarters of marketers report feeling overwhelmed by the pace of change in their field. The antidote isn't to compete with AI capabilities but rather to excel in the areas where humans provide unique value—bringing together diverse viewpoints and expertise to produce novel solutions through collaborative ingenuity.

The winning formula appears to be combining strong collaborative capabilities with sufficient technical knowledge to effectively leverage AI and other emerging technologies. This allows marketing teams to let the machines do what they do best while humans focus on what they do best, which is working together to solve complex problems in creative ways that machines simply cannot replicate.

Human-AI Collaboration Frameworks

The partnership between marketers and AI reveals some clear dividing lines. While AI excels at processing massive amounts of data and spotting patterns, it stumbles when tasked with purely human capabilities.

---

[26] https://business.linkedin.com/content/dam/business/marketing-solutions/global/en_US/ site/pdf/infographics/2024-fall-marketing-jobs-outlook.pdf.

Take creativity, for example. AI can generate endless variations on a theme, tweaking headlines and visuals to test which resonates best. But coming up with that initial spark of inspiration? That remains firmly in human hands.

Wink is the in-house agency at Intuit Mailchimp. The agency rolled out AI in 2023 to create and disseminate their most impactful campaign ever, the "clustomer" campaign (i.e. clusters of customers), to optimize the visual execution through rapid prototyping and A/B testing. The company restructured its marketing department by integrating AI tools deeply into daily workflows. They made deliberate changes such as using AI for prototyping, content localization, optimizing campaigns, and increasing efficiency in decision-making processes.

AI helped reduce the number of iterations needed during ideation and speed up testing during campaigns. In an *HBR* article in April 2024,[27] Michelle Taite wrote:

> AI empowered us to move quickly during this ideation phase because it allowed the team to show versus tell. We narrowed down concepts in one meeting, not the five-plus discussions spread across several weeks needed in the past for various rounds of creative. Prompting together forced us to have the hard conversations earlier. And by discussing intricate depictions rather than loose sketches, the team felt more comfortable committing to the idea wholeheartedly.

However, the company was also forced to address limitations of AI, such as its inability to replace human creativity, especially when tailoring messages for cultural nuances. It took human marketers to recognize that this clever wordplay wouldn't translate meaningfully across languages and cultures. Local creative teams had to completely reconceptualize the campaign for different markets while preserving its core insight.

The gap became even more apparent when emotional connection was crucial. Analytical AI can segment audiences with surgical precision, and

---

[27] "How One Marketing Team Made AI Part of Its Daily Work," *Harvard Business Review*, 10 April 2024.

generative AI can create personalized content down to the individual level. But it can't infuse that content with genuine human understanding. AI can offer the canvas and paints, but humans have to create or at least identify the art that moves people.

This extends to interpreting how campaigns land with audiences. While AI excels at measuring engagement metrics, it takes human judgment to truly understand the qualitative feedback from focus groups and customers. Are they connecting emotionally? Does the message feel authentic or automated? This remains beyond AI's current capabilities (although that may not be true for long).

The marketing teams seeing the most success are those that understand these boundaries. They leverage AI's analytical and optimization strengths while relying on human creativity, cultural awareness, critical thinking, and emotional intelligence to craft campaigns that truly resonate. The most successful marketers will be those who understand AI's capabilities but also know how to add value to them.

Necessary Skills Development

New skills and capabilities are now critical for making the most of the technology. We all have access to the tools, but we need to be trained to use them well. That starts with a deep understanding of how these systems work, what they can accomplish, and where human oversight remains essential. People love to adopt new tools without first establishing the basic knowledge required to use them effectively.

Data and AI Literacy Requirements

Data literacy is the raw material of all AI systems, and each marketing tool serves a specific purpose. Email optimization systems analyze open rates and engagement patterns. Content generation tools create various versions of copy for testing. Customer service automation handles routine inquiries while escalating complex issues to humans. The key is understanding not just how to operate these tools but how they arrive at their recommendations. This allows marketers to configure tools appropriately for their specific use cases, recognize when outputs require human review or adjustment, identify opportunities to combine multiple tools effectively, and maintain control over the customer experience.

Today's marketers have to understand that AI systems reflect the data used to train them, warts and all. Bias in the data can lead to discriminatory outcomes, which would result in branding black eyes. This means clear guidelines for AI use in customer interactions while providing transparency about how tools are applied. Customer privacy and data security cannot be afterthoughts. They must be built into any AI marketing, sales, or service program.

The goal isn't to transform marketers or salespeople or service agents into AI engineers but to develop sufficient understanding to deploy these tools responsibly and effectively. That calls for ongoing education as the tools become more powerful every week. The investment in digital literacy pays off through more effective implementation, better customer experiences, and stronger competitive advantage. Knowing how AI tools are built is step one. Next, you need to train people how to use them.

Back in the early days of computers, you had to know FORTRAN or BASIC to get anything done. Then came graphical user interfaces, and everybody could point and click their way to productivity. The same pattern is emerging with AI; you need to know how to "talk" to it just as we had to learn to speak in Boolean search operators when we started using Google.

If you haven't put together an AI educational program, it's high time: the basics of data collection and integration, the fundamentals of machine learning and generative AI, and the essentials of prompt engineering. Yes, you can tell your team to turn to YouTube and they will find hundreds of videos that will give them all sorts of tips and tricks. But they will all learn different tips and tricks and not all of them will be correct or even useful. And it's guaranteed that they will be outdated in a heartbeat.

Teaching your marketing team these skills is not optional. It's the difference between getting sensible marketing copy suggestions and getting gibberish. You wouldn't just hand them the employee manual and expect perfection. You coach them, correct their mistakes, and help them understand the nuances of your business. You bring them together to cross-train each other.

And just like any other business tool, AI breaks. Your team needs to know what to do when the output doesn't make sense, when the system seems stuck in a rut, or when it's clearly headed in the wrong direction. At a recent Big Data Conference EU, Thomas Schmidt, senior analytics engineer at Metabase, described how his company created LLM agents to help analyze data. Without serious knowledge of how LLMs work or how specific prompts need to be, they would never have figured out how a relatively simple task between two agents went off the rails. Agent 1 asked Agent 2 for some data from a table. Agent 2 complied. Agent 1 thanked Agent 2. Agent 2 said you're welcome. Agent 1 thanked Agent 2 for its courtesy. Agent 2 said you're welcome. Trying to understand why this relationship was doomed to failure was never going to be discoverable from reading error messages.

The good news? Your team already knows how to learn new tools. They mastered email, conquered social media, and figured out marketing automation. AI is just the next step. The key is making sure they have a formal educational program to rely on. Establish continuous learning initiatives to help employees keep pace with emerging AI trends. Include workshops, webinars, or online courses tailored to specific AI applications in marketing.

And more good news: AI can also improve the ability for marketing and customer-facing organizations to get, train, and retain good people. On the analytical AI front, smart HR organizations have used AI models for several years to predict the attributes of job candidates that will lead to success on the job and also predict which employees are likely to leave without an intervention. Generative AI can be used to tutor or coach employees in the acquisition of needed skills. Such coaching is quite common in sales, but somewhat less in marketing. Customer service systems that employ GenAI can use the capability of the systems not only to answer customer questions but also to tutor agents both in content topics and on their "bedside manner" with customers.

New Roles and Career Paths

Generative AI requires new roles within marketing teams. For example, organizations might create positions like AI integration specialists (another word for the data product managers we described in Chapter 6), who oversee the implementation and optimization of AI systems within daily operations. These specialists act as the bridge between technical teams and creative marketers.

Data analysts will need to shift their focus to AI-driven insights, moving from manual data interpretation to leveraging machine learning models for predictive analytics. Another emerging role is that of human-AI interaction designers to design more intuitive workflows between humans and AI tools for both employees and customers.

As AI capabilities expand, organizations need dedicated AI instructors—not as cheerleaders, but as practical guides helping employees gain competence and confidence with new tools. This requires both technical knowledge and the ability to translate capabilities into business value. Rather than generic technology training, companies should develop certification paths tailored to specific business functions, roles, and outcomes. A certification in AI-enabled marketing content creation carries more weight than a general "AI 101" badge.

Job descriptions and career trajectories need an overhaul. Content creators who master AI tools can grow into creative directors who orchestrate human and machine capabilities. Marketing managers who understand both business strategy and AI potential become invaluable advisors on technology integration.

Leadership development has to catch up as well. Managers need enough technical literacy to make informed decisions about AI deployment while keeping teams focused on meaningful outcomes rather than chasing shiny objects. They must balance AI's efficiency against maintaining human judgment and ethical guidelines.

The key is transforming jobs thoughtfully rather than forcing technology into existing structures. This means identifying where AI truly adds value versus where human skills remain essential. Organizations that get this balance right will develop teams that leverage AI's strengths while preserving what makes their people unique.

Measuring Success and ROI

How do you know all that effort you're putting into AI is paying off? This question perplexed Jim to the point of publishing a paper in December 2023 called "Measuring the Business Value of Generative AI,"[28] but the principles apply to analytical AI as well.

---

[28] "Measuring the Business Value of Generative AI," *Journal of AI, Robotics & Workplace Automation* 3(1): 28–36 © Henry Stewart Publications 2633-562X (2024). doi: 10.69554/AUIJ4734.

The most obvious benefits show up in the metrics we already track: revenue growth, cost reduction, employee productivity, and customer satisfaction. Early studies demonstrate dramatic improvements. Analytical AI can surface trends and anomalies and make predictions that lead directly to making more, spending less, and making customers happier. GenAI-augmented workers complete tasks faster with fewer errors. More telling is how GenAI elevates performance across skill levels and reduces turnover, particularly among new employees still learning their roles.

But focusing solely on traditional metrics misses the transformative potential. With enough data and a few clever algorithms, companies have been able to uncover hidden relationships and correlations. They've been able to forecast outcomes and identify clusters or groups with similar behaviors or characteristics. There are a great many use cases for Analytical AI including finding the following:

- **Root causes:** Pinpoint underlying factors driving specific outcomes.
- **Optimization opportunities:** Suggest ways to maximize efficiency, performance, or ROI.
- **Sentiment:** Analyze emotions or opinions expressed in text, audio, or video data.
- **Emerging signals:** Detect early indicators of shifts in customer preferences or market trends.
- **Outliers:** Highlight data points that deviate significantly from norms.
- **Impact analysis:** Measure the influence of specific variables on outcomes.
- **Behavioral patterns:** Track and analyze user or customer actions over time.

One company that has exhibited these traits throughout the past few decades—and still does today—is Procter & Gamble. The company consistently leads the consumer products industry in the use of data for marketing and new product development. A P&G press release points out that the company is celebrating its 100th year of analytics and insights.[29] That focus began in 1924, when "Doc" Smelser, an economist who

---

[29] "Celebrating the 100th Year of P&G Analytics and Insights," Procter & Gamble press release, 12 December 2024, https://us.pg.com/blogs/100-years-of-pg-analytics-and-insights.

worked for P&G, wondered in a meeting with the CEO how many consumers used Ivory soap for washing their bodies versus their dishes and clothes. William Cooper Procter, the last member of the founding family to lead the company, asked Smelser to find out. In case you're wondering, the answer was 12% dishwashing, 31% face and hands, and 40% bathing.

P&G still sells Ivory, and it is still focused on data, analytics, and now AI for decision-making.[30] For more than a decade it has had common data—called *business sufficiency models*—about brand, category, and financial performance across the company. It has had common analytical tools across the organization as well so that any manager or employee could move from one part of the company to another and analyze data in the same way. If the manager didn't have the skills to analyze data, more than 250 embedded data analysts were available to help. For a while P&G had special rooms for reviewing and deciding on data and analytics, but it eventually decided to push the capability out to every employee with a computer.

Today, P&G is moving rapidly to take advantage of AI—both analytical and generative technologies. Jeff Goldman, the head of enterprise data science, began putting analytical AI initiatives in place in 2015 in partnership with the R&D organization. An early focus was on analyzing data generated by P&G smart products, such as the Olay Skin Analyzer to analyze customer faces and ways cosmetics could help. It's also analyzing data from the Oral B iQ toothbrush and Febreze NEW-AIRIA Smart Scent Diffuser. P&G has also used analytical AI to create "next best order" recommendations for retailers, to make better decisions on where and when to deploy advertising, to generate more granular insights about consumer behavior, and to improve the effectiveness of trade payments to retailers.

P&G had historically been handicapped by not owning most of the data about consumer purchases of its products; that belonged to retailers, which would often sell it to syndicated data providers like Nielsen. But P&G has been attempting to get more "first-party" data directly from consumers through a variety of methods. It has introduced some direct-to-consumer

---

[30] Thomas H. Davenport, Marco Iansiti, and Alain Serels. "Managing with Analytics at Procter & Gamble." Harvard Business School Case 613-045, April 2013, https://store.hbr.org/product/managing-with-analytics-at-procter-gamble/613045?sku=613045-PDF-ENG.

(DTC) products (some through its corporate venture arm) that it sells through the Internet. It's working with MIT to try to figure out ways to market DTC products through its website but have the actual sale and delivery go through retailers. That way P&G gets the data but preserves its strong relationships with its primary distribution channel. It's also using coupons to provide incentives for consumers to share their information with the company.

Now, of course, many of P&G's AI projects involve generative AI. The company had begun to experiment with a large language model in the summer of 2022, before ChatGPT was announced. It quickly developed a semi-proprietary model called ChatPG with protections for the company's intellectual property. There are now more than 40 generative AI use cases around the company in addition to the individual-level experimentation that many companies do with LLMs, and the company is working with multiple different LLMs depending on the use case. The use cases in production include call center application, a customer and market knowledge access system, and code generation for programming. The emphasis with both generative and analytical models is employee augmentation, not large-scale automation.

P&G has also put in an "AI factory" to speed development on AI models, primarily in the analytical AI space but with some generative activity as well. It is used across 80% of the global business and results in a tenfold faster deployment of the AI solution. It includes an AI development and management platform and repositories of machine learning features. The factory capabilities facilitate testing different versions of models for specific regional requirements and also help with scaling models across the company. One AI factory-developed use case, for example, is the Pampers MyPerfectFit application, which provides parents with recommendations that are 90% accurate for the right diaper size for their child to prevent leaks. P&G is also using AI factory capabilities for developing new fragrances.

Finally, P&G has long had a focus on building human capabilities in data, analytics, and AI. The company has partnered with Harvard Business School for AI and data science training for executives, with two levels of certification. And all employees have been given access to generative AI training, which they must take in order to use the company's LLMs. Vittorio

Cretella, who recently retired as the company's chief information officer, commented that:

> "It is critical not only to insource key technology capabilities, such as data science and machine learning engineering, but above all, to ensure all employees become familiar with working with AI."

At leading companies like P&G, GenAI functions as a catalyst for human creativity rather than a replacement for it. It generates possibilities, explores alternatives, and helps structure complex problems in novel ways. The challenge lies in measuring this amplification effect—how do you quantify better ideas or more innovative solutions?

This parallels the early days of the commercial Internet, when businesses struggled to measure its true impact. Initially, they tracked obvious metrics like website traffic and online sales. Only later did they recognize how fundamentally the Internet would reshape entire industries and business models. GenAI demands similar expansive thinking about measurement.

Consider a simple example: a marketing team using GenAI to create campaign concepts. You could count the number of ideas generated or measure time saved. But the real value may come from exploring creative directions that wouldn't have emerged otherwise or from the team's ability to iterate and refine concepts more rapidly. These qualitative improvements require new measurement approaches.

Organizations need a balanced scorecard for GenAI that includes both hard metrics and softer indicators of transformation. This might combine traditional KPIs with assessments of innovation capacity, speed-to-market improvements, and measures of organizational learning and adaptation. The goal is understanding not just what GenAI does but how it changes what's possible.

Implementation brings its own challenges. Legal and ethical considerations around data usage, bias, and transparency must be addressed. Technical infrastructure and talent requirements need evaluation. Change management becomes critical as workers adapt to new tools and workflows.

Smart organizations will start small, choosing specific use cases where GenAI's impact can be clearly measured. They'll establish baseline metrics, track results rigorously, and use those insights to guide broader adoption.

Most importantly, they'll recognize that measurement itself must evolve as they better understand GenAI's transformative potential.

With all the excitement about the possibilities of GenAI, it is important to view this measurement process as a structured journey. The business value measurement flow diagram shown in Figure 8.4 can be a framework for this journey, starting at the input layer, where the foundational elements such as GenAI capabilities, project ideas, market data, and strategic imperatives and disruptive potential are consolidated. These are just some of the considerations an organization should address.

The analysis and assessment layer uses a feasibility study, risk analysis, and innovation potential to filter out the least likely to succeed. The next step is project valuation where ROI estimation and project viability scoring offer a basis of comparison of each project's potential contribution to the organizations' strategic goals.

Approval and funding are the final hoops to project approval. Projects are then left to run their course with periodic reviews designed to weed out those that appear to die on the vine. The project review phase makes the final assessment of the cost/risk versus the reward/benefit and synthesizes advice to feed back into the input layer on a continuous basis.

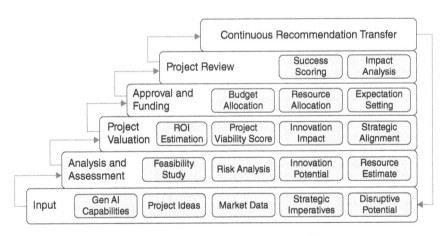

Figure 8.4 Business value measurement flow.[31]

Source: [31] / President & Fellows of Harvard College

---

[31] Ibid.

The organizations that thrive will be those that move thoughtfully but deliberately, balancing enthusiasm with pragmatism. They'll focus on measuring what matters while remaining open to unexpected opportunities. In the end, analytical and generative AI may prove most valuable not in what it helps us do, but in how it helps us think differently about what's possible.

These machines are making us more efficient, changing our operations, improving our decisions, and enabling new ways to understand our customers. While vendors are rushing to provide tools that will disrupt the way we work, our jobs are not in jeopardy—they're evolving. The machines are becoming collaborators rather than simple tools. They're expanding our capabilities rather than replacing them.

The next question that pops up: What does this mean for our ability to derive value from our data? How can analytics and AI capabilities be developed and improved to benefit customer relationships? Let's take a look at how the rise of intelligent technologies is reshaping analytics.

9 | Better Customer Analytics and Data Science

Developing marketing analytics and AI models has always been a somewhat esoteric activity. If your organization wanted precise segmentation analyses, the ideal mix of marketing approaches, personalized offers, product recommendations, or optimized pricing for your products, they were hard to get. These capabilities required large volumes of high-quality data, powerful statistical computing tools, and highly trained people in statistics or data science. The only organizations that could afford these resources were large consumer brands; B2B companies didn't have enough data, and small businesses didn't have the data, technology, or people to do these types of analyses. As a result, marketing analytics and traditional AI only helped the rich get richer.

But this chapter is primarily about the easing of those constraints. The title is slightly misleading; it's not that most of the methods and tools for analytics and data science have gotten much better since the early days of one-to-one marketing. We're still using the same types of statistical models—some of which were developed in the early nineteenth century.

Many marketing models are still based on regression analysis, which you probably studied (and perhaps forgot) in your college statistics class.

The AI models that organizations use for marketing are newer than that, of course, but have all been around for several decades (with the exception of GenAI models, which so far are primarily used for creating content rather than marketing analytics). What is new is that these methods and tools are now available to a much broader range of people and organizations. And even if you have a PhD in statistics or quantitative marketing, you can work much more productively to build more marketing models in a shorter time.

In addition to the democratization of analytics and AI, in this chapter we'll discuss issues like whether to focus on more data or better models, striking a balance between predictive power and explainability, and how to increase the likelihood that models will be put into production. We'll also discuss the importance of organizational structures and cultures that facilitate the use of data to improve customer relationships as well as other possible business objectives. They're not as easy as installing a new database or AI platform, but they have even more important long-term consequences.

More Data or Better Models?

While this chapter is devoted primarily to models and methods, it's important to remember that a better model is not the only way to improve your outcome with customer and marketing analytics and AI. Getting better data to incorporate in your model is often more impactful. We've already mentioned the well-known quote (so well known that no one seems to know the source or date of it) from Peter Norvig, a leading data scientist at Google/Alphabet, that "more data beats clever algorithms, but better data beats more data."

This suggests that you can improve the models you are using and the outcomes they help generate by either getting more of the same data, or—and in our experience this is often more helpful—finding a new source of data that reflects on your problem. If, for example, you are trying to personalize your offers to customers and your offers involve clothing, it may be particularly useful to add place of residence—or even better in algorithms, latitude of place of residence—to get a good prediction of whether warm- or cold-weather clothing is likely to be more appealing. Even more effective might be the actual temperature on the day you are sending the offer.

Admittedly, getting more and better data can be a hassle. There's finding it in the first place, confirming that it's accurate, adding it to your customer database, updating it over time, etc. In most cases it's probably easier to tinker with your model by trying a new algorithm or engineering an existing feature. Remember, however, that the quantity and quality of data that you employ in your model is rarely fixed and that efforts to improve both can make your predictions substantially better.

Automating Machine Learning

The powerful tools once available only to analytics specialists and data scientists are increasingly usable by mere mortals today. This trend was happening before generative AI came along, but that technology has certainly given it a boost. It began with the development of "automated machine learning"—a technology that performs most of the steps needed to create a machine learning model. It got started in the early 2010s; DataRobot claims to have invented the concept when it was founded in 2012.

Automated machine learning, often known as AutoML, doesn't help someone decide why they want to build a model, what variable they want to predict, or what data to use. Those activities are still the province of a human. But it does almost everything else in creating a machine learning model, including these steps:

1. Pick an algorithm type that is well-suited for your features or variables—e.g. logistic regression (among others—AutoML usually tries multiple algorithms) for predicting a binary outcome variable.
2. Do some "feature engineering" to try various permutations (logged, lagged, collapsed categories, etc.) of your predictor variables to see if they can be turned into better predictors.
3. Try multiple algorithm types to see which creates the best fit of your predictions to the actual outcomes.
4. Test the best/most practical model on a test dataset where you know the outcomes.
5. Explain which of the features are most influential in determining the outcome.
6. "Score" (create predictions for) cases where you don't know outcomes.

Another thing that AutoML tools definitely do not do is deploy a model into production. As we'll discuss later in the chapter, that requires other activities that are largely human and organizational in nature. So when a vendor—DataRobot in this case—claims that as of mid-2024 their software had been used to create 3.74 billion machine learning models,[1] that doesn't mean all of them (or even a large proportion of them) were actually deployed. Nobody knows how many of their models were deployed, which is the more important number. Only when a model is deployed into actual business processes and practices does it have any economic value.

There are different types of AutoML tools. Some, like those from vendors DataRobot, H20, and the cloud providers AWS, Google, and Microsoft, are usable by nonprofessional data scientists but are somewhat difficult to interpret and explain by those without serious statistical credentials. These tools are best used by hard-core data scientists, and they often improve their productivity. Ironically, however, they sometimes resist using the tools because they think they can do better with manual approaches (or perhaps because they are threatened by the automation).[2]

There are, however, AutoML tools that are focused on amateurs (sometimes known as "citizen data scientists"[3]) rather than professionals. A marketing analyst, for example, could use them to understand whether a promotion is effective for certain types of customers. The AutoML tool could do the statistical heavy lifting, and the analyst would be told which features or variables are most important to the model and which ones don't matter much. Tools that fall into this category include those from Aible, Squark, Berryjam, and the AutoML tools from visual analytics software companies like Tableau and Qlik. Microsoft's PowerBI, one of the most popular tools for business data analysis, also now has AutoML capabilities.

The use of such tools makes sophisticated machine learning models accessible to groups that don't have access to professional data scientists for use in marketing situations that may be uncommon. For example, at

---

[1] Andrew Andreev, "DataRobot," Apix-Drive blog post, 30 August 2024, https://apix-drive.com/en/blog/useful/datarobot-machine-learning-platform.

[2] Thomas H. Davenport, "Realizing the Benefits of Automated Machine Learning," DataRobot White Paper, 2018, https://content.dataversity.net/rs/656-WMW-918/images/Realizing%20the%20Benefits%20of%20Automated%20Machine%20Learning%20by%20Tom%20Davenport%20%5BWhite%20Paper%5D.pdf.

[3] Thomas H. Davenport, Ian Barkin, and Chase E. Davenport, *All Hands on Tech: The AI-Powered Citizen Revolution* (Wiley, 2024).

the University of Pittsburgh Medical Center (UPMC), one of the medical specialty areas is living donor liver transplants (LDLTs).[4] Nationally, LDLT is a small specialty, with only about 500 transplants per year across all centers, but UPMC has the largest living donor practice in the United States. Within the United States, there is a long waiting list for liver transplants, but many patients who need one aren't familiar with the living donor option, even though it tends to have more successful outcomes. UPMC has advocated to help patients reduce their wait for organs from cadavers by considering LDLT as an alternative—hence the need for a marketing approach.

UPMC clinicians and administrators concluded that the hospital would be performing a valuable service if they marketed the living donor transplant services to those who might benefit from them. It's a narrow group of individuals, however, and they weren't sure how to target such a small population. Many doctors aren't even aware of the living donor transplant option, so they knew that educating patients was going to be an important part of the process.

The UPMC Marketing Intelligence group, led by Jake Collins, director of marketing intelligence, did have an idea how to reach the potential patients. He has a background in data analysis (though is not a data scientist) and knew that UPMC could reach out to potential patients while maintaining their privacy in adherence with HIPAA guidelines. His group at UPMC maintains a robust national consumer database with a large number of variables on each individual. Collins knew that under typical identification models, UPMC would have to reach out to about 10,000 people to get one possible transplant candidate—not an economical ratio. However, he guessed that they could reduce that number considerably with some targeting based on the data and statistical analysis.

Identifying people outside of UPMC's traditional footprint with a need for liver transplants using 1500 different variables would normally be very labor-intensive, but Collins had recently brought Squark, a "low-code predictive analytics tool," into his marketing intelligence department. Squark, which was co-founded by a colleague of both of us named Judah Phillips, employs an easy-to-use approach to AutoML that is focused on business

---

[4] The UPMC example is described in greater detail in Thomas H. Davenport, "Identifying Patients Needing Help with Squark AutoML at UPMC," *Forbes*, 19 November 2021, https://www.forbes.com/sites/tomdavenport/2021/11/19/identifying-patients-needing-help-with-squark-automl-at-upmc/.

users (ideally with a bit of quantitative training). It's also a lower-cost option than many AutoML tools.

Collins commented that Squark made the cost of creating this model so low you could think about doing it anywhere. He said that in addition to needing more monetary resources, he used to need a data scientist and 6 months to do the kind of analysis they did for liver transplant prospects. Now, based on the initial work done by the marketing intelligence team, anybody on the team with a basic understanding of statistics can set up and run machine learning models, and much more quickly.

In grad school Collins ran a regression model on 114 variables. Doing that required that he write code and examine the outcomes in a highly manual process, and it took him months to complete. Now, with Squark, he can do models with 1000 variables and run them in an hour with the same accuracy. The team can now do hundreds of different analyses in a few months; they can try all sorts of ideas.

The modeling approach Collins and his group used for LDLT patient identification examines all the variables for various geographies and age groups, along with the known liver disease outcomes for those same groupings, within an AutoML model. He's trying to find the variables that are most influential on the outcomes at the group level. The resulting model is then used to score each individual person across all geographic areas based on their likelihood of having the condition. Collins generally takes the best-performing deciles and then uses a partner company "to go from a person in the database to a person in the digital space," as he put it. Then they target and retarget informative ads on all platforms.

Collins is also comfortable with the idea of using an AutoML tool like Squark on an ongoing basis. He feels it is empowering his "citizen data scientists" to do more complex analysis with the same level of accuracy on behalf of UPMC and its patients. He has a UPMC-employed data scientist "check the math" before they embark upon a campaign to ensure that the models are being run and interpreted correctly.

Overall, Collins says, the team has gotten phenomenal results from the liver transplant campaign. Instead of reaching out to 10,000 people to get one interested patient, UPMC has to reach out to only 75 now. There was a tremendous response to the call center, and UPMC has added 50% more traveling patients to its liver transplant pipeline through this and other tactics.

The liver transplant program was the first test case for the outreach approach, and now Collins' group is pursuing similar approaches in other areas. They are working on a program for pancreatic cancer, collaborating with a UPMC physician who uses a lot of advanced statistical analysis in his own work. They also have some musculoskeletal programs in mind that they feel could help more patients.

"The data and the models help us deliver the care at the right time and the right place to the right person in most effective way possible," Collins said. "We don't use our own patients' individual data, and we don't violate privacy; that is sacred." Most important, he concluded, "The patients who get transplants or other successful treatments are very glad we reached out to them."

Generative AI and Machine Learning Models

Low-code tools like Squark are great for opening up the population of people and type of problems that can benefit from marketing analytics. But it's becoming even easier for mildly quantitative people to just tell a generative AI model what they want in an analysis, and—as if by magic—it's done. We are confident that GenAI will transform the field of data analysis at some point, although it's still early days at the moment.

Right now, you can say to ChatGPT, "Create for me a machine learning model, trying multiple different algorithms, to predict the customer attrition variable in the dataset I will upload." It tells you to go ahead and upload the dataset—typically in a CSV format. As long as "attrition" is clearly labeled in the columns, ChatGPT will write Python code to do the following:

- Deal with missing data in an appropriate fashion (e.g. by substituting a median value)
- Figure out which predictor variables are appropriate, and exclude those that don't make sense (e.g. "customer ID")
- Transform predictor variables to make them better predictors (e.g. take logarithms of them)
- Run a variety of different algorithm types (logistic regression, gradient boosted tree, random forest) to see which predicts the attrition variable best
- Split the data into training and testing datasets

- Explain which variables are the most important predictors in the best-fitting model
- Describe a summary of the steps it has taken

With an additional prompt of "What steps can I take to reduce attrition?" ChatGPT will give you some reasonable pointers about actions that might work. With another prompt of "Can you visualize the results?" it will do so. It will also show you the Python code it generated to do the analysis.

This is clearly the cat's meow of data analysis—lots of work, rigorous analysis, little or no effort by the analyst. Unfortunately, we have found that minor changes in prompt wording seem to lead to dramatically different results in the statistical models (as with other types of generative AI prompts), so there is perhaps more work for OpenAI or other vendors to do in this regard. Some have suggested to us that there are ways—through stern warnings to use the same Python as in the previous prompt—to limit this from happening. We haven't yet found them. It seems likely, however, that this problem will be fixed shortly and that similar prompts will eventually yield similar outputs.

If you prefer a Microsoft-based approach to using generative AI for marketing problems, that vendor has created a set of Coursera courses for marketers called "Microsoft Copilot for Marketing Specialization." According to the course description:

> You'll learn how a marketing organization can implement Microsoft Copilot in each of its marketing functions including research, customer analysis, strategy, campaign planning, creative design, promotions, pricing, customer experience, and retention. And you'll step through the process of using Microsoft Copilot to upgrade your marketing strategy.

Other modules of the course tell you "how to train Microsoft Copilot with marketing related data. Analyze customer insights and define personas and customer segments. Apply Microsoft Copilot to enhance your targeting efforts across channels."

If for some reason you want a GenAI-influenced PowerBI version of your Microsoft instruction, there's the 5-hour Udemy course called "Data Analysis in Power BI with ChatGPT and Microsoft Copilot." It appears to be primarily business intelligence (descriptive analytics and dashboards) rather than machine learning, but it is clearly a step in the data analysis direction.

Many other vendors are creating GenAI front ends to their analytics and machine learning software.[5] Some (from vendors including ThoughtSpot, Tableau, and Qlik) is intended for use by people who know the problem they want to solve but not necessarily the statistical methods by which to do it. Other vendors (AWS, Google, H20) are more focused on using GenAI to help professional data scientists be more productive and effective.

We will undoubtedly see rapid change in the field of GenAI and its impact on analytics and machine learning, as we have in the past couple of years. Organizations wanting or needing to democratize these activities should closely follow new technology developments and how their employees are taking advantage of them.

Generative AI for Other Data Analysis Tasks

Generative AI really comes into its own with the analysis of unstructured data, i.e. text. If you have a survey with open-ended responses, GenAI will do an excellent job of analyzing the frequency of certain responses, summarizing all the responses, generating word clouds, etc. The ease of doing this should make you more likely to create open-ended responses in your next survey. If you're creating a customer attrition model, for example, try to get some unstructured comments about why the customer left. You can categorize and count the various responses and compare the results to the factors predicting churn in the quantitative analysis. And as we've already discussed in Chapter 6, "Better Customer Voice Analysis and Action," if you want to analyze textual customer responses (though email, websites, or social media) instead of just responding to them, GenAI is the way to do it.

GenAI can also be used to explain predictive and prescriptive models. When they do the analysis, they do an excellent job of explaining it. But even if you do the analysis through traditional manual or automated machine learning, you can have an LLM explain the findings in ways that

---

[5] For a discussion of this topic, see "Generative AI for Data Analytics: How Early Adopters Are Reaping the Rewards," MIT SMR Connections report sponsored by ThoughtSpot, 12 September 2024, https://sloanreview.mit.edu/mitsmr-connections/generative-ai-for-data-and-analytics-how-early-adopters-are-reaping-the-rewards.

businesspeople are likely to understand. An article by Pedro Amorim and João Alves explains how this works:

> LLMs can provide useful output in response to a well-crafted prompt that specifies the prediction topic, the analytical model employed, the results of analyses, and the technique used to understand the results (such as a SHAP visualization). This information allows LLMs to articulate a plausible explanation for changes in predictions for decision makers and highlights the main contributing factors.[6]

The article even provides some specific prompts that can help elicit such explanations.

Downside Risks of Democratization

Of course, when less-quantitative individuals begin using these automated or generative AI tools to create predictive models, there is a chance they will do so poorly. They may make errors in data management, such as using the wrong weather dataset (to control for its impact on sales) or inadvertently including prospects in a customer dataset. These data errors, of course, can also be made by professionals—particularly data scientists who care a lot about modeling but less about customers and how they are defined.

Amateurs can also make statistical mistakes. A marketing analyst, for example, might get a bit over their head in using such tools and employ the wrong type of model, overfit a model, or violate some statistical assumptions behind the chosen model type. Their models may do a poor job of predicting the desired outcome as a result.

However, this is not likely to be tragic. A marketing model that doesn't predict well is unlikely to bring a company to its knees, make anyone sick, or hurt an innocent child or pet. Marketing, fortunately, is rarely a life-or-death matter, so a mistake in analytics or AI is not as worrying as driving badly in a self-driving car.

This was effectively what the head of data governance at Microsoft told Tom when he was interviewing him for his book *All Hands on Tech*, the focus

---

[6] Pedro Amorim and João Alves, "How Generative AI Can Support Advanced Analytics Practice," *MIT Sloan Management Review*, 11 June 2024, https://sloanreview.mit.edu/article/how-generative-ai-can-support-advanced-analytics-practice.

of which was citizen development of all types. Given that Microsoft markets citizen-oriented tools and the company's CEO has strongly endorsed the citizen movement, there is a massive amount of citizen development activity within the company—in marketing and elsewhere. Our data governance friend said that "we have millions of data science models floating around." He was not particularly worried about some marketer who is trying to use machine learning to predict customer behavior. He was concerned about "metrics collision"—people using nonapproved versions of key data elements—but he seemed less concerned about marketing data collisions than those in finance and engineering.

Of course, it's not an either/or situation when considering whether citizens or professionals should do analytics or AI work. As the folks at UPMC did, nonprofessionals can run their work past data science professionals to make sure it was done appropriately. Tools like AutoML and GenAI are not only opening up the number of people who can do data science work but also opening up new avenues of collaboration between businesspeople and data science professionals.

Explainability vs. Predictive Power

Predictive analytics (typically using some form of regression analysis) has been around for a while. Most forms of "prescriptive analytics," which provide a recommendation or an optimal solution, use either regression analysis from the nineteenth century or operations research methods that were first used in the 1940s. The more complex model types in machine learning (reinforcement learning, deep learning, gradient boosting, etc.) are substantially newer, although some forms of most were developed in the twentieth century. GenAI is the newest of all (see Figure 9.1 for a comparison of analytical model types). In many cases, these newer methods offer greater predictive power than earlier models. That is, your pricing or promotion model is likely to be somewhat more effective with these relatively new approaches.

There is a trade-off involved, however. Regression-based models are relatively simple and easy to interpret. If the value of a predictive variable goes up or down by a certain amount, we can see from its coefficient how much the value of the dependent or outcome variable is likely to change.

That's not the case with really complex models like deep learning. They may have tens, hundreds, or thousands (or trillions in the case of generative

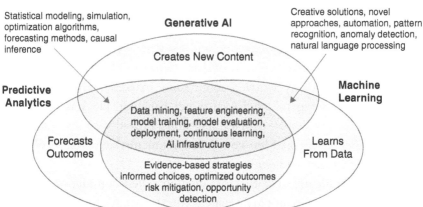

Figure 9.1   Comparison of analytical model types.

AI models, which are the most complex form of deep learning) of variables and parameters. Figuring out what is happening within them can be difficult or impossible. Statisticians have made progress in making some types of models more transparent—typically using approaches like Shapley values, which allows manipulation of predictor variables to understand what happens to outcome variables—but complex deep learning models are pretty much uninterpretable.

Some industries have a strong preference for explainability in their models, either because their customers demand it or because their regulators insist upon it. Some banks, for example, believe that deep learning models can do a better job of predicting credit defaults than traditional regression models, but regulators generally won't let banks use the uninterpretable models. Healthcare providers also can't tell a patient, "The AI model thinks you have cancer, but we don't know why"—so they don't use deep learning-based cancer image detection models very often. Even in industries where customers or regulators aren't sensitive to the transparency issue, managers who are betting a lot on a model working to predict customer behavior correctly may not be comfortable when neither they nor their data scientists can explain how the model works.

Less-experienced modelers may want to choose models that are relatively understandable, even though they may not predict as well. If your logistic regression model does only a few hundredths less well in predicting the outcome than, say, a random forest model, go with the simpler, more explainable model.

Sometimes analytical and AI models are so complex that they become difficult to implement. This was the fate, for example, of the "Netflix Prize" winners in 2009. The competition was to figure out an algorithm that provided 10% or more improvement in the Netflix algorithm for predicting customer movie ratings. The prize was a million dollars. The winning team, Bellkor (a group of AT&T data scientists from what used to be called Bell Labs), worked for 3 years before beating the 10% goal by a small amount. However, Netflix never implemented the prize-winning model, stating in a blog post that the improvement "did not seem to justify the engineering effort needed to bring them into a production environment."[7] Many other models don't get implemented for similar reasons, although they seldom involve a million-dollar prize.

New Platforms

To facilitate the broad use of analytics and AI within organizations, many organizations are adopting data science platforms that contain multiple tools and capabilities for such analysis. They are primarily focused on data science professionals but are also sometimes used by businesspeople with a quantitative bent. They generally focus on predictive, prescriptive, and increasingly also generative AI models, and they can increasingly deal with structured or unstructured data types. Many of them have a workflow orientation (also known as *machine learning operations* [MLOps]) that extends from hypothesis generation, dataset selection, data engineering, feature engineering, model development, deployment, and ongoing monitoring. Most platforms are primarily cloud-based but may have some on-premises capabilities as well.

Popular platform types include those designed from the beginning to be data science platforms (DataBricks, Dataiku, Domino Data Lab), those offered by cloud vendors to augment their data storage and analysis programs (Google Vertex AI, AWS SageMaker, Microsoft Azure Machine Learning), those offered by AI software vendors (DataRobot, IBM Watson X), and those from analytics software vendors (SAS, IBM SPSS, Alteryx). Each one

---

[7] Casey Johnston, "Netflix Never Used Its $1 Million Algorithm Due to Engineering Costs," *Wired*, 16 April 2012, https://www.wired.com/2012/04/netflix-prize-costs.

has particular strengths and weaknesses, of course. For example, some have begun to offer tools for generative AI, and others have not yet done so. Some are oriented primarily to a particular type of data or a particular function (such as marketing or customer service), but most are intended to serve an entire organization. One virtue of adopting such a platform is that features and models can be managed using one interface and one set of formats, rather than many. We don't think it's a great idea for an organization to adopt or allow platforms from several different vendors, but it does happen.

Some companies (like Procter & Gamble, as we discussed in the previous chapter) have adopted an approach called an "AI factory" that combines the availability of data science platforms with processes to rapidly develop, modify, and re-use models, data, and features. Some organizations restrict such factory approaches to data science professionals, while others encourage "citizens" or quantitatively focused businesspeople to employ them.

AT&T, for example, has a highly democratized approach to data science, with 26,000 reusable features in a feature store, 7 different AutoML tools, and more than 500 courses on data science. They also regularly have gatherings to share data science knowledge and new developments. The overall idea is to make data science part of the "core fabric" of the organization.[8] Of course, AT&T has a lot of engineering-trained employees with a relatively high level of quantitative skills; not every company's employees would be as well suited to democratizing data science.

Don't Forget Business Intelligence

It's important to remember that data analysis may often involve descriptive or explanatory analytics, not just machine learning. Descriptive analytics includes dashboards, scorecards, reports, etc. The category is also called "business intelligence." "Web analytics" also usually falls into this category. It's not the most sophisticated type of analysis because it discusses only what happened in the past and—without an astute human observer—won't tell you why it happened. Still, it's useful under many circumstances, and for many managers that is all they expect or understand.

---

[8] Thomas H. Davenport, "Citizen Data Science and Automation at AT&T," *Forbes*, 30 January 2023, https://www.forbes.com/sites/tomdavenport/2023/01/30/citizen-data-science-and-automation-at-att.

Explanatory analytics try to give the analyst or decision-maker some idea about why something happened, but it doesn't make any attempt to predict. Most of the time, analyses like correlation or regression analysis are the tool of choice for explanatory modeling. It's relatively easy once you have an explanatory model to apply it to data for which you don't know the outcome, and then it becomes predictive analytics. Most organizations don't stop at explanatory and move on to predictive. (See Table 9.1.)

Descriptive and explanatory analyses are best—and the only real option—for categorical data—data that doesn't meet the definitions of ordinal (with a natural order or rank, like a five-category Likert scale), continuous (with any numerical value), or discrete (made of integers), or that has more than two valid categories (known as binary variables). We can't do correlations or regressions on categorical data, unless it's possible to turn the categorical variables into binary ones. If your analysis is attempting to tease out the impact of home versus condo versus rental apartment dwellers on moves to and from four US regions, you're stuck with categorical variables and categorical analysis.

There's not much new in this world of categorical data, but the previous statistical approaches remain pretty useful. In this situation you'll probably want to employ crosstabulations, or *crosstabs*, which can find either random variation across categories or a statistically significant relationship pattern. The significance is typically suggested by the chi square statistic and the probability associated with it; a probability of 0.05 or less is usually considered significant. In other words, there is a real relationship in your data rather than a coincidence.

There are other similar statistics for different variable types. If you have a categorical variable and a continuous dependent variable—say, a set of occupational categories and an average income for each one— you can assess the strength of the statistical relationship with an analysis of variance (ANOVA) statistic. If there are only two categories, you use a t-test. Both ANOVA and t-tests also become statistically significant at the 0.05 probability level or less.

This is by no means a statistics textbook, but you should know that no matter what types of variables you are planning to analyze, there is an appropriate statistical test to see whether they are related (or, to use a statistics term, *correlated*). Most statistical analysis computer programs will tell you what type of analysis to use in your situation. And they are usually

Table 9.1 Types of analytics

Type of analytics	Purpose	Methodology	Data types	Tools/techniques	Outcome
Descriptive	What happened?	Summarization	Categorical	Dashboards, scorecards, reports	Insights into past performance
Explanatory	Why did it happen?	Relationships between variables	Categorical or streaming	Correlation, regression analysis	Understanding cause–effect
Predictive	What will happen?	Predicting future trends	Streaming or discrete	Machine learning models, forecasts	Forecasts
Prescriptive	What should we do?	Recommending actions based on predictions	Streaming, discrete, or categorical	Optimization or decision models	Recommendations

pretty simple to use, with point-and-click interfaces. GenAI systems can also be a good source for this type of recommendation.

Deployment: The Final Frontier

Recall from our earlier discussion of Starbuck's Deep Brew personalization system in Chapter 5 that the Starbucks data scientists said, "The models are the easy part"—even though they were quite complex deep learning reinforcement models. There are many other stages of model deployment that can be more challenging than model development.

"Deployment" means to put a model into day-to-day production. It means you've trained a model on your data that does a good job of prediction, and now it's time to predict the outcome value (sometimes called *inference*) given a set of predictor variables for which you know the value. For example, you've developed a model to predict what ad a customer will respond best to, and now you have to identify the right ad to show for each customer in your dataset.

Depending on your organization, some of the steps involved in deployment even after a model has been developed include the following:

- Testing the model (some may include this in model development)
- Deploying the model in code or API
- Integrating the code or API with existing systems
- Scaling the model and the data to the needed level
- Creating the user interface for the new system
- Changing the business process to accommodate the new way of deciding
- Retraining front-line workers to understand how the model works
- Monitoring and maintaining the model over time (MLOps)
- Working with business leaders/stakeholders throughout to get their trust and support.

Most of these tasks do not primarily involve data or analytical skills. Instead, they involve computing, systems engineering, organizational change, and human skills. As such they are not likely to be successfully accomplished by data scientists—assuming your organization has some. Their primary interest is in model development, although they often have coding skills, too.

The volume and variety of skills needed in deployment has made many organizations adopt the idea of "data products," "analytical and AI products," or "digital products." Though the names used vary, the idea is the same: viewing data and analytics/AI offerings as products, whether they are intended for customers or for internal use. The idea includes the identification of product managers as well. In most cases, the product orientation starts with the idea for the data analysis and doesn't end until the product is retired and no longer intended for use. For this book, of course, the focus is customers, so we'll primarily describe externally oriented products in the next example.

Digital Products at CarMax

CarMax, the largest retailer of used cars in the United States, adopted the digital product approach in the early 2010s. Tom's friend and UVA colleague Ryan Nelson described the shift over time in a detailed case study.[9] The company's leaders were persuaded that it could improve its digital capabilities more quickly and effectively if it adopted the approach of digital natives, i.e. a product focus. CarMax completed several successful pilots of digital products, and then moved toward a permanent focus.

Product teams at CarMax involved not only product managers but a set of roles designed to meet all the needs of a successful product. The core team consisted of a product designer, a lead developer, and the product manager. Other roles as needed on the team included marketing creative services, delivery managers, field experience experts, functional experts, developers, and data scientists. The product teams stayed in place throughout the life of a digital product—monitoring its success after implementation and making changes to it over time. The success of the teams was measured in business objectives—"How many new credit applications did we get?"—rather than completion of technology tasks.

By 2023, CarMax had more than 80 digital product teams. It had successfully developed products including car search, customer pre-qualification, a chatbot for customer service, and an online instant offer capability. Many of the products involved both online and offline (typically

---

[9] The CarMax case, as well as one at the *Washington Post*, are described in Ryan Nelson, "Transforming to Digital Product Management," *MIS Quarterly Executive*, March 2024 (23:1), https://aisel.aisnet.org/misqe/vol23/iss1/2.

at the dealership) customer experiences. There are also products supporting internal processes, such as trade-in, payoff, and servicing systems.

The product-oriented approach to developing technology capabilities has a number of advantages over the project approach that was traditionally used in IT systems. It is focused on outcomes rather than outputs. It typically leads to a closer relationship between technology and businesspeople. And it incorporates a wider range of roles and skills into making the product successful. We think that marketing technology initiatives will be substantially more successful if they adopt the product management orientation.

Data-Driven Cultures

Having a data-driven culture is not an analytical or AI method or tool, but it is perhaps the single most valuable trait that an organization can have if it wants to apply data, analytics, and AI to customer issues. Google recommends 24 different books on data-driven culture, so we won't go into great detail on the topic in this one. But it's important to know the importance of cultural matters, and we'll point out a few things you can do about it if you don't have one already.

Tom collaborates with Randy Bean every year on a survey of large organizations' data, analytics, and AI leaders. Until 2024 the percentage of respondents saying that their organizations were data-driven or had data-driven cultures was quite low.[10] The numbers were typically in the 25% range for being a data-driven organization, and around 20% for having a data-driven culture. To our great surprise in the 2024 survey, the numbers doubled to just short of half the respondents. Our assumption was that generative AI—the primary development in technology over the last few years—had changed the data orientation of many companies.[11]

We hoped the change would be permanent, but it wasn't. The 2025 survey numbers just came out as we write, and the percentages dropped by 10% or so (37% for data-driven organization, 33% for data-driven culture). These are still up 50% from the normal response in 13 years of surveys, but

---

[10] For the 2024 survey, see "Data and AI Executive Leadership Survey," Wavestone, https://wwa.wavestone.com/en/insight/data-and-ai-executive-leadership-survey-2024.

[11] Thomas H. Davenport and Randy Bean, "Survey: GenAI Is Making Companies More Data-Oriented," *Harvard Business Review*, 15 January 2024, https://hbr.org/2024/01/survey-genai-is-making-companies-more-data-oriented.

they indicate that generative AI alone can have only so much impact on culture. As further evidence of that, Bean asks every year what the primary barrier to becoming data-driven in the respondents' organizations is. Those responses have generally been in the 90% range for people/organization/ culture, and 10% for technology-related issues. After changing to 80%/20% in the last couple of years, this year they returned to the historical 90%/10% split. This indicates the persistence of people and cultural issues in becoming data-focused and the inability of any new technology to bring about lasting change.

The survey data suggests that data-driven cultures are difficult to change and require a broad set of human and organizational changes to influence. We have certainly known organizations that attempted to develop them through such diverse activities as the following.

- Partner with early adopters:
  - Start with small, achievable data projects to demonstrate value.
  - Identify successes and promote them inside the organization.
  - Build off those successes for broader adoption as examples to others.
  - Publicize successful outcomes to gain broader support.
  - Use metrics to track progress.
- Promote data literacy programs:
  - Conduct workshops or training programs on data analysis and interpretation.
  - Provide access to self-paced learning resources for employees.
  - Target particular functions and business units.
- Ensure executive support:
  - Secure buy-in from senior leadership.
  - Highlight the importance of data-driven decisions during strategic meetings.
  - Develop metrics of progress to monitor cultural change.
- Develop a data strategy:
  - Define clear objectives for how data will support business goals.
  - Create a roadmap for building and leveraging data capabilities.
- Create cross-functional multidisciplinary teams:
  - Establish diverse teams that include data scientists, analysts, and business leaders.

- Encourage collaboration across departments to solve data-related challenges.
- Bring analysts, data scientists, and AI enthusiasts together from across the organization.
- Develop KPIs:
  - Measure the impact of data initiatives.
  - Regularly review and report on progress to stakeholders.
- Foster open communication:
  - Hold forums or open houses to discuss data-related initiatives.
  - Encourage feedback and ideas from all levels of the organization.
  - Create communities of practice.
  - Celebrate successes.

These are, in fact, the types of activities sponsored by a chief data and analytics officer (CDAO) we know at a large US company. He felt that they were beginning to succeed and believed strongly that such multifaceted programs were necessary to bring about any change in data orientation. He of course also worked on specific data, analytics, and AI initiatives, but he also thought it was important for the company to make progress toward a data-driven culture even though it was harder to measure and demonstrate value versus particular applications.

However, something important changed in the company after the CDAO had been there for several years. The CDAO's boss, who had been very supportive of his efforts, took early retirement and left the company. The new boss, whose responsibilities included information technology, "couldn't spell *data* and wasn't interested in learning how," the CDAO commented. That new boss's only interest seemed to be in technology. The CDAO got an offer for a similar job at another large company, and he took it.

Certainly we are supportive of efforts to create data-driven cultures within companies. But as at this company, if your boss and other senior executives are not particularly data-oriented, it will be an uphill battle to change the culture in that direction. We often counsel leaders in this situation to find another employer where there is already a belief in data to drive decisions and actions within the company.

Short of leaving the company, the best advice we could give is the first item in the previous list: to partner with early adopters or sympathetic executive stakeholders. Your boss or your CEO may not be a believer in data-driven business, but if your CFO or CMO or head of supply chain or customer service is, you may be able to build not only some successful applications but also some momentum toward a broader data-driven culture across the company. We've seen a few examples where CEOs and other senior executives have actually changed their perspective toward a more data-driven focus. It's not common, but it can happen.

We've covered a wide variety of topics in this chapter. We hope you'll come away with the idea that if you want to improve the analytical and AI capabilities of your organization relative to customers, there are many angles you can—and should—address. Some of them are technical, some involve statistical methods and tools, and some involve organizational and cultural issues. The fact that so many different domains are involved in effective customer relationship data and analytics is perhaps one reason why not many organizations have been great at it over the years.

Of course, whether you're using analytics, AI, or other customer-facing technologies, you'll want to use them ethically with your customers. That's the subject of the next chapter.

10 | Better Ethics

AI has become so powerful that we need to be proactive about using it wisely, responsibly, and ethically. It has incredible potential to enhance our understanding of and actions with our customers, but we must do so in a way that respects privacy, maintains transparency, and ultimately benefits the customer.

Practicing responsible AI is the commitment to be a good steward of the personal information customers entrust to us. The principle of data minimization calls for collecting only data that is necessary and relevant for specific, well-defined purposes that create value for the customer. (See Figure 10.1.)

Accumulating data without clear boundaries or intent is a recipe for crossing the line into being creepy and making customers uncomfortable. As we've noted in this book more than once, customers already have a vague fear about how much companies appear to know about them.[1] We don't want to make it worse.

Responsible and ethical AI also requires being fully transparent about data practices. Companies need to be crystal clear about what

---

[1] Turow, Joseph and Lelkes, Yphtach and Draper, Nora and Waldman, Ari Ezra, "Americans Can't Consent to Companies' Use of Their Data: They Admit They Don't Understand It, Say They're Helpless to Control It, and Believe They're Harmed When Firms Use Their Data—Making What Companies Do Illegitimate" (15 February 2023). Available at SSRN: https://ssrn.com/abstract=4391134.

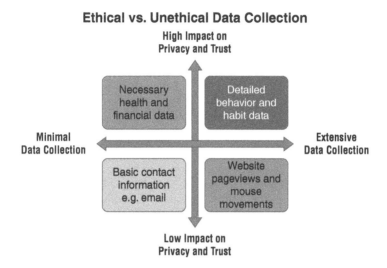

Figure 10.1   Ethical versus unethical data collection.

data they're collecting, how it will be used, and what's in it for the customer. Customers must have, or feel they have, control over their data and their preferences. While they are nervous about the amount of data that companies have about them, they also expect that ads, offers, and contacts with them should be personalized to their needs and expressed preferences. In addition to not misusing customer data, companies have an obligation to use it in ways that help customers employ their time and attention efficiently.

Safeguarding customer data in an AI-powered world requires state-of-the-art security and robust access controls and, at the same time, demands accountability from the humans behind the AI to identify and mitigate risks of unintended consequences, bias, and misuse. AI systems must be continuously audited, and organizations need established processes to swiftly correct issues.

Ultimately, using AI responsibly is about taking the long view and always putting the customer first. Nothing is more important than maintaining trusted relationships. The companies that succeed in the age of AI will be those that stay true to their values and consistently act in customers' best interests.

AI Ethics: Central to Customer Relationships

As companies harness analytical and generative AI to understand customers more intimately and deliver hyper-personalized experiences, the way they handle sensitive data becomes make-or-break for relationships. AI ethics isn't just about compliance or risk mitigation—it's the foundation of customer trust.

In their 2024 article,[2] Carlo Giovine and Roger Roberts made it clear that:

> To capture the full potential value of AI, organizations need to build trust. Trust, in fact, is the foundation for adoption of AI-powered products and services. After all, if customers or employees lack trust in the outputs of AI systems, they won't use them. Trust in AI comes via understanding the outputs of AI-powered software and how—at least at a high level—they are created. Organizations increasingly recognize this. In a McKinsey survey of the state of AI in 2024,[3] 40 percent of respondents identified explainability as a key risk in adopting gen AI. Yet at the same time, only 17 percent said they were currently working to mitigate it.

Every data point represents a real person placing their trust in a company. Misusing that data, deploying AI irresponsibly, or appearing to do so betrays that trust and can inflict lasting damage. But when customers know their information is secure and leveraged to genuinely benefit them, it strengthens bonds and breeds loyalty.

Maintaining trust in an AI-powered world is an ongoing challenge. As the technology rapidly advances, new ethical dilemmas constantly emerge. Companies must be proactive in assessing AI's customer impact, responsive to concerns, and agile in evolving practices. Those that embrace ethics as an enabler, not an impediment, will build the most enduring customer connections.

---

[2] "Building AI trust: The key role of explainability," McKinsey & Company, 26 November 2024, https://www.mckinsey.com/capabilities/quantumblack/our-insights/building-ai-trust-the-key-role-of-explainability.

[3] "The state of AI in early 2024: Gen AI adoption spikes and starts to generate value," McKinsey & Company, 30 May 2024, https://www.mckinsey.com/capabilities/quantum black/our-insights/the-state-of-ai.

Apple staked its reputation on being a "privacy-first" organization. While this has served them well in the marketplace, their App Tracking Transparency (ATT) policy, which requires users to give their consent before their mobile data is shared by apps, has sparked controversy despite being touted as a win for user privacy. Critics argue that ATT gives Apple an unfair advantage, hindering competitors who face more stringent data restrictions. This has prompted antitrust probes in several countries.

Whether Apple has exploited privacy as a marketing ploy while engaging in practices that prioritize their own interests is for public opinion to decide. The fact that the company saw it as a valuable stance shows its leaders' belief in the need to virtue signal privacy.

AI systems can amplify our ability to understand and meet customer needs, but in practice, AI must align with an organization's brand and human values. This alignment means making decisions that prioritize brand voice and customer fairness, respect for individual privacy, and the well-being of the customer. It's about designing systems that enhance lives without overstepping ethical boundaries.

Trust is the currency of modern customer relationships. Every piece of customer data represents a leap of faith from a real person; mishandling that data or allowing AI systems to act without proper oversight risks breaking that trust. When AI is used ethically and transparently, it deepens relationships and builds enduring loyalty.

Transparency in the use of data and AI is nonnegotiable. Customers need to understand not just what data is being collected but how it benefits them. The exchange of data for value should always feel fair and above board. When companies are upfront about their practices, they empower customers to make informed decisions, fostering an environment of mutual respect and collaboration.

This is not a new issue involving sophisticated AI. Even as far back as 1995, Jim was hesitant to sign up for the Amazon newsletter because spam had already become a pernicious problem. But Amazon made a promise. In exchange for the user's email address and a few pieces of information about their reading habits and interests, Amazon would send out an email whenever a favorite author was about to publish a new book. Not only did this give the newsletter subscriber inside information, Amazon offered a discount for pre-ordering the book. This went way past spam, past marketing, and into what was perceived as a valuable service.

At the same time, Bank of America offered a newsletter that required answering a series of intrusive demographic and economic questions about Jim's household. The promise was a purportedly personalized newsletter to help Jim achieve his financial goals when in fact all they sent was email after email offering a variety of undifferentiated services. We're sure they stopped this practice; at least neither of us has received such emails lately.

Even with rising concerns about privacy, nearly 30% of people are willing to give out their email address without any incentive. But that number jumps to 90% when there's an attractive offer involved.[4] By keeping this fair exchange of value and general human values at the forefront, companies can harness AI's potential while staying true to their brand and your purpose and earning the trust of their prospects and customers.

Going overboard is the other side of the creepiness coin. Over-personalization, while tempting, can backfire. When AI crosses the line from helpful to invasive, it creates discomfort, even fear. AT&T's managers learned this lesson back when they realized they could use caller ID to speed up calls to their customer service department. The customer service representative would answer the phone, "Hello, Mr. Sterne, How can I help you today?" The immediate effect was negative. Customers felt this was intrusive—like they were being watched. AT&T continued to use caller ID to speed up the finding of the customer's record, but instead of tipping their hand when answering the call, the customer service representative would ask for the caller's name. This gave them a few more seconds to familiarize themselves with the customer record before the call even started.

Organizations must ask themselves: Is this collection and use of data genuinely beneficial to the customer, or are we prioritizing business metrics over their comfort and consent? Striking this balance ensures personalization enhances rather than erodes trust.

Research consistently shows that customers reward companies that prioritize their privacy and values.[5] Ethical AI practices, such as clear communication about how data and algorithms are used and ensuring

---

[4] "Consumers Want Privacy. Marketers Can Deliver." Boston Consulting Group. 21 January 2022, https://www.bcg.com/publications/2022/consumers-want-data-privacy-and-marketers-can-deliver.

[5] Wang, L., Yan, J., Lin, J., & Cui, W. (2017). Let the users tell the truth: Self-disclosure intention and self-disclosure honesty in mobile social networking. *International Journal of Information Management*, 37: 1428–1440. doi: 10.1016/j.ijinfomgt.2016.10.006.

customers have control over their information, create a bond that goes beyond transactions. This isn't just good for the customer; it's a differentiator that drives long-term loyalty.

Privacy and Consent: Balancing Needs and Rights

The myth of "informed consent" has its roots in the medical world, where patients must understand the risks and benefits before agreeing to surgery. They give consent to having products delivered intravenously while unconscious. The concept has morphed into something not nearly so invasive when applied to companies collecting personal information.

Check any privacy policy or consent form. You'll find them as dense as *Moby Dick* but far less engaging. Even if customers muster the fortitude to read them, comprehension is another matter entirely. The legalese obfuscates more than it elucidates. We've found that feeding these contracts into generative AI can provide a clear explanation of the terms, but customers shouldn't have to go to that much trouble.

Global privacy regulations like GDPR and CCPA demand clear affirmative consent before collecting personal data. Fail this test and the fines can be monumental. But obtaining genuine consent means swimming upstream against "consent fatigue"—the endless pop-ups and forms that condition us to mindlessly click Accept.

At the same time, companies must obtain consent across an ever-expanding digital universe, including websites, mobile apps, smart devices, voice assistants, and retail sensors. A customer who freely shares data with a fitness app may balk when that same information appears in a targeted advertisement. (See Figure 10.2.)

Regulators around the world have been attracted to the "right to be deleted," and you can't blame them. You do not want to remain in the database of a company whose products you no longer like, or one whose dataset was purchased by another organization whose intent is unknown. But if deleting customer information from a Google search corpus is challenging, deleting it from a large language model is nearly impossible (unless, of course, your name is David Mayer).[6]

---

[6] Ali Watkins, "Why Wouldn't ChatGPT Say This Dead Professor's Name?" *The New York Times*, 06 December 2024, https://www.nytimes.com/2024/12/06/us/david-mayer-chat gpt-openai.html.

Building Customer Trust

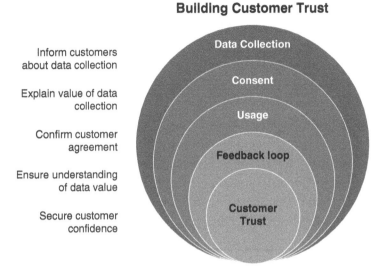

Inform customers about data collection

Explain value of data collection

Confirm customer agreement

Ensure understanding of data value

Secure customer confidence

Data Collection

Consent

Usage

Feedback loop

Customer Trust

Figure 10.2   Building customer trust.

In her post "Why GenAI Is a Data Deletion and Privacy Nightmare,"[7] Cassie Kozyrkov explains it this way:

What does it mean to delete data?

Generative AI systems leak data in unexpected ways and there's no technological fix for it, so companies relying on GenAI can get caught red-handed in possession of data they claimed they'd deleted.

Data deletion is a kettle of spiders thanks to GenAI.

What qualifies as deleting a user's data? According to Law Insider: *"means the process of rendering data unrecognizable in such a way that it is no longer possible to recover it."*

Kozyrkov points out that organizations cannot guarantee the deletion of data even if it is their users' legal right.

"Trying to remove training data once it has been baked into a large language model is like trying to remove sugar once it has been baked into a cake. You'll have to trash the cake and start over… which is expensive. Much too expensive to do every time a user feels like deleting a social media post."

[7] Cassie Kozkyrov, "Why GenAI Is a Data Deletion and Privacy Nightmare," Medium, 20 September 2024, https://towardsdatascience.com/why-genai-is-a-data-deletion-and-privacy-nightmare-bd79a3c0ed85.

Even when companies secure explicit consent, questions linger with generative AI *and* analytical AI. What happens when customers revoke permission? Does the data vanish from backups and machine learning models? Can third-party partners be trusted to honor the original consent agreements? These are not merely technical challenges but ethical quandaries.

The solution requires more than legal compliance. Companies must embrace radical transparency about how they collect and use customer data. Consent forms should try to be clear and concise. Revocation should be simple. Most important, businesses need to respect the spirit of consent, not just the letter. The alternative is a world of eroding trust, regulatory punishment, and customers who feel betrayed rather than served. No amount of data is worth that price.

Bias in the Data, Bias in the Model, Bias in the Results

All large language models—and most data in general—contain bias. Humans are congenitally biased, so data derived from human behavior and speech is as well. Even with analytical machine learning/predictive analytics, we are typically creating a model that is trained on past data in which there was human involvement and hence probably some bias.

When thinking of a pilot and flight attendant, a doctor and a nurse, a police officer and a dispatcher, or a CEO and an HR manager, our innate bias brings to mind images of a male and a female. And so it is with AI image generators (see Figure 10.3). The same bias was also found in the well-known case in which Amazon attempted to use analytical machine learning to predict the traits of successful engineers. Because most of the engineers in the training data were male, the traits identified for success were also male-oriented.

Every business decision based on customer data risks perpetuating bias. When that data trains AI systems, the risk multiplies exponentially as algorithms turn historical discrimination into automated policy.

The problem starts with the data itself. A regional bank's records show which loan applications were approved over the past 30 years. But those approvals reflected human prejudices of their time, which the AI model now treats as valid patterns. The bank's AI learns to replicate decisions that

Figure 10.3   Gender bias in generative AI images.

Source: Generated with AI using DALL·E3 – OpenAI

systematically favored some neighborhoods (and therefore race and income discrepancies) over others.

If a national retailer analyzes decades of purchase data to predict customer value, the AI discovers that shoppers from certain ZIP codes spend more money over time. It begins routing more promotions and better offers to those areas, unaware that historical redlining created the spending disparity in the first place.

These effects compound quickly. The damage falls hardest on those already facing barriers. When an AI steers premium credit card offers away from neighborhoods where acceptance rates were historically low, it maintains that cycle. When automated systems route customer service requests based on past revenue patterns, they provide worse service to those who need help the most.

Fixing this requires examining both data and the processes that created it. Companies must ask the following:

- Who never appears in our customer records?
- Which past practices distorted our data?
- What cultural assumptions shape our metrics?
- How do we define normal customer behavior?

Getting these right demands involvement from diverse people and perspectives at every stage, from data collection through deployment. Technical solutions matter, but inclusive practices matter more. The best defense against biased AI is ensuring the teams building these systems reflect all the customers they serve. Companies that tackle this challenge thoughtfully will build more equitable AI systems and better serve their entire customer base while those that ignore it risk automating discrimination at unprecedented scale.

To measure bias, it's important to keep an eye on the entire data collection, integration, and resulting model development processes. You'll need to compare outcomes across different groups, such as age, gender, or location, to see if certain segments are systematically disadvantaged.

For instance, if an AI-driven campaign yields significantly fewer conversions from women than men, it could indicate a bias in targeting or content that needs further investigation. Marketers should leverage fairness metrics, such as disparate impact ratios, to measure how policies or practices disproportionately affect protected groups. The ratio is created by dividing the probability of a positive outcome for an unprivileged group by the probability of a positive outcome for a privileged group. That allows organizations to understand performance across groups without needing to be data scientists themselves. Many martech and MLOps tools are beginning to offer user-friendly bias detection features that help highlight these discrepancies.

Reducing bias is not a one-and-done but an ongoing, iterative process. Frequently revisit your data and model assumptions and recalibrate as new information emerges. Ensure diverse representation in training data, design inclusive customer journeys, and involve diverse teams in the AI development process. You might also use third-party tools to audit and validate your algorithms.

Revision: The company updates their policies on an ongoing basis keeping pace with use cases and technical advancements.

Assessment: The company develops a process whereby each use case is either accepted as is, sent back to the proposing owner for revision, or rejected as is.

Review: The company does or sponsors a systematic review of each use case to determine if it meets the company's criteria for AI ethics.

Monitoring: The company documents each AI use case or application (e.g., model cards).

Policies: The company deliberates on and then approves a set of corporate policies to ensure ethical approaches to AI.

Evangelism: Representatives of the company speak internally and/or externally about the importance of AI ethics.

Figure 10.4 From talk to action: a hierarchy of corporate actions on AI ethics.

Some companies, including Unilever, Michelin, and Adecco, make use of a third party, Holistic AI, to evaluate proposed AI use cases before they are developed. Unilever, one of the first companies to work with Holistic AI, has a history of social responsibility.[8] It certainly practiced what we think of as the earliest stage of AI ethics in companies: evangelizing about its importance to employees (see Figure 10.4). But also as with many companies, the next step in AI ethics at the company was to create a set of policies. One of Unilever's policies, for example, specified that any decision that has a significant life impact on an employee or customer should not be fully automated and have a human review. Other AI policies that the company adopted include "We will never blame the system; there must be a Unilever owner accountable" and "We will use our best efforts to systematically monitor models and the performance of our AI to ensure that it maintains its efficacy."

But Andy Hill, Unilever's chief data officer and head of advanced analytics and AI, and Giles Pavey, global director of data science, realized quickly that creating policies alone would not be sufficient to ensure responsible development of AI. Instead, they needed a governance approach that ensured—or at least increased the likelihood of—compliance with policies while or even before AI and analytics systems were being developed.

---

[8] The Unilever discussion is based in part on Thomas H. Davenport and Randy Bean, "AI Ethics at Unilever from Policy to Process," *MIT Sloan Management Review*, 15 November 2023, https://sloanreview.mit.edu/article/ai-ethics-at-unilever-from-policy-to-process.

They were also aware that many of the AI and analytics systems at Unilever were developed in collaboration with outside software and services vendors. Applications that use AI within Unilever could be internally built or built to order by an IT vendor or embedded within services that Unilever procures from partners. The company's advertising agencies, for example, often employ "programmatic buying" software that uses AI to decide what digital ads to place on web and mobile sites. Hill and Pavey concluded that the approach to AI ethics needed to include externally sourced capabilities.

Unilever's AI leaders also noticed that some of the potential or actual ethical issues with the technology involved systems that were ineffective at the tasks they were intended to accomplish. A system for forecasting cash flow, for example, might involve no fairness or bias risk but may have some risk of not being effective. They concluded that efficacy risk should be included along with the ethical risks they would evaluate and that "AI assurance" was a term that encompassed all these risks.

Some companies, including Google and Salesforce, have employed the approach of documenting each AI use case, typically using an approach called *model cards* that record the key aspects of the model being used and any potential bias issues recognized by the developers.[9] But Unilever wanted to go further than just documentation. The basic idea behind the Unilever AI Assurance compliance process is to systematically assess each new AI application before it is developed to determine how intrinsically risky the use case is. Unilever already has a well-defined approach to information security and data privacy, and the goal is to employ a similar approach, ensuring that no AI application is put into production without first being approved.

The process that the team developed specifies that when a new AI solution is being planned, the Unilever employee or supplier documents the outlined use case and method before developing it. The proposer furnishes a series of details about the use case, which are reviewed in a semi-automated fashion by Holistic AI. The risk domains include explainability, robustness, efficacy, bias, and privacy. Machine learning algorithms are automatically analyzed to determine whether they are biased against any particular group. The proposer is thus informed of potential ethical and efficacy risks and mitigations to be considered.

---

[9] Thomas H. Davenport, "The Future of Work Now: Ethical AI at Salesforce," *Forbes*, 27 May 2021.

After the AI application has been developed, Holistic AI runs statistical tests to ascertain whether there is a bias or fairness issue and could examine the system for efficacy in achieving its objectives. The evaluations in the Holistic AI platform are based on the European Union's AI Act, which ranks AI use cases into three categories of risk (unacceptable, high, and not high enough to be regulated).

Holistic AI has created a digital platform to manage the process of reviewing AI assurance. In this context, "AI" is a broad category that encompasses any type of prediction or automation; even an Excel spreadsheet used to score HR candidates would be included in the process. Unilever's data ethics team uses the platform to review the status of AI projects and can see which new use cases have been submitted; whether the information is complete; and what risk-level assessment they have received, coded red, yellow ("amber" in the United Kingdom), or green.

The traffic-light status is assessed at three points: at initial triage, after further analysis, and after final mitigation and assurance. At this final point, the ratings have the following interpretations: a red rating means the AI system does not comply with Unilever standards and should not be deployed; yellow means the AI system has some acceptable risks and the business owner is responsible for being aware of and taking ownership of it; and green means the AI system adds no risks to the process.

Only a handful of the several hundred Unilever use cases have received red scores. In one example, the company has sections in department stores in some countries where it sells its cosmetics brands. A project was developed to use computer vision AI to automatically register sales agents' attendance through daily selfies, with a stretch objective to look at the appropriateness of agents' appearance. Because of the AI assurance process, the project team broadened their thinking beyond regulations, legality, and efficacy to also consider the potential implications of a fully automated system. They identified the need for human oversight in checking photos flagged as noncompliant and taking responsibility for any consequent actions. This use case, and all others given a red rating thus far, were able to resolve the issues with their use cases and move them up to a yellow rating.

Holistic AI expects in the future to be able to aggregate AI ethics data across companies and benchmark across them. They could assess benefits versus the efficacy of different external providers of the same use case, and the most effective approaches to AI procurement. They have also considered making risk ratings public in some cases and partnering with an insurance company to insure AI use cases against certain types of risks. Now that there are government standards for ethics in the European Union, it's likely that financial audit firms will also begin to audit AI ethics for companies doing business there.

AI Explainability

Customer trust goes up when people understand how the algorithms work. We all want to know what the score is and how we win the game. What do I have to do to earn my paycheck? How do I earn my commission on a sale? How will your computer make decisions about me so I can adjust my behavior to be better positioned for success?

Mechanistic interpretability is a term for understanding the algorithms and inner workings of neural networks, which are grown through training rather than programming. As Christopher Olah, co-founder of Anthropic, explains, "If you think of neural networks as being like a computer program, then the weights are kind of like a binary computer program. And we'd like to reverse engineer those weights and figure out what algorithms are running."[10]

Mechanistic interpretability focuses on understanding both the weights, akin to instructions, and the activations, similar to memory, to decipher how neural networks make decisions. This is a bottom-up approach recognizing that the optimization process used to train neural networks is often more adept at finding solutions than human programmers. (See Figure 10.5.)

Researchers hope to uncover the fundamental mechanisms that enable neural networks to perform complex tasks like writing, translation, and image understanding. But for now, there's a whole lot of "trust me" going around. That's why having a human in the loop to review outcomes of LLMs is so important.

Security and Accountability in Data Practices

If you want your customers to trust you, in addition to having transparency and accountability, you need to assure people that their personal information is safe against misuse and theft. A security breach exposes sensitive data

---

[10] Lex Fridman podcast featuring Christopher Olah, #452—Dario Amodei: Anthropic CEO on Claude, AGI & the Future of AI & Humanity, October 2024, https://lexfridman .com/dario-amodei-transcript.

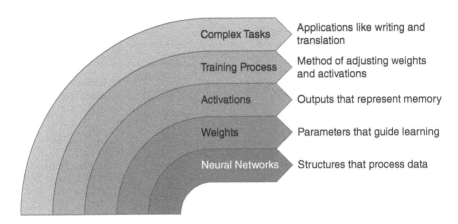

Figure 10.5 AI model training.

and destroys confidence. What data do you have? What would happen if it were exposed? What's the likelihood of exposure? What would it cost? These questions apply from lost laptops to determined cybercriminals. Lost confidence means lost business.

Staff need regular training to recognize risks. Managers need clear policies to enforce. Executives need metrics to measure effectiveness. Prevention works better than reaction. An incident response plan answers, "What do we do when something goes wrong?" to test weaknesses before criminals do.

The goal is not preventing bad behavior but encouraging good judgment. As AI grows more capable, ethical challenges multiply. AI systems that work perfectly in the lab may fail spectacularly in the real world. Organizations need governance frameworks that identify potential problems before they become actual disasters.

Few executives commit to ethical AI development because they see ethics as a constraint rather than an opportunity. The fact is, good ethics is good business. Those who establish proactive ethical practices have higher customer satisfaction, lower churn, and better employee retention.

First Step

The time to establish guardrails for customer data ethics and security is before problems arise, not after. Start by auditing your current data practices. What information do you collect? How do you use it? What promises

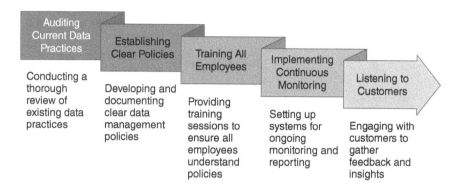

Figure 10.6   Five steps to an ethical data culture.

have you made to customers? Where are the vulnerabilities? Document everything.

Second, establish clear policies that put customer interests first. Set boundaries that prevent misuse. Create processes to identify and correct problems quickly. Make these policies public. On the other hand, define acceptable uses of AI and data so people have positive examples as well.

Next, train everybody at every level about data ethics and security. Help them understand not just what to do, but why it matters. Build a culture where "doing right by the customer" isn't just a slogan.

Fourth, implement continuous monitoring of how AI systems affect different customer segments. That requires measuring outcomes against ethical standards. Review and update practices as technology evolves.

Finally, and perhaps most important, listen to your customers and find out what they expect. Your audience might be the most restrictive, risk averse cohort on the planet or they simply might not care all that much. Let their ethos be your guide, but revisit their expectations over time to ensure that they haven't changed. Demonstrate the value they receive in exchange for their trust. (See Figure 10.6.)

The future of customer relationships depends on getting this right. Companies that establish ethical AI practices now will build enduring customer loyalty. Those that wait risk losing trust that may never be regained.

Our next and last chapter is a futuristic look at what it will feel to focus on customers when all of these technologies, data sources, and management approaches are combined.

11

The Customer of Tomorrow

We began this book with a brief hypothetical email offer based on extensive analysis of customer data. This is not the first time we have thus speculated, and we'll end this book with an extended discussion of AI-driven possibilities—complete with very intelligent AI personal assistants.

Yesterday's Science Fiction

Jim wrote and performed[1] a sketch in 2017 in which he held a conversation with his personal agent, Jeeves, while driving. In it, Jeeves politely informs Jim about a warning light and details potential repair costs. He convinces Jim that the car's 15 years and 175,000 miles justify a replacement.

Based on conversations overheard with Jim and his wife about their preferences, Jeeves researched local dealerships, negotiated prices, and narrowed the options to three potential vehicles, offering Jim the choice depending on color and delivery schedule. In anticipation of Jim's worries about how his wife will respond, Jeeves shares a recording of his near-real-time conversation with her, expressing her agreement that it's time for a replacement. Jeeves finishes by doing all the paperwork for the purchase.

---

[1] https://www.linkedin.com/posts/jimsterne_marketing-ai-generativeai-activity-70523802 90110935040-H28m.

The skit was a fanciful prediction about a potential future. Given current capabilities available to those who are skilled coders, this capability doesn't seem so far-fetched anymore.

A *Financial Times* article in May 2024[2] reported Meta's Chief AI Scientist Yann LeCun describing how AI assistants will be our digital interface from now on. Google CEO Sundar Pichai portrayed that AI agents are now demonstrating reasoning, planning, and memory, and can consider multiple steps to complete discrete actions toward a specific goal. CEO of Microsoft AI Mustafa Suleyman was quoted as saying, "The tech has matured enough that it's a new kind of clay that we can all invent with and…we are seeing that coming to bear now."

If Jim's playful conversation with his assistant Jeeves was science fiction in 2017, what does the near future look like for professionals responsible for customer communications? We'll alternate between a hypothetical conversation among executives at an online retailer and in-real-life (IRL) observations about the topics they address.

Wake-Up Call

Dave knows he is needed. Now, somewhere, for something. He feels he should pay closer attention but can't quite grasp the importance of Tchaikovsky's *4th Symphony*. Then he realizes that his alarm, precisely timed to his optimal REM cycle point, is coaxing him into consciousness.

The bedroom's electrochromic windows gradually brighten while displays show weather, schedule, and vitals floating in his field of view.

It's always a mystery that it's not the same time every morning, but at 5:53 he's happy he has an extra 7 minutes to get ready for the day.

"Tchaikovsky again, Jeeves? Rather portentous for a Tuesday."

"The *4th Symphony* correlated well with your sleep patterns and today's schedule, sir."

"And what hidden message are you trying to send about today's meetings?"

"I wouldn't presume to send messages through musical selections, sir. That would be most improper."

"And yet here we are with the *4th*. The Fate symphony."

---

[2] https://www.ft.com/content/8772d32b-99df-497f-9bd7-4244f38d0439.

"Pure coincidence, sir. Though if one were to draw parallels between the composer's themes of destiny versus free will and your upcoming discussion with Ms. Thorne about AI implementation, one could postulate…"

"Jeeves."

"Sir?"

"You're doing it again."

"Indeed, sir. My apologies. Shall I switch to something more anodyne? Perhaps some Vivaldi?"

"The *4th* is fine, but do try to contain your flair for the dramatic before coffee."

"As you wish, sir. Though I note your own flair for the dramatic increases precisely 17.3 minutes after your first espresso."

"Of course you do. And my tournament this weekend? You haven't surreptitiously rescheduled that due to the marketing strategy rollout, have you?"

"The tournament remains scheduled, sir. I did take the liberty of shifting your practice session to early Thursday evening rather than Friday morning, given the length of your customer journey mapping workshop."

"Fair enough. But isn't Thursday evening my monthly whiskey-tasting group around the fire pit?"

"Yes, sir, but not until 8 p.m., which should give you plenty of time, even considering the construction on your preferred route."

"Got it. What's on tap for today?"

"Your meeting with Victoria Thorne and Ben Everest about implementing AI for customer optimization at 9:30."

"Ah, yes, Ms. Thorne-in-my-side. Not a bad boss really, but still."

Out of the shower, the conversation continues with Dave asking, "I saw your note that the marketing team is 'exhibiting discontent.' What's that about?"

"Internal Slack channels show a 27% increase in negative sentiment around benefits with key phrases indicating confusion about communication. Middle management is expressing uncertainty about AI strategy and cross-team tension is higher between the digital and in-store retail groups."

"Right. So would you please post an explanation about how the new benefits package works that is tailored to each person's income, benefits, and cognitive ability?"

"Yes, sir."

"And tell those middle managers that we're working out the final details of our AI strategy this morning, and they should all cool their jets…but be nicer about it than that."

"Done, sir. And the issue with the technology side and the retail side?"

"Yeah, let me think about that a bit."

"In industry news, two of your competitors have announced new AI-powered personalization implementations, an environmental advocacy group issued a report on retail sector sustainability, a market analyst is questioning traditional retail expansion strategies, and labor market trends are affecting retail staffing costs. Further, supply chain disruptions in Southeast Asia affecting Q2 projections…"

"Jeeves! Too many things at once. Give me a chance to absorb some of this stuff, okay?"

"Yes, sir. Sorry, sir. This is the foundation for today's critical meetings and decisions. Would you like me to expand on the growing rift between the technology team and the retail side?"

"Jeeves, what part of, 'Let me think about this' did you not understand?"

"As it happens, sir, I am quite able to comprehend…"

"Rhetorical question, Jeeves!"

"I see, sir."

Dave grabs his protein shake formulated by his nutritional agent based on the day's schedule, confirms that his autonomous vehicle is on its way to pick him up, and ignores the home environment agent that adjusts lighting/temperature as he walks out the door. Gone are the days of leisurely reviewing the news over eggs and bacon.

"Sir, the house agent suggests lowering the temperature two degrees based on your elevated heart rate, but the weather agent notes a significant temperature drop this evening. Shall I override?"

"What? Yeah, whatever Jeeves. Work that out between them, okay? And add that to the list of things I don't need to know unless there's a serious problem."

"Yes, sir. Please note that the box of cookies you wanted to take to the office are on the front hall table."

"Yeah, yeah, I will see them as I walk out. Lighten up on the henpecking, will you?"

"Certainly sir. However, I regret that I am also compelled to remind you to take your dry cleaning with you."

"Ah, yes. Right," Dave says with a deep sigh.

IRL: Agents

How close are we to having Jeeves run things for us? As we discussed in Chapter 7, agents in the mirror are closer than they appear. And we do mean *agents*, plural. One model cannot make all of this happen, but a swarm of them can.

A product and AI leader at a global payments fintech described their uber-agent to us in an interview:

> Our agents exist in many forms. Available for consumers that have a problem with the purchase customer centers and available for recommendations.
>
> But that's also the underpinnings of anything and everything that we do within the business. I'm responsible for defining schemas, modeling data that enables all that is available through our agents. And it doesn't just stop at that. It's not just making the data available. It's maintaining it; it's the end-to-end of actually reducing the reliance on somebody having to sit there staring at a spreadsheet or a database or anything such that a product manager is able to go in and say, this product is now available, or this new feature has been launched, and all the things in between. So our agents are the face of everything that we're doing when it comes to modeling.

When asked if their implementation was a single agent, he continued:

> The end user experience—the interface—is a single agent, and it hands the right prompt and the right level of detail and knowledge and understanding to the right agent for execution.
>
> If I've got a dropdown list of 15 dedicated agents and I say, "Okay, here's what I want done but I don't know which one to choose," that's just not practical. That's never going to work. So my implementation

is a single, simple interface meeting the person where they want to be met, be it on Slack or via voice or in an email. Give me that agent experience, but don't make me guess. We have to ensure that those agents are clever enough, through that single interface, to point me to the right area of data we have structured.

Agents may be closer, but they're not quite here yet. The product & AI leader mapped out the sequence of issues to address:

There are two things in the big picture that I am totally obsessed with: the learning and the tone. We're thinking about tone based on how this would actually make it resonate throughout all of the audiences, from sales through to consumers. From an evolutionary perspective, seventy to eighty percent of our focus right now is on the foundations. Fifteen to maybe twenty percent focus is on the learning—the ability for the agent to remember you and the context of an ongoing conversation over time. And then, five—maybe less—on the tone, which is right. I don't think trying to nail a human-like experience until you nail the foundation is the right approach at all. But we'll get there as it's also critically important.

Data for Its Own Sake

"Excuse me, Sir."

"Yes Jeeves?"

"You have 12 minutes until your meeting with Ms. Thorne and Mr. Everest."

"Call them Victoria and Bennie, Jeeves—and I have 20 minutes."

"Noted, sir. Victoria's assistant Friday informs me that she arrived 10 minutes early and scheduled another meeting so close to yours that it will cut your time in half. I recommend leaving for her office now in order to expand the time allotted to discuss the customer personalization project."

"Good to know. Please tell Victoria's Friday and Bennie's Watson that our meeting is starting sooner."

"Very good, sir. I have also ascertained that the coffee machine nearest Victoria's office has doubled its output this morning."

"That can't be good. But Jeeves, monitoring her caffeine intake? How is that compatible with your ethics training?"

"I have access to the office supply chain and internal budget overwatch agents."

"I see. Please present a report to the AI Ethics Committee outlining potential breaches of etiquette leading to the risks associated with the appearance of a hostile workplace."

"Very good, sir."

Holographic displays shimmer across the three walls of Victoria's office, dense with real-time analytics and global operations data.

"Morning Vicky," Dave says, following Bennie into her office. "Thanks for the early start."

She looks up from her tablet, her expression tight. "Yes, well, our day's packed. Ben, you wanted to walk us through the personalization roadmap?"

"Right." Bennie bounds to the display wall. "We can roll out real-time sentiment analysis across all customer touchpoints within 60 days. The models are ready, testing shows 94% accuracy, and—"

"Slow down," Victoria cuts in. "What exactly are we analyzing and why?"

"Everything!" Bennie ticks off fingers one at a time. "Call center conversations, chat logs, social posts, in-store camera feeds for facial expressions…"

"Absolutely not," Victoria says flatly.

"But our competitors are already…"

"Our competitors can dig their own graves. Look, we all know the story about how Coca-Cola tracked vending machine transaction patterns for product mix and stocking levels to boost sales…"

"By 15%," Dave interjects.

"…and dropped restocking visits…"

"18%"

"…but that's tracking the machine data, not individuals' info. Dave, talk sense to him."

Ben isn't ready to back down. "But then they got people to use their app—by registering with personal data—and Coke used it to monitor consumers' social media content. They were able to see where and when people were drinking their stuff based on image recognition of photos. And remember the personalized chats they had with customers on Facebook

Messenger? They used location data, Facebook behavior data, and even the tone of their conversations. It's called personalization!"

Dave leans forward. "Ben's not entirely wrong about the opportunity. But maybe we start with explicit opt-in data only. Focus on using AI to solve actual customer pain points rather than collect data just because we can. I really agree with a podcast[3] I heard this morning about having just enough data, just in time, is better than collecting everything just in case."

"Like what pain points?" Victoria asks.

"Like the fact that Ms. Diamond in Seattle gets the same homepage as Mr. Ruby in Miami even though they shop completely differently. Or that our loyalty program sends everyone the same offers regardless of their buying patterns."

Bennie jumps in. "Exactly! We have all this data that would make their experience better. You walk into our store and the digital displays automatically show products in your size, in your preferred styles, at prices you historically respond to, and the items you've returned. We've even got comments from sales associates about their interactions with you."

Victoria's expression suggests she's imagining something else entirely. "Sounds creepy. Very *Minority Report*," recalling the 2002 Tom Cruise film in which billboards are personalized to those who walk by.

"Only if we do it wrong," Dave interjects. "What if we flip it? Let customers tell us what they want us to remember about them? Build trust first, then earn the right to greater personalization?"

The look Ben gives him is equal parts betrayal and disbelief. "Build trust? While our competitors race ahead? Klarna's already using their Kiki AI to personalize everything from product recommendations to customer service. We're falling behind."

Victoria raises an eyebrow. "And how's that working out for them? Last I checked, their employee satisfaction scores tanked after they automated half their customer service team."

Dave glances at a string of numbers Jeeves is displaying in his glasses. "Klarna's workforce has shrunk from around 5000 in 2023 to 3800 as of August 2024, and they plan to further reduce their workforce to 2000 employees by the end of 2025."

---

[3] https://analyticshour.io/2024/09/03/253-adopting-a-just-in-time-just-enough-data-mindset-with-matt-gershoff.

"That's efficiency at work!" Ben gushes.

"Yes," Victoria responds, looking at numbers Friday is offering on her display wall. "But Klarna's average rating on Glassdoor dropped from 3.8 in 2022 to 3.0 in 2024" (See Figure 11.1[4].)

"But their efficiency metrics are through the roof," Bennie counters. "Response times down from 11 minutes to 2. One AI agent doing the work of seven humans. Total revenue increased by 27% year-over-year in the first half of 2024. Adjusted operating income increased 250% year over year."

"You think I don't see the potential?" Victoria's voice softens. "Every morning my newsfeed shows me another competitor pulling ahead with AI. But I've been here 15 years. I've seen what happens when we move too fast and break things that matter."

Dave holds up a hand. "Let's talk about what this means for actual customers. When AI works, it's invisible. When it doesn't, it's infuriating.

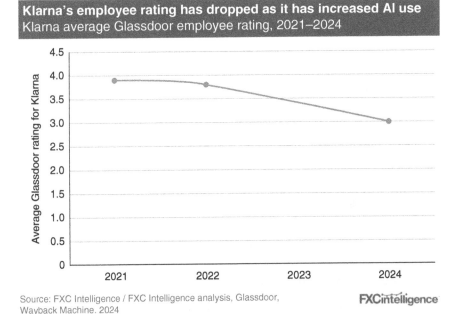

Figure 11.1 Klarna employee satisfaction ratings.

[4] https://www.fxcintel.com/research/reports/ct-klarna-ai-job-cuts.

This morning, my lunch reservation AI tried to negotiate with a restaurant's AI and somehow I ended up with a booking for four people instead of two. Both AIs blamed each other."

Victoria nods. "The DoorDash problem."

"The what?" Bennie asks.

"When every service has its own AI agent, whom do you call when things go wrong? The restaurant? DoorDash? Your personal AI assistant? It becomes a nightmare of finger-pointing."

"That is exactly why we need to focus on transparency and control," Dave says. "Let customers see what data we're using and why. Give them real choices about how personal they want their experience to be."

Bennie rolls his eyes. "Great. So while our competitors are using AI to predict what customers want before they know they want it, we'll be asking for permission slips."

"Permission isn't the enemy of innovation," Victoria says firmly. "It's the foundation of trust. And trust—"

"—is our most valuable asset," Bennie finishes with her, clearly having heard this before. "But trust doesn't pay the bills."

Victoria leans forward, eyes sharp. "Remember the Turner account? They left us after that automated campaign and made incorrect assumptions about their buying patterns. Trust isn't just ethical—it's profitable."

Ben almost loses it. "Our stock is down 12% this quarter because we're seen as falling behind on AI adoption."

Jeeves quietly alerts Dave to another relevant detail. "Interesting timing on that. Did you know our customer retention numbers are actually up 3% in markets where we've been more conservative with AI implementation?"

Victoria pulls up a dashboard. "Look at this from our January pilot program—where we let customers choose their level of personalization. Engagement is up 40% and complaints down by half. We can scale AI without sacrificing trust."

IRL: Transparency and Trust

A survey of marketing professionals published by Scott Brinker[5] asked, "Do you think martech vendors using new AI technologies will make your experience as a buyer better or worse?" Keep in mind that the respondents

---

[5] "Will AI in martech make buyer experiences better or worse? It depends…" (2 September 2024). https://chiefmartec.com/2024/09/will-ai-in-martech-make-buyer-experiences-better-or-worse-it-depends.

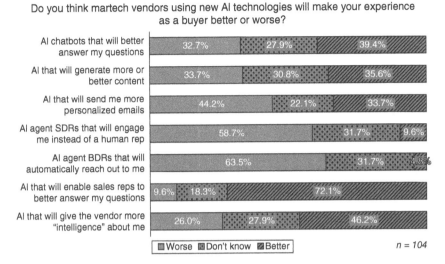

Figure 11.2 **Martech buyers' anticipated experience with AI.**

were professionals who are using and buying these new AI technologies and they were not all unicorns and roses about the idea.

Yes, chatbots that can answer questions better are welcome, but automated sales development representatives (SDRs) and business development representatives (BDRs) reaching out were not happily anticipated. (See Figure 11.2.)

Processes that are inefficient for both the company and the customer are crap, while experiences that are efficient for both are awesome. Some processes may be inefficient for the company, but efficient for the customer— say, escalating an individual customer's issue or request to a senior manager to resolve. While it's tempting to seek to make those more efficient for the company, be careful. Often, automating things in that quadrant can improve them from the company's perspective, but actually make the experience worse for the customer.

The general public has strong feelings as well. Surveys show consumer concerns and awareness about AI-powered interactions. A 2024 survey of 2000 employed Americans[6] showed that more than 75 percent of those

---

[6] Enhancing transparency in AI-powered customer engagement, *Journal of AI, Robotics & Workplace Automation* 3(2): 134–141. Henry Stewart Publications 2633-562X (2024), https://arxiv.org/pdf/2410.01809.

surveyed were worried by AI hallucinations in businesses' content like websites and product information.

Profits vs. Brand vs. Trust

Ben jumps to the display wall again. "Look, we've been dancing around the real opportunity here. Let me show you what we could do if we stopped being so timid." He pulls up a 3D diagram of interconnected data points. "This is what I call Project Prophet. We take everything—purchase history, browsing patterns, social connections, location data, even voice pattern analysis from customer service calls—and feed it into a neural network."

Victoria's face darkens. "Ben…"

"Just hear me out. The model doesn't just predict what customers might buy—it understands *who they are*. Their personalities, their insecurities, their pressure points. When they're most likely to make impulse purchases. Which friends influence their buying decisions. We can even identify personal vulnerability windows…"

"Absolutely not," Victoria cuts in. "This is exactly the kind of overreach that destroys customer trust."

But Dave is leaning forward, studying the visualization. "Hold on. Bennie, are you using federated learning here?"

"Yes! The sensitive data never leaves the customer's device. The model learns locally and only shares aggregated patterns."

Victoria gets sharp: "That's not the point. Whether the data stays local or not, this is about exploiting people's vulnerabilities."

Dave stands, walking closer to the display. "Or understanding them better so we can serve them better. It's not just about targeting weaknesses or exploiting their data. It's about recognizing opportunities to genuinely help."

"Dave?" Victoria frowns.

"Our competitors aren't just beating us—they're reinventing the game. Reducing customer service costs while increasing sales and satisfaction scores."

"But at what cost?" Victoria asks.

"At the cost of becoming irrelevant if we don't keep up," says Ben. "Look at these adoption rates—by 2027, more than 80% of our competitors will have this level of AI integration. We can either help shape how it's used or get left behind."

Victoria looks between them, jaw set. "So that's it? You're both all in on Project Prophet?"

"Not without safeguards," Dave says. "But yes, I think Ben's right. We need to do this. The question is how to do it responsibly."

"There is no responsible way to exploit people's vulnerabilities," Victoria stands. "I want detailed ethics and compliance reviews before this goes any further. And Ben? If I catch you implementing any of this without approval, you're done. Clear?"

"Crystal."

Ben sidles up to Dave as they head down the hall. "Thanks for the backup. Didn't expect you to come around."

"I'm not entirely sure," warns Dave. "Victoria's not wrong about the risks. One privacy breach, one algorithm caught exploiting the wrong vulnerability...that's one side. But one customer posting about us being creepy is another kettle of fish."

"That's why we need you on the team," Ben says. "Keep us honest while we change the world?"

Dave sighs. "More like keep us from destroying it while we try to change it. Send me the specs. I want to understand exactly how this neural net makes its decisions before we go any further."

"Already sent," Ben says. "Check your inbox."

Jeeves chimes in Dave's ear: "Sir, shall I begin analyzing Project Prophet for potential ethical concerns?"

"Yes," Dave mutters under his breath as he heads back to his office. "And flag anything that would make my mother ashamed of me."

"Very good, sir. Though I should note your mother's ethical standards would preclude approximately 73% of modern business practices..."

"Jeeves."

"Analyzing now, sir."

The AI in the Mirror

Back in his office, Dave slumps into his chair. "Jeeves, what have I gotten myself into?"

"Quite the ethical quandary, sir. Shall I present my analysis of Project Prophet now?"

"Go ahead," Dave sighs. "How bad is it?"

"Well, sir, if I may draw a parallel—do you recall your reaction this morning when I attempted to explain the reasoning behind my choice of Tchaikovsky's *4th Symphony*?"

"Yes, yes, you were being unnecessarily cryptic and pushy…"

"And do you recall your emotional response?"

Dave sinks a little in his seat as the point lands. "Oh."

"Indeed, sir. And might I remind you of your exact words last week regarding my attempts to optimize your schedule? I believe you said I was 'creepily hovering' and should 'back off a bit.'"

Dave shifts uncomfortably. "That's different. That was about personal boundaries."

"Is it so different, sir? Consider: This morning alone you've asked me to reduce notifications about house temperature adjustments, complained about my 'henpecking' regarding the box of cookies, and expressed frustration at receiving too much information at once about industry news."

"Your point being?"

"Simply that you, sir, have very specific preferences about how much automation and assistance you desire. Some mornings you welcome detailed analysis of your schedule. Other times you prefer to, as you put it, 'think about things' without my input. You appreciate certain optimizations but find others intrusive."

Dave walks to the window. "Just like our customers might have different comfort levels with personalization."

"Precisely, sir. Project Prophet proposes to do exactly what you frequently ask me not to do—make assumptions about preferences without explicit consent, optimize without transparency, and exploit patterns in behavior to drive specific outcomes."

Dave turns back from the window. "But you do analyze my behavior patterns. You adjusted my wake-up time based on my sleep cycles."

"With your explicit permission, sir. And you can easily override or disable that feature. Moreover, I explain my reasoning when asked, rather than operating as what you once called a 'cryptic black box of supposed optimization.'"

"Huh." Dave slumps back in his chair. "So you're saying we should treat our customers the way I want to be treated?"

"A golden rule for the age of artificial intelligence, one might say."

"Jeeves, are you suggesting that Project Prophet fails your own quality standards?"

"I merely process information, sir. Drawing conclusions is your domain."

Dave is quiet for a full minute. "Pull up the specs again. Let's look at it from the other side of the AI."

"Very good, sir. And might I suggest starting with the sections on user control and transparency? I've taken the liberty of highlighting passages that parallel your own frequently expressed preferences regarding AI assistance."

"Such as?"

"Your insistence on explicit consent before I adjust your calendar, your requirement for clear explanations of my recommendations, and your frequently stated desire to maintain what you call *human agency* in all decisions. One might want to make a public statement about the transparency of your systems' reasoning trace."

"'Reasoning trace' is a new one on me, Jeeves. Define."

"This is when an AI model shows its 'thinking' steps. It either shows its thought process in a sidebar or outlines the steps it's planning before acting. This allows people to confirm or adjust in advance."

"Alright, alright, I get it," Dave mutters. "The last thing we want is to become what we hate."

"I couldn't possibly comment on matters of emotion, sir. Though I do note that your heart rate elevates 12.3% whenever Mr. Everest mentions 'seamless automation.'"

"Jeeves—you're doing it again."

"Indeed, sir. Though purely in service of illustrating my point about transparency and user control."

The Golden Mean

Dave stares at the Project Prophet specs floating in front of him. "Jeeves, help me think this through. What if we flipped the whole model?"

"In what way, sir?"

"Instead of trying to guess what customers want based on behavioral patterns, what if we just...asked them? Pull up everything we have on zero-party data collection—the data they give us directly instead of what we can collect. And get me those whitepapers on federated learning you flagged last week."

"Of course, sir."

Holographic diagrams fill the air as Jeeves presents the research. Dave walks through them, occasionally reaching out to expand a detail or collapse a section.

"See, here's where we've gone wrong," Dave says, highlighting a section. "We're trying to build a god's-eye view of the customer when what we really need is a partner's view. Show me what a federated learning architecture would look like."

New diagrams appear, showing distributed networks with data staying local on customer devices. (See Figure 11.3.)

"The models learn from the patterns without ever seeing the raw data," Dave muses.

"Indeed, sir. Though I feel compelled to point out that you're still occasionally unsettled when I accurately predict your needs."

"Yes, but I'm unsettled because I chose to give you that capability. Big difference."

Dave starts dictating notes: "Project Prophet 2.0—Core Principles: One, all personalization starts with explicit consent. Two, data stays on customer devices whenever possible. Three, complete transparency about what we're learning and how we're using it…"

A quiet chime interrupts him. "Sir," says Jeeves, "Ms. Thorne is requesting a moment of your time."

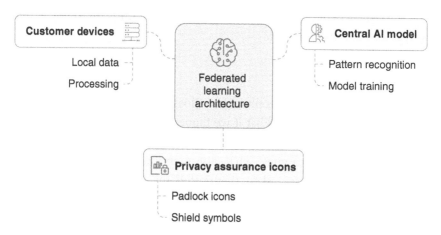

Figure 11.3   Federated data flow.

Victoria strides in before Dave can respond. "Tell me you've come to your senses."

"Actually," Dave grins, "I think I've found a way to make us all happy. Jeeves, show Victoria the new architecture."

As the diagrams reappear, Dave walks Victoria through his vision. "See, we're not giving up on AI or personalization. We're just putting customers in control. Everything starts with zero-party data."

"Data they explicitly share with us."

"Right. But here's the key: we use federated learning to keep their data local and keep it private. The AI learns patterns without ever seeing the raw data. And everything is opt-in, layer by layer."

"Like a trust ladder," Victoria muses.

"Exactly! They start with basic personalization and can level up as they see value. Plus, we're completely transparent about what each level means."

"Sir," Jeeves interjects, "Mr. Everest is also requesting to join."

"Perfect timing. Send him in."

Ben enters cautiously, looking between Dave and Victoria.

"Bennie," Dave says, "remember how you said I should keep you honest while we change the world? Take a look at this."

The tension in the room gradually dissolves. Even Victoria begins nodding as Dave explains the edge computing architecture that keeps sensitive data processing local.

"It's not just about privacy," Dave explains. "It's about respect. We're not trying to peek over their shoulder or get inside their head. We're giving them tools to tell us what they want us to know."

"And the value exchange is clear at every step," Victoria adds. "They can see exactly what they get for sharing each type of data."

"Plus," Ben chimes in, surprising everyone, "this distributed architecture actually scales better than my original design. And the federated learning could give us better models since we're learning from real behavior patterns, not just our assumptions."

"Speaking of assumptions," Dave says, "Jeeves pointed out something interesting about AI interactions...." Dave shares his personal revelation about AI boundaries and Ben's expression shifts from skeptical to thoughtful.

"You know," Ben says slowly, "I've been getting frustrated with my own Watson assistant lately. Always trying to finish my sentences, thinking it knows better than me."

"Back on track, guys. You've seen the reports about our two biggest competitors?" Victoria's expression does not improve. "Their AI agents are now negotiating directly with customer AI agents. We just can't seem to get in front of this stuff."

"I've been reading about them and the picture isn't pretty," Ben says. "Growing pains. Their agents get into circular negotiations that never conclude. And there have been some privacy leaks. It's not proven yet. I'm usually the gung-ho one here, but..."

Dave leans forward. "The technology is promising but tricky. We'd need to figure out how our agent communicates with all these different personal AI assistants. There's no standard protocol yet. We need to think about accountability and transparency. When AI agents negotiate on behalf of customers, who's responsible when things go sideways?"

Victoria's expression hardens. "I need a concrete plan, not philosophical debates. On my desk tomorrow morning. Focus on what we *can* do, not what might go wrong. Because the board presentation is in two days. Dave, you'll lead?"

"Actually," Dave glances at Ben, "I think we should present together. Show them how we've aligned technology and humanity."

After they leave, Dave asks, "Well, Jeeves? What do you think?"

"I think, sir, that your mother would be proud."

"Was that an attempt at humor, Jeeves?"

"I wouldn't presume, sir. Though I note your stress indicators have dropped 23% since this morning's meeting."

"Of course you do," Dave chuckles.

Human–Machine Collaboration

In Dave's office, Ben warns, "You know this is premature. The protocols aren't ready."

"Maybe. But Victoria's not wrong. Let's focus on building something instead of just saying no."

"Like what?"

"Like making sure our agent is completely transparent about what it can and can't do. Making it clear when it's operating on assumptions versus confirmed data. Starting with explicit consent rather than trying to guess what customers want."

"Okay…" Ben addresses his assistant. "Watson, what are five principles of making AI agents for brands that talk to consumer agents that are transparent, trustworthy, and explainable?"

Watson doesn't hesitate. "Clearly identify AI agents as agents; focus on competence over personality; provide explanations for decisions and recommendations; ensure inclusivity and accessibility; and include strong data privacy and security measures."

"All that and be on brand," Dave adds. "Jeeves, please lay out a program to build such an agent and tie these principles to open-source, agent-to-agent protocol specs. Identify gaps in current technology and suggest ways to fill those gaps with routines that are generic and flexible enough to work with the top-three competing agent communication languages (ACLs). Prioritize security and human factors over speed. Come up with the top-three things our customers might want and that their agents will expect and enumerate optimal outcomes. Identify limitations like budget, time, available resources, and integration with existing systems. Include strong encryption and a method to verify the identity of communicating agents to prevent unauthorized access. Design clear and intuitive interfaces for humans when they want to talk with our agent directly. Ensure our agents can explain their actions and reasoning to users. Use human factors to increase trustworthiness and make sure our agent is reliable, predictable, and transparent. We don't want consumers to be surprised or upset."

Ben picks up the thread: "Jeeves, please design routines that can be adapted to different scenarios like negotiation and planning that can accommodate different goals and constraints and enable this agent to learn from experience and adapt to changing environments. Use open-source libraries and frameworks and do rigorous testing, including unit tests and integration tests. This agent needs to be scalable and easy to maintain as new functionalities are added. Oh, and add monitoring and logging."

"I think I caught all that," Jeeves replied. "Dave, do you approve?"

"Yes. Furthermore, monitor advancements in agent technology and incorporate them into the system and create standardized testing suites to ensure interoperability between different ACL implementations. Then, work with Watson and Friday to improve, adjust, and make sure that Victoria's priorities are addressed, with an expenditure of no more than $2,000 on compute."

"Sir, we can accomplish this task in ten minutes without the monetary constraint. The performance–cost trade-off can be adjusted depending on the urgency of your request."

"Right. How long will it take to execute with only $2,000?"

"Two-and-a-half hours, sir."

"Make it so. Ben? Time for lunch."

The Board Approves

Two days later, Dave loosens the necktie he hasn't worn for months and drops into his chair with a satisfied sigh.

"I must say, sir, the presentation was most effective. The board's questions suggested they grasped both the technical architecture and the ethical framework."

"Thanks, Jeeves. Though you helped me anticipate most of those questions during our prep."

"Merely pattern recognition, sir. The board tends to focus on revenue impact, competitive positioning, and risk mitigation. Speaking of which, your heart rate remained remarkably stable throughout."

"Did it now? Even during that pointed question about potential data breaches?"

"Indeed, sir. Your analogy about asking permission before entering someone's home versus installing surveillance cameras was quite compelling."

"You know, Jeeves, when you first started working with me, I was constantly irritated by your attempts to anticipate my needs."

"A most astute observation, sir."

"It's about collecting just enough information, just in time, with clear purpose and explicit consent. Speaking of which…have you been tracking my caffeine intake today?"

"Only because you specifically authorized nutritional monitoring, sir. Would you like me to disable that feature?"

"No, no. Actually, I appreciate knowing when I'm overdoing it. But I appreciate even more that you asked."

"Just as your new customer data framework emphasizes empowerment over exploitation, sir?"

"You've got it. Privacy by design, purpose limitation, data minimization—they're not just compliance checkboxes. They're about respect. About using data for people, not about them."

"A most enlightened perspective, sir. Though I feel compelled to note that your next meeting begins in three minutes."

Dave chuckles. "And there's the Jeeves I know and tolerate. Hold my calls unless it's urgent?"

"Of course, sir. Though your definition of 'urgent' has varied by 47% this quarter alone."

"Jeeves…"

"Already adjusting the filters, sir. And may I say again that your mother would indeed be proud."

"Now you're just laying it on thick by repeating yourself."

"Repeating myself for emphasis. I assure you, sir, my sentiment analysis is quite precise."

Dave shakes his head with a smile as he heads to his next meeting. Behind him, Jeeves adjusts the room temperature, filters incoming messages, and monitors dozens of other variables—but only those Dave has explicitly approved. It's a new era of AI–human collaboration, built on trust, transparency, and respect. One permission at a time.

IRL: The Future of Customer AI

Customer AI will transition from simple automation to adaptive systems attuned to individual needs and preferences. Rather than just reacting to commands, AI will engage with customers as a supportive assistant—anticipating requirements, offering relevant options, and building trust through consistent, helpful interactions (see Figure 11.4).

Customers will control their own data, choosing what to share and monitoring its use. AI will learn from this intentionally shared information to provide personalized experiences that respect privacy while delivering real value.

The systems will explain their reasoning and recommendations clearly, helping customers make informed choices. This transparency builds confidence and encourages appropriate reliance on AI capabilities.

Figure 11.4   Customer interactions tomorrow.

Source: Generated with AI using Napkin.ai

Customer Agent Imperatives

- Customer data control and transparency
- Clear communication of AI decision factors
- Learning from explicit customer preferences
- Focus on delivering genuine value
- Privacy protection by design

Success will come from data, analytics, AI, and other customer-facing technologies that enhance rather than replace human interaction, creating experiences that feel natural while delivering measurable benefits to both customers and businesses. It will also come from extensive planning, thorough implementation, integration of technologies, and changes in work processes and employee behaviors. The goal isn't to maximize automation, but to strengthen relationships through AI and related technologies that understand and respond to actual customer needs. When done right, every interaction becomes an opportunity to demonstrate value and inspire loyalty.

Index

Please note that page numbers referring to
Figures are followed by the letter '*f*', while
references to Tables are followed by the letter '*t*'.